*Action under Planning*

# McGRAW-HILL SERIES IN INTERNATIONAL DEVELOPMENT

# Action under Planning:

## The Guidance of Economic Development

Bertram M. Gross, Editor

McGraw-Hill Book Company

NEW YORK   LONDON   SYDNEY   TORONTO

*General Editor*

FRED W. RIGGS
Chairman
Comparative Administration Group

# *Preface*

Back in 1945 Stuart Chase, one of the most vigorous of all polemicists in favor of national planning, presented his "mountain view" vision of how to prepare a plan for America's future. He would assemble people from many walks of life and have them meet "in some high, quiet place" where, insulated from narrow pressures, they could "think in terms of the whole community."[1]

As a government planner at the time, I thought the idea silly. A few years later, in the more academic language I was then learning to use, I said so rather sharply:

> A delightful prospect! Particularly for the participants! But the keenest minds in America could get together and prepare a general program for America or even a little program dealing with a single problem and, unless the participants represented important groups in the social conflict, or had guidelines for conveying their ideas to these groups, their proposals would be neglected. Insofar as the proposals really tied up with the interests of organizations with power, they would themselves be another incident in the group struggle. Actually, many conferences of this type have taken place and no more can be expected from them than the production of occasional reading matter . . .[2]

Today, two decades later, I am still willing to defend, with a few minor amendments, my earlier skepticism. I am still not

[1] Stuart Chase, *Democracy under Pressure*, Twentieth Century Fund, New York, 1945, p. 133.

[2] Bertram M. Gross, *The Legislative Struggle*, McGraw-Hill Company, New York, 1953, p. 29.

willing to propose "mountain view" conferences as a way of getting better and more realistic plans for any country. Indeed, upon examination, too many of the development plans for countries in Asia, Latin America, and Africa look as though they had been prepared high on the Himalayas, the Andes, or Kilimanjaro —well insulated from the harsh facts of life in the countries to which they are alleged to refer.

Today I know much better what a delightful experience for the participants a mountain view conference may be. This volume was born at a month-long residential seminar conducted at Syracuse University's Minnowbrook Conference Center on the edge of Blue Mountain Lake in the Adirondack mountains. Together with the other authors, I believe the Chase vision should be amended to provide for a quiet lake near the "high, quiet place."

Moreover, some of the conditions I had suggested for the success of any such conference were partially met at the Minnowbrook Conference. The quiet of the lake and the mountain merely provided the background for the sharp clash of conflicting viewpoints. Although "interest groups" in the ordinary sense of the term were not represented, we all went through the "meat grinder" of trying to understand and reconcile the divergent interests and premises of people coming from such diverse fields of inquiry as economics, political science, organization theory, sociology, psychology, psychiatry, history, and regional planning. We experienced many trials, tribulations, and misunderstandings stemming from the diversity of our national backgrounds; we came from India, Poland, France, Britain, Pakistan, and Tanganyika, as well as the United States. Somewhat less clear—but no less important—were the divergencies and conflicts stemming from our major roles in life: academic observer, dedicated reformer, practical administrator, graduate student, technical adviser. For all the participants this was a meaningful and memorable learning experience. It is hoped that some of the things we learned are communicated in this volume.

Also, the ideas herein presented are unquestionably "tied up with the interests of organizations with power." Our "supradisciplinary" analysis of what is involved in translating development plans into reality deals directly with the interests of Chiefs of State, development administrators, industrial managers, and planning technicians in every one of the preindustrial countries now seeking to escape the clutch of poverty through planned economic development. It deals directly with the vital interests of the many weak national planning commissions that as yet have little power to influence events and are therefore seeking new and better ways to mobilize, maintain, and use power.

Yet can anything more be expected from a meeting such as the Minnowbrook Conference than "the production of occasional reading matter"? I think so. Even before publication, the germinal ideas in this volume have contributed immensely to the flowering of the new literature on national planning which is, at a higher theoretical level, both more empirically rooted and more action-oriented than the "grand debates" of previous decades. The volume will be read with interest by leading national planners and development administrators in many countries—for whom even occasional reading may be highly important. It will be discussed at international conferences and in the sessions of special training institutes. It will enter into the continuing explorations fostered by the Comparative Administration Group of the American Society for Public Administration. It will serve as one of the intellectual springboards of INTERPLAN (the International Group for Studies in National Planning). After being born on the shores of Blue Mountain Lake, INTERPLAN is now carrying forward, through international conferences in Warsaw, Caracas, and elsewhere, the development of the germinal ideas presented in this volume.

On behalf of all the authors, I voice our deep indebtedness to three of the conference participants whose wisdom and perceptive critiques contributed to all of the chapters: Eric Trist and David Armstrong of Britain's Tavistock Institute of Human Relations (who also served as members of the committee under Michel Crozier which prepared Chapter 11), and S. S. Khera, formerly Cabinet Secretary of the Government of India. We are also highly appreciative of the ideas and stimuli contributed by our guest commentators and advisors: Douglas Ashford, Stephen

K. Bailey, Edwin Bock, Harlan Cleveland, Milton Esman, Gerard Mangone, A. H. Maslow, Paul Meadows, S. M. Miller, Nenad Popovic, Fred Riggs, Sidney Sufrin, and Irving Swerdlow. We are indebted to the graduate students who not only summarized our discussions and criticized our drafts but also chaired most of our sessions: Wendell Brown, Savithri Chari, Nikos Georgulas, David Hutchinson, Thomas Rasmussen, and Tariq Saddiqui. We are indebted to the Ford Foundation, whose generous financial support made this volume possible.

We are also highly indebted to Nora F. Gross, who served on the committee that, under the chairmanship of Peter Wiles, produced Chapter 10, and who did the detailed final editing of all the chapters. To her we quickly assign all the credit and the blame that authors—or even general editors like myself—are willing to dodge.

Above all, we express our profound appreciation of the indispensable support and encouragement given us by two scholar-administrators who have been pioneering in new and more fruitful approaches to public administration in the modern world: Prof. Stephen K. Bailey, Dean of the Maxwell Graduate School of Citizenship and Public Affairs, Syracuse University; and Prof. Fred W. Riggs, Chairman of the Comparative Administration Group of the American Society for Public Administration.

*Bertram M. Gross*

# The Authors

**Zygmunt Bauman:** Professor of Sociology, University of Warsaw (Poland); Editor, *Sociological Studies;* member, governing body, Polish Sociological Association; Ford Foundation Scholar, London School of Economics, 1957; author of *Class Movement Elite, Problems of Modern American Sociology, Outline of Sociology: Problems and Concepts* (Zary's Socjologii, Warsaw).

**Fred G. Burke:** Professor of Political Science and Director of the Program of East African Studies, Maxwell Graduate School of Citizenship and Public Affairs, Syracuse University; author of *Africa's Quest for Order, Local Government and Politics in Uganda, Tanganyika: Preplanning,* as well as articles in professional journals.

**Lynton K. Caldwell:** Professor of Government, Indiana University; member, Executive Committee, Committee on Comparative Administration; Director, Institute of Training for Public Service and Coordinator, Thailand and Indonesian Public Administration programs, 1958–1963; United Nations Co-director, Public Administration Institute for Turkey and the Middle East; Director of Research and Publications, Council of State Governments; author of *Administrative Theories of Hamilton and Jefferson, The Government and Administration of New York,* and "Environment: A New Focus for Public Policy," *Public Administration Review,* September, 1963.

**Michel Crozier:** Director, Groupe de Recherche de Sociologie des Organisations at the Centre National de la Recherche Scientifique, Paris; Fellow, Center for the Advanced Study in the Behavioral Sciences, 1959–1960. Author of *Usines et syndicats d'Amérique,* 1951; *Petits fonctionnaires au travail,* 1956; "Human Relations at the Management Level in a Bureaucratic System of Organization," *Human Organization,* May, 1961; "The Cultural Revolutions," in *Daedalus: New Europe,* December, 1963; *Le Phénomène bureaucratique,* Editions du Seuil, Paris, 1964, translated into English as *The Bureaucratic Phenomenon,* The University of Chicago Press, Chicago, 1965; and *Le Monde des employes de bureau,* Editions du Seuil, Paris, 1965.

**John Friedmann:** Director, Ford Foundation Program for Urban and Regional Development in Chile; formerly, Associate Professor of Regional Planning at the Massachusetts Institute of Technology; consultant to the Venezuelan Guayana Development Corporation and the Inter-American Development Bank; author of *Regional Policy for Developing Areas, Venezuela: From Doctrine to Dialogue,* coauthor of *Regional Development and Planning: A Reader;* contributor to professional journals, including the *Journal of the American Institute of Planners, Comparative Studies in Society and History, Land Economics,* and *Papers of the Regional Science Association.*

**Bertram M. Gross:** Professor of Political Science and Director of National Planning Studies, Maxwell Graduate School of Citizenship and Public Affairs, Syracuse University; and first Chairman, National Capital Regional Planning Council; formerly Executive-Secretary, Council of Economic Advisers to the President; Fellow, Center for Advanced Study in the Behavioral Sciences, 1961–1962; Visiting Professor, Harvard Graduate School of Business Administration, University of California, Berkeley, Cal., and Hebrew University, Jerusalem. Author of *The State of the Nation: Social Systems Accounting,* 1966; *Space-Time and Post Industrialism,* 1966; *The Managing of Organizations: The Administrative Strug-*

*gle*, 2 vols., 1964, and *The Legislative Struggle: A Study in Social Combat*, 1953.

**Robert Shafer:** Professor of History, Syracuse University; Visiting Professor, University of California at Los Angeles; author of *The Economic Societies in the Spanish World* (winner of the H. E. Bolton prize of the Latin American Conference of the American Historical Association), coauthor of *Contemporary Civilization*.

**Peter J. D. Wiles:** Professor of Russian Studies, London School of Economics; former Professor of Economics, Brandeis University; author of *Price, Cost and Output* and *The Political Economy of Communism*, 1962.

**Executive Committee, International Group for Studies in National Planning (INTERPLAN).** Bertram M. Gross, Chairman; Peter Wiles, Secretary; Zygmunt Bauman, Michel Crozier, Eric Trist (Staff Convenor, Tavistock Institute of Human Relations, London).

# Contents

# 1

# Planning the Improbable

### Bertram M. Gross

How to get action under planning?

"We have had lots of advice from experts on how to make economic plans," Prime Minister Nehru of India is reported to have complained. "But when shall we hear something on how to implement them?"

With the spread of national planning such questions are asked with increasing force. When development planning is first undertaken, it seems relatively simple to get the plans started—particularly for their most fervent proponents. But soon the planners themselves find shocking gaps between plans and performance. Their self-confidence is rudely shaken. Their supporters' hopes may be quickly replaced by disillusion with the planners, if not with planning itself. Disillusion is magnified by well-intentioned rescue missions based upon econometric irrelevancies or the stale folklore of "classical" public administration.

In an effort to provide some fresh responses to Nehru's lament, an intensive research seminar on national planning was conducted during July, 1964, at Syracuse University by the Comparative Administration Group of the American Society for Public Administration. Papers were prepared in advance, dissected intensively during heated seminar sessions, and rewritten in subsequent tranquillity. In addition, informal working parties produced a number of other documents. One of these, completed after a second international conference in Warsaw in 1965, will be discussed at subsequent international conferences under the auspices of the International Group for Studies in National Planning (INTERPLAN). We hope that this book, the product of all this activity, will promote ever-widening attention to the factors determining the extent to which the planners' dreams are shattered or consummated.

Although many different viewpoints are presented by the authors of the subsequent chapters, the entire volume is closely related to the following underlying themes:

1. Most of the people and nations in the world are poor.
2. To overcome poverty quickly national planning faces tremendous obstacles.
3. One of the serious obstacles is inadequate attention to the noneconomic aspects of economic development.

With these themes in mind the authors of the chapters in Part 1, as individuals from different disciplines and countries, have tried to develop an interdisciplinary and international approach to the "web of implementation." In this effort we have been seriously limited by the still primitive state of both research and theory on this subject.

Our awareness of these limitations has led us, in turn, to appreciate the other side of the coin, namely, the remarkable opportunities for widening and deepening social science research and theory on national planning. In Part 2, accordingly, we have worked together in developing certain "starting point" concepts and questions for use by the scholars in many countries who are beginning to explore this great new vista of the social sciences.

Brief statements of the underlying themes and a summary of the approaches taken in Parts 1 and 2 are presented in this chapter.

## THE CLUTCH OF POVERTY

In previous periods of history, it was assumed that "the poor will always be with us." The aim of abolishing poverty was little more than an idle dream. But today, planned attacks on poverty, backed by public and private programs for harnessing science and technology, are underway throughout the world.

For the minority of the world's population who live in the rich countries, the attack on poverty can be compared to a "mop up" operation. In a country like the United States, where considerable affluence is already enjoyed by a large part of the population, the alleviation or elimination of poverty is only a part of a drive toward a greater affluence. For the majority of the world's people, however, the attack on poverty is a major issue of overwhelming importance.

*Poverty* may be defined simply as an insufficiency of material assets and of currently available services or goods. For individuals and families this involves three interrelated forms of insufficiency: *asset poverty, income poverty,* and *public service poverty*.[1]

The poor, first of all, are those with few assets that they can call their own. They have little or no property or savings. They are often burdened by debt. They have little furniture, household equipment, or clothing. They are the modern-day sans-culottes.

The incomes of the poor are low, irregular, and undependable. They are often pieced together from the earnings of various family members or by charity, dole payments, or begging. Hence, the poor suffer from unsanitary and overcrowded housing, insufficient or unbalanced diets, insufficient medical care, inadequate education, and meager opportunities for recreation, culture, or travel.

The public services enjoyed by the poor are minimal. The poor habitually live in areas with the poorest public facilities in the form of water supply, public utilities, sewage disposal, flood protection, police protection, schools, hospitals, libraries, recreation facilities, and parks. The services of "welfare agencies" are often designed less to promote the welfare of the poor than to keep poverty within the limits of political tolerability.

Statistics on these three forms of poverty are always deficient. Personal and family assets cannot be readily evaluated. Data on the distribution of disposable personal and family income [2] are notoriously inaccurate; even in those countries with the best statistics, they are usually out of date. Data on the availability of public facilities and services by groups of beneficiaries are rarely collected. Sometimes the best way to calculate the extent of poverty is to focus on certain indirect indicators. These concern social phenomena to which poverty is a contributing (although by no means a completely determining) factor: infant mortality, illiteracy, malnutrition, disease, juvenile delinquency, crime, and preventable epidemics, droughts, and floods.

But no statistics, good or bad, direct or indirect, can ever reveal the human—or rather the inhuman—aspects of poverty. The poor eke out lives of insecurity, apathy, and despair. In the Latin-American phrase, they are *los rotos*—"the broken ones." To see poverty in terms of human misery one must walk through the teeming slums of Calcutta and brave the stares of jobless men, haggard mothers, and hungry children.

Statistics on the poverty of nations are also inadequate. On the asset side, aggregate measures are not available. Indeed, national accounting for economic wealth has barely been initiated in any country. One can merely point to specific deficiencies in one or another form of natural resource—water, mineral, or agricultural—or to resource potentialities that lie unexplored or undeveloped. With respect to currently produced services and goods, the best measures are per capita gross national product (GNP) or national income. Yet these data suffer from major inaccuracies.[3] They provide averages only, with no attention to the pattern of distribution below and above the average. While including both personal and family income and services provided under public services, they do not show the balance between the two or the composition of the various services and goods produced. Nevertheless, they provide important—albeit somewhat impressionistic—perspectives on the state of the world.

As shown in Table 1, three-quarters of the world's people are in countries with about one-quarter of the world's annual output. Half of the world's people are in countries with less than $100 per capita output per year and less than 10 percent of the world's annual output. For these people it would be a tremendous advance merely to reach the higher levels of the "poor" category, let alone to pass the $600 per capita level and enter the "middling" category. Poverty, of course, exists in all these countries, even those classified as "middling" and "rich," but the types of poverty in these different countries differ in at least four ways.

**Table 1.** *Estimated World Distribution of GNP and Population, 1961*

| GNP per Capita | Percent of World Population | | Percent of World GNP | |
|---|---|---|---|---|
| | group | cumulative | group | cumulative |
| **Poor countries:** | | | | |
| Less than $100 | 50.1 | 50.1 | 8.5 | 8.5 |
| $100–$300 | 15.7 | 65.8 | 6.1 | 14.6 |
| $300–$600 | 10.7 | 76.5 | 10.1 | 24.7 |
| **Middling countries:** | | | | |
| $600–$1,200 | 16.7 | 93.2 | 35.3 | 60.0 |
| **Rich countries:** | | | | |
| $1,200 and more | 6.8 | 100.0 | 40.0 | 100.0 |

SOURCE: Max Millikan and Donald L. M. Blackmer, *The Emerging Nations*, Little, Brown and Company, Boston, 1961, Table II, "Estimated Distribution of World Income, 1961." This table, in turn, is derived from P. N. Rosenstein-Rodan, "International Aid for Developing Countries," *The Review of Economics and Statistics*, May, 1961. The various GNP estimates are converted into dollars at the currently effective foreign-exchange rates. As with all data on GNP (which is composed of national income plus depreciation allowances and indirect taxes), the GNP figures are higher than any comparable figures for national income in the same year.

First, *in the poor countries a much larger percentage of the population is poor.* Poverty is the way of life for the overwhelming majority.

Second, *in the poor countries the gap between poor and rich is often larger than in the rich countries.* Inequalities in income distribution are often tremendous. Often there are unbelievable contrasts between the destitution of the masses and the conspicuous opulence of a tiny minority of privileged rich.

Third, *in the poor countries the poor are much poorer.* In countries such as Mexico and Tunis, to say nothing of India and Tanzania, millions of people live under conditions of deprivation and squalor that would be unthinkable among the poor in Western Europe or the United States, or even Israel. The rising levels of output and assets in the middling and rich countries have raised, and will continue to raise, the accepted conceptions of minimum living standards. As these countries progress on their path toward more and more affluence, not only will the numbers of the poor decrease, but the living conditions of the poor will unquestionably rise.

**Table 2.** *Distribution of World Population and Income, 1938–1961*

| Area | 1938 Percentage Distribution | | 1961 Percentage Distribution | | 1938–1961 Change in Percentage Distribution | |
|---|---|---|---|---|---|---|
| | popu-lation | in-come | popu-lation | in-come | popu-lation | in-come |
| **Rich:** | | | | | | |
| Overseas descendants of Western Europe | 7.1 | 29.6 | 7.3 | 41.3 | + 3 | +40 |
| Europe | 26.4 | 46.6 | 21.4 | 38.8 | −19 | −17 |
| Total | 33.5 | 76.2 | 28.7 | 80.1 | −14 | + 5 |
| **Poor:** | | | | | | |
| South and Central America | 6.0 | 4.2 | 7.0 | 4.7 | +17 | +12 |
| Asia | 53.2 | 17.3 | 56.9 | 13.1 | + 7 | −14 |
| Africa | 7.3 | 2.3 | 7.4 | 2.0 | + 1 | −13 |
| Total | 66.5 | 23.8 | 71.3 | 19.8 | + 7 | −12 |

SOURCE:  Table of similar title in Phyllis Deane, "The Long Term Trends in World Economic Growth," *Malayan Economic Review*, October, 1961, pp. 14–22, reprinted in Gerald M. Meier, *Leading Issues in Development Economics*, Oxford Unversity Press, Fair Lawn, N.J., 1964, p. 6.

Fourth, *the gap between the poor countries and the rich countries has tended to grow wider*. While the poor countries have made progress in recent years, the rich countries have progressed more rapidly. As Meier and Baldwin have pointed out, "International differences in per capita income are now absolutely greater, and probably also relatively greater, than they were a century ago. . . . We may broadly estimate that in the richest countries the rate of increase in national income is now about 25 percent to 30 percent every 10 years, whereas in poor countries it is generally less than 15 percent every 10 years." [4] This tendency is illustrated by the broad estimates in Table 2. Thus between 1938 and 1961 the countries roughly classified as rich declined by 14 percent in their proportion of world population but increased their proportion of world income by 5 percent. During this same period the United States, Australia, and other overseas descendants of Western Europe increased their population proportion slightly and their income share by 40 percent. South and Central America were the only poor areas to increase their income share, but their population share increased more rapidly in the same period. The largest increase in population share, along with the largest decrease in income share, took place in Asia.

## THE MYSTIQUE OF CENTURY SKIPPING

The present wealth of the rich countries has been the result of uneven and tortuous growth. The early Industrial Revolution was rooted in the innovating dynamism of the Renaissance, the Protestant ethic of the Reformation, the scientific spirit of the Enlightenment, and centuries of painful nation building. Modern science and technology, though now developing at an extremely rapid pace, have evolved through centuries of laborious pioneering. Modern institutions, from large corporations, and government agencies to banking systems and "multiversities," developed over many decades of trial, error, and accretion.

In the poor countries of Asia, Africa, the Middle East, and Latin America the political and intellectual leaders of today are committed to achieving similar results in a much shorter period. Most of them have in the past been exposed, at least temporarily, to the material benefits of industrialized societies: balanced diet, modern medical care, modern plumbing and sanitation facilities, decent clothing, higher education, and modern modes of travel and recreation. They want more of these for their own countries, not only for themselves, but for the masses living under devastating conditions of poverty, disease, and illiteracy. They have attained their positions of authority or prestige partly by offering bright visions of better living conditions. They have made great promises, rather vague at first but increasingly concrete. They know that if they fail to translate vision and promise into reasonable reality, they will be replaced. Hence the slow processes of change that brought economic development in the rich countries will not do. They are committed to "century skipping." The number of countries led by would-be century skippers is growing rapidly. By 1970 it will surely include nearly every poor country in the world.

For the century skippers national economic planning is the indispensable instrument of rapid change. Some may be committed to it because they believe in some form of socialism or Marxism and see planning as part of the Socialist or Marxist creed. Some see it as a way to build the public infrastructure for private enterprise. Many see in it an opportunity for the use of their technical skills or for personal advancement to national positions of power and prestige. For all, national economic plans and national economic planning agencies are invaluable symbols of rapid achievement in the future, symbols that are all the more valuable when the present is dismal and progress is slow. As stated by a former president of Venezuela, "Planning is the myth and mystique of our time. . . . Today, the thesis of state intervention in the economic processes, in order to channel and lead them toward goals of social betterment and national independence, constitutes the ABC of all modern Government policy." [5]

As the mystique of century skipping, national economic planning is based on the idea that *national government can and should assume and discharge certain responsibilities for the guidance of economic development.* This means that various agencies of national government must do, in a necessarily looser way, what the managers of any single organization do in trying to guide its future: (1) develop commitments to sequences of objectives, that is, commitments to future action, (2) activate people and groups to perform in accordance with these objectives, and (3) evaluate both objectives and performance as a basis for improved objectives and more effective activation.[6]

The central idea manifests itself in a great variety of forms. Different national governments assume greater or lesser degrees of responsibility. Their attitudes differ on the role and control of markets and of private government, of mixed and foreign enterprises. Often, indeed, the central idea is itself blurred by an overidentification of economic guidance with the more limited and technical processes involved in calculating possibilities for desirable objectives. This may detract attention not only from activation and evaluation but from the very process of *commitment* to objectives.

Despite the great variety of forms, however, there are certain common elements in the economic plans of all the century skippers. The would-be century skippers are frequently utopian planners. Impossible items, particularly in terms of the time span at first envisaged, often become embodied in their plans. This may help kindle the enthusiasm of the planners and even develop popular support, most markedly at the outset of planning endeavors. But as they got down to business in their planning activities, the utopianism tends to filter out. The planners soon learn that extravagant promises can boomerang.

The easiest plans to fulfill are those with exceedingly modest aims. Indeed, plan implementation can be guaranteed by setting one's sights at what is about to happen anyway. This has been called *epiphenomenal planning*.[7] At times, the century skippers are epiphenomenal planners. The inclusion of a few small items that are about to happen helps create the impression that progress is being made. This may help to counterbalance the disillusion resulting from the unrealizable promise of utopian planning.

Between these two extremes lies a broad stretch of planning for objectives that can be attained only by tremendous effort and with considerable luck; they are possible but not highly probable. This kind of planning may be called *planning the improbable*. For the most part, the would-be century skippers are planners of the improbable. Rather than be misled by wild dreams or blandly accept the slow pace of the most probable, they seek to perform modern miracles by trying to achieve objectives of tremendous difficulty.

## ECONOMIC PLANNING MORE THAN ECONOMICS

Because their plans deal primarily with *economic* activities, they invariably focus attention upon economics, economic planning agencies, and the services of economists and econometricians. It is often taken for granted that economic development is a process to be analyzed by the tools of economics alone. It is widely assumed that economists must be the master minds in century skipping.

This concentration upon economics and economists has had many interesting effects:

First of all, it has greatly oversimplified the processes of change. By focusing attention on economic factors, it has detracted attention from the institutional, political, and cultural obstacles to change. It has diverted attention from the noneconomic or transeconomic objectives that are sought through economic development. Thus, a bleak air of unreality hovers over many serious discussions of economic development. By some mysterious form of common consent the texts of plans and treatises are watered down to exclude many critical variables and issues that cannot be expressed in the language of economics.

Secondly, this economic orientation has been of tremendous benefit to economists and economics. It has provided economists with previously unprecedented access to influential leaders and groups. It has promoted the training of more economists. It has brought economists away from the make-believe world of "perfect competition" and prompt marginal utilities into closer contact with real-life problems of public policy. It has enabled modern economists to free themselves of the limitations of Keynesianism (now properly regarded as somewhat old-fashioned) and to initiate new and imaginative inquiries into the economics of development and growth.[8]

Thirdly, it has led more and more of the best economists to the difficult conclusion that *economics alone, no matter how much it is broadened, cannot provide an adequate understanding of economic development.* Thus, in recent writings on economic development, we find such statements as these:

By Edward S. Mason:[9]

> The class composition of the population and divergent geographical interests will inevitably affect the character of the plan. All this does not mean, however, that democratic planning must inevitably be an economically irrational compromise of divergent political interests. But it does mean that the economic calculus operates within a fairly severe set of limitations. From the point of view of development, it is the economics of the second best, and the fourth best, that is the real concern of the planner.

By John P. Lewis:[10]

> Despite the contentions of economics textbooks, consumption is not the end purpose of human existence, and the Indians do not regard it as such. . . . On balance, it would be better for us to think of Indian development as an essentially political phenomenon requiring major economic implementation than to put the matter the other way around.

By Everett E. Hagen:[11]

> If we observe the process of change, we may be able to note the repercussions among personality, culture and social structure that deter change as well as the forces causing it. . . . Economic theory has rather little to offer toward an explanation of economic growth, and . . . broader social and psychological considerations are pertinent.

By Albert O. Hirschman:[12]

> When economists build models of growth, they typically do not give explicit independent roles to the ability or motivation to solve problems of public policy.

In keeping with this recognition of the noneconomic aspects of economic planning, Mason has surveyed the role of government and political leadership in promoting economic develop- ent. Lewis has analyzed important problems in public admin- istration as they bear on economic planning. Hagen has studied the role of innovational personalities as they bear on the initiation of modernization. Hirschman has reviewed economic develop- ment in terms of strategies of "reform mongers" and their opponents. In addition, Neil W. Chamberlain has used concepts from his previous work in business administration and collective bargaining to interpret national planning as the management of national assets.[13] Charles Lindblom has exploited some of the best ideas in political science in analyzing the mutual-adjustment decision making which is inevitable in large-scale planning.[14]

With no particular stimulus from the economists, political sci- entists have also moved into the study of guided processes of modernization in developing nations. A major force in this di- rection has been the Social Science Research Council's Committee on Comparative Politics. Its work has led to such important vol- umes as *The Politics of Developing Areas,* edited by Almond and Coleman,[15] *Communications and Political Development,* edited by Pye,[16] and *Bureaucracy and Political Development,* edited by LaPalombara.[17]

Another major force has been the Comparative Administration group of the American Society for Public Administration. The work of Fred W. Riggs, as illustrated by his *Administration in Developing Countries,*[18] has stimulated renewed interest in the exploitation of ideas from sociology and anthropology. The group itself has brought forth an important series of publications.

Although the bulk of its work has centered around the social and political background of guided economic change, the Com- parative Administration Group has also decided to deal directly with national economic planning. For this purpose discussions were opened with the Maxwell School, where a series of separate studies on national planning in many countries had been under- taken as a preliminary to subsequent comparative analysis.[19] It was decided to enlist some of the authors of these country studies in a probe of national planning processes. Thus this volume came into being.

## THE WEB OF IMPLEMENTATION

The authors of this volume started with the deceptively simple question "What can national leaders and administrators do to convert economic development plans into reality?" We soon reached agreement on the proposition (stated in the first paragraph of Chapter 7, "Activating National Plans") that "The problem of implementing plans in any country at any particular period is always a unique problem. . . ." We then set ourselves the task of identifying the many variables that combine in myriad ways to produce the unique characteristics of specific countries. This led us far beyond the original question. We found that in order to address ourselves to plan implementation, we must also deal with plan formulation. On the one hand, the nature of the formulation process is often a major factor in implementation. On the other hand, as Peter J. D. Wiles succeeded in convincing most of us, many plans may be highly undesirable; their implementation may impede economic development, and their failure may be helpful. Accordingly, in order to deal more effectively with the process of implementation, we restated the original question in terms as broad as "What are the major factors involved in the formulation and implementation of national development plans?"

One of the greatest dangers in any effort to study plan implementation is the use of routinized, oversimplified analysis along narrow channels of traditional thought. Indeed, such conventional approaches to the subject have led to serious misconceptions concerning the entire planning process. Among the most misleading—and hence the most dangerous—of these are the "seven sins" of ignoring the institutional context in which planning decisions are made, failing to appreciate the significance of the cultural context, failing to consider relations with the biophysical environment, irrationally assuming that perfectly rational planning is possible, positing some simplistic relation between national planning and social and political freedoms, assuming that controls and propaganda can be enough to get plans implemented, and neglecting the need to develop the capacities of the national planners themselves. Apart from whatever positive virtues they may promote, the seven chapters in Part 1, "The Web of Implementation," may at least help national planners avoid these sins of omission.

In Chapter 2, "The Institutional Context," John Friedmann discusses the "style" of development planning in seven Latin-American countries: Argentina, Brazil, Chile, Columbia, Mexico, Uruguay, and Venezuela. The feasibility of development plans in these countries is directly affected by certain institutional factors peculiar to their transitional-modern reconciliation systems (TMR). The attempt to adapt rationally to these factors results in planning that tends to be "fragmented, focused, short-range, . . . little-coordinated." Increased capacity for rational choice, he suggests, requires action to enlarge the area of stable consensus, strengthen public administration, reduce vulnerability to external market fluctuations, and develop effective central planning agencies. To this end he would greatly encourage communication between divergent groups and improved information processes.

In Chapter 3, "The Cultural Context," Fred G. Burke identifies a profound dilemma facing the national planners of the new African states. Being in most cases also the leaders in the so-recent struggle for independence, they have promised to achieve Western-style political freedom and economic well-being while simultaneously trying to satisfy demands for racial equality and cultural continuity. While most acute in Africa today, this dilemma is everywhere inherent in developmental planning. Each individual culture, of course, is the product of its own unique history and environment, but there are, in general, very far-reaching differences between Western-type cultural elements and those prevailing in the various African states. And since "national planning and its operative administrative institutions are themselves aspects of Western culture currently being diffused throughout Africa," it becomes imperative to study those elements in African daily life and traditions which affect most directly, and are most affected by, the needs of national planning. Some of the more resistant elements of traditional culture, such as the cyclic concept of time, the unspecialized nature of social organization, "with authority tending to cluster about the elders," the frequent preference for nonnational techniques, and the more limited cognitive range, come into inevitable conflict with their counterparts in the borrowed Western culture. Burke concludes that such cultural conflict must be recognized "as a major variable affecting national planning" and calls for "bold and innovative research in this neglected area."

In Chapter 4, "The Biophysical Environment," Lynton K. Caldwell maintains that we are in danger of incurring great damage in the future through the injudicious manipulation of our biophysical environment. Many of our currently serious problems are the result of insufficient, faulty, or misguided planning with respect to natural resources. There is an enormous lag between man's increasing ability to affect swift and massive changes and his understanding of the marvelously complicated ecological relationships that are involved.

Caldwell feels that national planning agencies have shirked their responsibility to study the biophysical ramifications of their work and to assemble a solid body of meaningful, hard knowledge. They have based their decisions on more easily quantifiable economic criteria and done very little research. He strongly recommends reversing this trend and feels that a national planning agency should serve as a clearinghouse for the great diversity of research pertaining to national development and environmental relationships. He further notes that international organizations must play a very active role, since no one agency or even country can mount a sufficiently large program to "cover all aspects of environmental relationships in which research is needed."

In Chapter 5, "The Limitations of 'Perfect Planning,'" Zygmunt Bauman presents briefly the basic requirements that have to be met if "perfect planning" is to be achieved. The most crucial ones are resource self-sufficiency, perfect access to all information by the planning agent, perfect rationality of the planners, no serious conflicts of interest in the society, and perfect hierarchic control by the planners. It seems quite clear, therefore, why perfect planning has not so far been achieved in any known social system. Moreover, when attempts have been made to achieve such perfect planning in a society that does not conform fully to the model, the result has only been to expose the limitations on effective planning that are inherent in that society.

Using the experiences of Polish planning as background material, Bauman describes the most important of these limitations: dependence on international trade (which is beyond the planners' power); priority of consumption goals; heterogeneity of interests in goal formulation (which includes conflict between collective and individual consumption); the contradictions between the requirements of goal formulating and the conditions of efficient goal attainment. The last problem, moreover, exists on three levels: the first level, or the area of macroeconomic decisions, is left entirely in the hands of the central planning agency; the so-called "middle level" decisions, which involve the enterprise, and the lowest level, that of the individual, are exceedingly complex, with any number of possible answers along a continuum of "manipulation by punishment" to "manipulation by reward." Finally, Bauman points out, "when economic growth is the sole guide in the decision-making process, the planners are likely very soon to be lost. . . ."

In Chapter 6, "Economic Activation, Economic Planning, and the Social Order," Peter J. D. Wiles scrutinizes the four economic planning models that are present, to varying degrees, in all political systems: free market (FM); regulated market (RM); joint initiative (JI); and central initiative (CI). They all use many private activators, both economic and "psychological," as well as "direct" and "indirect public activators," but these activators are all inefficient and limited to an appreciable extent. They can never, therefore, be the criteria for making planning decisions but only, hopefully, "stimuli for carrying them out."

Wiles takes the national planners in a CI economy step by step through their efforts to achieve an effective blueprint and assure its realistic implementation. The problems start with the drawing-up stage, become more acute in the centralization-decentralization struggle (with its subdivision of region versus enterprise), progress through the difficulties of the microrational allocation of resources from the top, and proliferate in the details of actual blueprint fulfillment. At each step, the solutions for one problem raise new ones in the next with "very likely a conflict between . . . two sets of activators. . . ." Wiles concentrates on the Soviet Bloc, which depends almost entirely on CI, but also refers to other attempted solutions drawn from various political systems.

Moreover, Wiles concludes, the command economy, in trying to achieve and enforce a coordinated economic blueprint, "is incompatible with the rule of law in the economic field." One of the results has been a large amount of blueprint evasion, or *economic crime*, as distinguished from such ordinary economic crimes as graft or theft, which occur everywhere. But far more serious, "no government dedicated to the command economy attempts to grant or preserve social freedom. . . ." However, he hopefully concludes that "nearly always when such governments slightly relax their grip in one field, they do so also in the other."

In Chapter 7, "Activating National Plans," I concentrate on the strategies of implementation. "Activating" is presented as interwoven into the seamless web of planning, activating, and evaluating. The obstacles to activation are varied. They include deficiencies in physical, human, and institutional resources, resistance and apathy, and defects in the planners' own approaches to planning, activating, and evaluating. I then discuss the necessity of building an "activation base" through the support of organized groups and unorganized opinions and attitudes. This leads to the desirability of a varying "activation mix," that is, a mixture of methods of wielding influence. A successful activation mix will usually include changing proportions of such different methods of persuasion, pressure, and promotion of self-activation. Since, in any case, complete victory for the planners is rather rare, implementation tends to be a stream of successive compromises punctuated by frequent instances of avoidance or deadlock, with occasional victories, defeats, and "integrations." Effective implementation, particularly where the obstacles are significant, requires the development of campaign strategies to exploit crisis situations, achieve proper timing, and maintain a "positive stance."

In these chapters of Part 1 it is blandly assumed that the national planners themselves have the personal capacity to take institutional, cultural, and biophysical variables into account, to understand the limitations of perfect planning, to use economic incentives without damaging the social order, and to develop effective campaign strategies. Chapter 8, "The Development of National Planning Personnel," brushes aside this assumption. Without belaboring the ignorance, stupidity, or questionable motives of planners they have known in real life, the authors insist that the Emperor very often has no clothes. The theme is that "The planners too must learn." Indeed, the "myth of infallibility and omniscience on the part of the people at the top may produce stultification and routinization throughout the lower levels. Too many national planning agencies think that the only people to be educated on the intricacies of plan formulation and implementation are junior technicians, but the authors feel that the "learners" should include senior specialists, group leaders, top executives, and even political leaders and interest-group leaders.

The substance of the learning process, moreover, should not be limited to traditional economic concepts. They should include the multidimensional analysis of planning and implementation problems, the uses and limitations of various specialized techniques, and the arts of conflict management. The specific educational methods must be adjusted to the requirements of individual areas and regions. Special consideration should be given in all parts of the world to problem-oriented workshops, seminars on the social system of a country or region, and conferences on social (as distinguished from economic) accounting. The various proposals in Chapter 8 were prepared not in an ivory tower but only after detailed discussion with experienced planners.

## VISTAS FOR RESEARCH AND THEORY

The authors of the first seven chapters in Part I are far from satisfied with the conclusions we have reached. Without exception,

we feel there is a serious need for more empirically based generalizations concerning the national planning process. Apart from
our personal research plans, we feel it desirable to promote the
formulation, testing, and reformulation of such generalizations
not only in economics but in administration, political science,
sociology, social psychology, anthropology, and history, as well.

But to present a master plan for research or a grand strategy
for theory building would be both utopian and presumptious.
The study of planning by social scientists is certainly high on the
list of things that cannot be comprehensively planned—at least,
not if one is at all concerned with implementation as well as with
rosy visions.

Accordingly, in attempting to influence the plans of other social
scientists, we have limited ourselves to the more modest task of
suggesting certain basic concepts and asking certain fundamental
questions.   This is done in the three chapters of Part 2, "Vistas
for Research and Theory."

To see these concepts and questions in proper perspective, let
us examine briefly the major currents of past social science involvement in this field.

### Ideology, Econometrics, and Empiricism

There have been three major currents in the literature on national planning:

The first has been ideological debate.   This was sparked by
Russia's initiation of the first Five-Year Plan in the mid-1920s.
National economic planning soon became identified with the
image of what the Russians were doing. This image, for both
supporters and opponents, usually included tight central control
and widespread nationalization or collectivization. During the
Great Depression of 1929–1939 not only Communists but many
progressives and socialists, as well, advocated Russian-style planning as the solution to sustained mass unemployment. This led
to a widespread debate on the "grand alternatives" of planning
versus *laissez faire* and socialism versus capitalism. During
World War II, as "capitalist" countries resorted to highly centralized wartime planning, the debate eased temporarily. As the
end of the war neared and decisions had to be made on the dis-

mantling or continuation of wartime economic planning, the debate became acute again. It probably reached its height with the attack of Hayek [20] and Von Mises [21] on any form of national economic planning as the "road to serfdom" and the sharp rebuttals by Finer [22] and Wootton.[23] The arguments on both sides were distinguished by their speculative nature and their looseness of connection between conclusions reached and behavior actually observed under any given system of national economic planning.

The second current is econometric technique. This got under way after World War II as attention shifted from debates based on a single, oversimplified style of planning to hard work on calculational tools to be used in many styles of planning The political scientists and philosophers left the scene, at least temporarily. The economists, building upon the order foundations of national economic accounting, made great advances in input-output analysis, linear programming, and computerized econometric models. One of the great by-products stemming from the use of these tools has been the escape from sterile ideologies concerning social and economic systems. In France, for example, the use of econometric projections of national growth has facilitated pragmatic and creative planning based on new forms of cooperation among key interest groups. In all the Western democracies, indeed, econometrics has made it easier for government officials to develop new forms of planning without being regarded as Socialists or Communists. In the Communist countries, econometrics has made it easier for planners to use price systems and profit calculations without being branded as agents of capitalism. These advantages, however, all stemmed from a concentration on presumably neutral techniques and a studied avoidance of the social, administrative, and political problems involved in making decisions on proposed plans and taking action to implement them.

A third current, empirical analysis, is now slowly forming. Although econometric technique is still highly valued (and indeed is receiving increasing rather than decreasing attention), the period of "oversell" is probably drawing to a close. There is increasing awareness that just as it takes more than a good economist or accountant to run a business, much more than economic calculation is required to guide an economy. Economists themselves are beginning to deal directly, albeit gingerly, with noneconomic factors in economic growth and development. Above all, they are beginning to examine the actual experience of various countries under various forms of national economic planning. A few scholars from other fields have joined in this fact-oriented exploration. We already have the beginning of a segnificant body of empirical analysis in the already published writings [24] of Bauchet, Hackett and Hackett, and Sheahan on France; Balassa on Hungary; Montias on Poland; Nove and Bergson on Russia; Lewis on India; Walinsky on Burma; Hirschman on Latin-American countries; Hagen and Waterston on various parts of the world; and Wiles on the Communist countries as a whole. While few of these studies go as deeply into the realities of bureaucratic life under planning as Devons's classic *Planning in Practice*, Hirschman's *Journeys toward Progress* has opened up the entire field of real-life planners' strategy. Wiles's *The Political Economy of Communism* has not only transcended economic analysis at many points but has also produced the first example of a genuinely comparative study of planning systems at different periods in time and in different countries. Scores of special studies in many countries are at the point of completion, under way, or getting started. By 1970, with the number of published studies probably more than tripling and a significant increase in comparative approaches, we should have a sizeable body of empirical literature in this field.

## Concepts and Questions

"What is national planning?"

This is an explosive question. The term *planning* is surrounded by so many emotional overtones that many people are afraid to ask it. They therefore answer it implicitly rather than explicitly. Even a cursory examination of the writings in the three currents referred to above will reveal that many of the debates in the field are cross-purpose arguments in which, no matter how they may feel about substance, people tend to use the term *planning* to refer to a great variety of activities.

"What should we try to learn about national planning? This

question is asked even less frequently. Too many researchers and theorists operate in well-worn routinized paths, seeking slightly new answers to old questions and investing too little energy in asking new questions.

In Chapter 9, "What Is National Planning?", Robert J. Shafer and his committee provide a certain kind of answer to the first question, one that also has profound implications for the second question. First of all, they define planning in general as "a process of formulating goals and developing commitments to attaining them . . . a process of intended adaptive rationality . . . usually intermingled with behavior which is spontaneous, inadvertent, or random or behavior which is directed by habit, tradition, previous decision, or external pressure." Indeed, six discrete propositions are used in this general definition. This is a far cry from the simplistic approaches that try to identify the phenomenon of planning in terms of a single phrase that "tells all."

Attention is then focused on national planning specifically, as distinguished from planning by individuals and organizations. This requires nine propositions, some of them rather complex. The heart of the approach is to identify national planning as "an effort through central planning institutions to promote or coordinate the activities of (a) intermediate bodies . . . (b) operating units. . . ." Still more important, the point is made that national economic planning always consists of efforts by these central planning institutions to develop some combination of aggregate, cross-sectoral, sectoral or subsectoral, enterprise, and spatial planning. Each of these five components is itself defined. Other variables that differentiate national planning in different countries are also identified. One of the most important propositions states that "many of the conscious objectives and unintended consequences, as well as many of the means required for goal formulation, implementation, and evaluation, are usually political, cultural, social, or biophysical rather than merely economic."

Finally, Shafer and his committee state that "In any country, national planning functions are performed by a variety of institutions rather than by a single agency. The subsequent propositions identify some of these functions and indicate that they "are usually institutionalized in different ways in response to the conditions prevailing in different societies."

This starting-point concept of national planning is then used by Peter J. D. Wiles and Michel Crozier in formulating a wide-ranging and profound set of questions.

In Chapter 10, "Some Fundamental Questions on National Planning," Peter J. D. Wiles and his committee break loose from the tight traditions of customary inquiry in this field. "Question propounding," they point out, is more important than "answer giving," particularly in a field where government officials are apt to focus too much attention on short-range technical matters. The questions they formulate cover five major categories of information: the social framework, goal formulation, decision making, implementation, and results. The questions on implementation cover the areas of activators and sanctions, campaigns, the obstacles to implementation, and correcting mechanisms. The questions on results cover goals, side effects, and the evaluation of both. Among the most probing of all the questions are those dealing with the impact of national planning upon the "rule of law," the Constitution, and politically guaranteed freedoms.

In Chapter 11, "Attitudes and Beliefs on National Planning," Michel Crozier and his committee deal with an area of inquiry only barely hinted at in the previous chapter. "National leaders and plan administrators," they point out, ". . . take special pride in their intuitive sensitivity to divergent and changing attitudes and beliefs as they are affected by specific plans." Yet there has been little effort to study these attitudes and beliefs explicitly. Accordingly, Crozier and his committee propose the kind of questions that "could form the basis for formal surveys in particular societies over time or in different societies at the same time." The first set of questions deals with the images people have of central government planning or policy making, including their perception of their own personal involvement and their judgments concerning the value of the plans. They then deal with the attitudes of people toward space, time, change, and social action. The sets of questions deal with attitudes of people toward social structure and conflict management. "The capabilities of a society to manage conflict," they point out, "constitute a boundary condition for the success of planning. . . . Since planning entails making decisions about conflicting interests, planners must learn to work with whatever types of conflict regulation are acceptable to, or can be learned by, those concerned." The questions propounded in this area, let it be stressed, have a significance far beyond their possible use in formal attitude and opinion surveys. Indeed, the authors wisely suggest that the "personal radar sets" of plan administrators "be tuned in to questions of this type."

At first glance it would seem that both the concepts set forth in Chapter 9 and the questions suggested in Chapters 10 and 11 are directed entirely toward the current of empirical analysis. Certainly, all the authors have been engaged in empirical studies of national planning and are committed to the extension of this approach. Nevertheless, this orientation is far from antagonistic to the current of econometric technique. The maturation of technique certainly requires more empirical research linking the *should be* of prescriptive decision making with the *was* and *is* of empirical observation. Indeed, with the broadening of planning theory to include noneconomic variables, it might be possible to broaden econometric models into sociometric models dealing with the structure and performance of the societies which national planners hope to change. Moreover, both the concepts and the questions utterly reject the ultrapositivist, pseudoscientific idea that national planning can be really understood in isolation from basic human values and moral standards. They thus touch upon many of the issues that have been involved in the earlier currents of ideological debate. We may yet see new and more fruitful debates on the human values that are served or betrayed by the actions of national governments committed to the guidance of major national change.

## APPLYING RESEARCH AND THEORY

A clear orientation toward *basic* research and theory is evident in both Part 1 and Part 2. How do we reconcile this with our avowed interest in action under planning?

If we are really interested in action to help developing nations escape the clutch of poverty, why have we not gone in for *applied* research and theory?

Our answer is absurdly simple:

Because of our interest in action, not merely in paper plans, we believe it essential to develop concepts, generalizations, and techniques that are *worth applying*.

We are convinced that only basic research and theory on national planning can provide the intellectual impetus and the tools for more useful applied research in more countries and on more aspects of planned economic development than has been possible until now. We are thus hopeful that this volume may contribute toward imaginative and far-reaching efforts to use social science more effectively in the service of human needs.

### NOTES

[1] This concept of poverty has been developed in close cooperation with S. M. Miller, of Syracuse University's sociology department, in the course of a graduate seminar on national planning against poverty in the United States. It represents a radical departure from the currently accepted definitions of poverty, most of which define poverty in terms of deviation from some minimum level of personal or family income. Thus the entire analysis of poverty in James N. Morgan et al., *Income and Welfare in the United States*, McGraw-Hill Book Company, New York, 1962, revolves around the idea of "poverty lines" and minimum budgets expressed solely in terms of monthly or annual income. A shift to the three-dimensional view of living standards in terms of assets, income, and public services would mean many significant changes in public policy with respect to welfare, social security, and antipoverty programs. It would also require a more sophisticated approach to data collection and the use of qualitative information.

[2] *Gross disposable income*, the best measure of income poverty, may best be defined as total money and nonmoney income after income taxes. For alternative definitions see James N. Morgan et al., *Income and Welfare in the United States*, McGraw-Hill Book Company, New York, 1962, p. 500.

[3] As pointed out by Oskar Morganstern in *The Accuracy of Economic Observations*, rev. ed., Princeton University Press, Princeton, N.J., 1963, particularly pp. 242–282, there are three general sources of inaccuracy in all national product and income statistics: (1) inadequate basic data, (2) improper fitting of the data to the concepts, and (3) the use of interpolation and imputation to fill gaps. Even with the data of the statistically most ad-

vanced countries, such as the United States and Britain, the weighted margin of error for such estimates may be estimated as ranging from 10 to 20 percent. In the poor countries, with less developed statistical devices, the margins of error are much greater. Also, the economists' market measures are not geared to dealing properly with the levels of economic activity in nonmonetized peasant agriculture or in the provision of nonmarketed government services, both of which loom large in most poor countries. Finally, international comparisons are impaired by the arbitrary calculations involved in converting formal exchange rates of various currencies into a common currency.

[4] Gerald M. Meier and Robert E. Baldwin, *Economic Development*, John Wiley & Sons, Inc., New York, 1957, p. 10.

[5] Romulo Betancourt, *Venezuela, Politica y Petroleo*, Fondo de Cultura Economica, 1962, p. 311.

[6] The definition herein presented is very close in spirit to the concepts presented in Chap. 9, "What Is National Planning?"

[7] The term *epiphenomenal planning* was introduced by Peter J. D. Wiles in his *The Political Economy of Communism*, Harvard University Press, Cambridge, Mass., 1963, pp. 72–75. See also Chap. 6.

[8] The range of new thinking embodied in the economics of development and growth is well illustrated in the excerpts from dozens of writers in Gerald M. Meier, *Leading Issues in Development Economics*, Oxford University Press, Fair Lawn, N.J., 1964.

[9] Edward S. Mason, *Economic Planning in Underdeveloped Areas*, Fordham University Press, New York, 1958, p. 66.

[10] John P. Lewis, *Quiet Crisis in India*, The Brookings Institution, Washington, D.C., 1962, p. 11.

[11] Everett E. Hagen, *On the Theory of Social Change*, Dorsey, Richard D. Irwin, Inc., Homewood, Ill., 1962.

[12] Albert O. Hirschman, *Journeys toward Progress: Studies of Economic Policy Making in Latin America*, The Twentieth Century Fund, New York, 1963.

[13] Neil W. Chamberlain, *Private and Public Planning*, McGraw-Hill Book Company, New York, 1966.

[14] Charles Lindblom, "Economics and the Administration of Planning," *Public Administration Review*, December, 1965, pp. 274–283.

[15] Gabriel Almond and James S. Coleman (eds.), *The Politics of Developing Areas*, Princeton University Press, Princeton, N.J., 1960.

[16] Lucian Pye (ed.), *Communication and Political Development*, Princeton University Press, Princeton, N.J., 1963.

[17] Joseph LaPalombara (ed.), *Bureaucracy and Political Development*, Princeton University Press, Princeton, N.J., 1963.

[18] Fred W. Riggs, *Administration in Developing Countries*, Houghton Mifflin Company, Boston, 1964.

[19] This is the National Planning Series of the Syracuse University Press, Syracuse, N.Y. Already published are John Friedmann, *Venezuela: From*

*Doctrine to Dialogue;* Douglas E. Ashford, *Morocco-Tunisia: Politics and Planning;* Fred G. Burke, *Tanganyika: Preplanning;* Robert J. Shafer, *Mexico: Mutual Adjustment Planning;* Benjamin Akzin and Yehezkel Dror, *Israel: High-Pressure Planning;* Everett E. Hagen and Stephanie F. T. White, *Great Britain: Quiet Revolution in Planning;* and Joseph LaPalombara, *Italy: The Politics of Planning.*

[20] Friedrich A. Von Hayek, *The Road to Serfdom,* The University of Chicago Press, Chicago, 1944.

[21] Ludwig Von Mises, *Planned Chaos,* Foundation for Economic Education, New York, 1947.

[22] Herman Finer, *Road to Reaction,* Little, Brown and Company, Boston, 1946.

[23] Barbara Wootton, *Freedom under Planning,* The University of North Carolina Press, Chapel Hill, N.C., 1945.

[24] Bibliographical references to the writers mentioned:

M. Bauchet, *Economic Planning, the French Experience,* William Heinemann, Ltd., London, 1964.

John Hackett and Anne-Marie Hackett, *Economic Planning in France,* Harvard University Press, Cambridge, Mass., 1963.

John Sheahan, *Promotion and Control of Industry in Postwar France,* Harvard University Press, Cambridge, Mass., 1963.

Bela Balassa, *The Hungarian Experience in Economic Planning,* Yale University Press, New Haven, Conn., 1959.

John M. Montias, *Central Planning in Poland,* Yale University Press, New Haven, Conn., 1962.

Alec Nove, *The Soviet Economy,* Frederick A. Praeger, Inc., New York, 1961.

Abram Bergson, *The Economics of Soviet Planning,* Yale University Press, New Haven, Conn., 1964.

Lewis, *op. cit.*

Louis J. Walinsky, *Economic Development in Burma, 1951–60,* The Twentieth Century Fund, New York, 1963.

Hirschman, *op. cit.*

Everett E. Hagen (ed.), *Planning Economic Development,* Richard D. Irwin, Inc., Homewood, Ill., 1963.

Albert Waterston, *Planning in Pakistan: Organization and Implementation* and *Planning in Morocco: Organization and Implementation,* both published by The Johns Hopkins Press, Baltimore, 1962, and *Development Planning: Lessons of Experience,* The Johns Hopkins Press, Baltimore, 1965.

Wiles, *op. cit.*

Ely Devons, *Planning in Practice,* Cambridge University Press, London, 1950.

PART 1

# The Web of Implementation

# 2

# *The Institutional Context*

## *John Friedmann*[1]

This chapter is concerned with the variety of institutional forms of national planning decisions. By planning decisions I mean decisions of the central government which are concerned with the management of the economy. Here I shall deal with only non-routine decisions of this kind. To the extent that means-ends relations are considered within a broad context of relevant information, such decisions can also be said to strive for rationality.

To facilitate analysis, the general form of a decision can be isolated from its specific content. This makes it possible to speak of policy or program decisions or of decisions leading, for example, to long-term commitments. There are many ways of describing the general form of planning decisions. One way is to look at the institutional forms which evolve out of the adaptation of planning decisions to the circumstances that prevail when the decision is taken. I shall refer to this set of relevant circumstances as the *environment for decision.*

## THE ENVIRONMENT FOR DECISION

This environment may be described quite concretely; ultimately, however, it refers to characteristic conditions of choice

31

behavior such as the relative ignorance of the deciders, the extent of their uncertainty about the future, the number of relevant interests and the need for reconciling them, and the ability of the deciders to influence the decisions (and actions) of others. At an appropriate level of generality, these conditions describe the social context of decisions.

When I abstract from the concrete environment of a particular decision to the environment for *all* innovating decisions within a given society, it is possible to show that the decision environment maintains considerable stability over time. As a result, planning-decision behavior becomes institutionally adapted to the structural characteristics of the environment. Since different social systems can be expected to vary according to the measure of ignorance, uncertainty, goal conflict, etc., that are typically encountered in planning situations, I shall expect to find a distinctive *style of national planning* in every society. The second part of this chapter is an exploration of the national planning style of a group of roughly similar Latin-American countries.

What is the wider significance of this subject? To start with, its importance derives from the observation that the manner of deciding will influence what it is that one *can* decide and thus is bound to influence the results of the decision. Where a variety of different interests must be laboriously reconciled through a drawn-out bargaining procedure, for instance, the outcome may be quite different from situations where a single will can be imposed by force. The current debate on the merits of competing planning systems in generating and sustaining rapid economic growth turns on this very issue.

In the second place, technical planners will benefit from becoming more fully aware of the relation between decisions and their environment. Where this leads to a more precise perception of the existing social capacity for rational action, it will be of immense value in the design of optimal planning systems. It will also be helpful in the design and evaluation of program proposals. The "best" proposal will always be one which in the accomplishment of ends, and in the very setting of them, takes full cognizance of the social context. Any tax scheme, no matter how justified it may be on theoretical grounds, will fail unless it is adapted to the capacity and efficiency of the revenue collection system. Agricultural programs must be tailored to the number and technical competence of available agricultural experts, irrespective of theoretically desired "balances" in the allocation of resources. Central aggregate planning linked to a system of direct controls is likely to yield suboptimal results in the United States. The "best" decision is always a feasible decision. Rationality is "bounded."[2]

Finally, the present study claims to have theoretical relevance. Many theorists of planning fail to take the feasibility of decisions into account. They operate with what Charles E. Lindblom has called a model of "synoptic" decision making in which the ends are given, all alternative courses of action are considered together with all their consequences, and an optimal solution is obtained on the basis of a simple preference function.[3] Operations research, while becoming ever more subtle in its application, is nevertheless closely adhering to the synoptic model of rationality.[4] Economic planners are equally prone to use it as a criterion for choice.[5]

Braybrooke and Lindblom[6] have criticized this model on the grounds that the synoptic ideal is not adapted to:

1. Man's limited problem-solving capacities
2. The inadequacy of information
3. The costliness of analysis
4. The absence of a satisfactory evaluative method (whether a rational-deductive system, a welfare function, or some other)
5. The closeness of the observed relationships between fact and value in policy making
6. The openness of the system variables with which it contends
7. The analyst's need for strategic sequences of analytical moves
8. The diverse forms in which policy problems actually arise

In response to these limitations, Lindblom proposes a decision model of "disjointed incrementalism." Although it is intended to be more realistic than the synoptic ideal, it appears to assume that the conditions which, in practice, limit the usefulness of this idea are universally present and do not substantially vary among social systems. Nowhere, to my knowledge, is this assumption treated explicitly in Lindblom's writings. But by making the contrary assumption, it may be possible to expand upon his original model. Accordingly, I shall assume that what I call the *social context of planning decisions* is significantly different among social systems. And since I shall further assume that the institutional form of planning decisions depends on defined characteristics of the decision environment, the following working hypothesis may be stated: *distinctive styles of national planning are associated with different combinations of system variables, including the level of economic development attained, the form of political organization, and historical tradition.* Before elaborating this hypothesis into a general model for research, further comment is necessary on the type of decision with which this chapter is concerned.

### Blueprints and Planning

Planning is often defined as the making and carrying out of plans or blueprints. Planning decisions are, therefore, decisions about blueprints, and a central problem, from this standpoint, is how to get the subjects of planning to act in accordance with the blueprint.[7] The model of the planning process which underlies this formulation has been stated as involving five discrete steps: [8]

1. Surveying total system resources to discover where the main effort is required, to estimate its cost, and to envisage the alternative courses of action
2. Taking a general decision between these alternatives
3. Drawing up the program
4. Executing the program
5. Adjusting the program to changing circumstances

These steps may be reduced to the more simple form shown in Figure 1. According to this model, planning is regarded as a three-phased process involving (1) design, or plan making, (2) plan implementation, and (3) feedback. The central feature in the model is the *plan,* which will formally consist of one or more goal statements that are successively reduced to more specific policies, programs, and projects, all spaced out over a limited period of time, and related to sets of priorities, standards, investment needs, and financial arrangements.[9]

In a more elaborate view, the single plan—the "master plan"—is replaced by a series of tightly interlocking specialized plans. According to the United National Economic Commission for Latin America, a fully developed national planning system, backed by an adequate information process, should consist of at least five types of plan: [10]

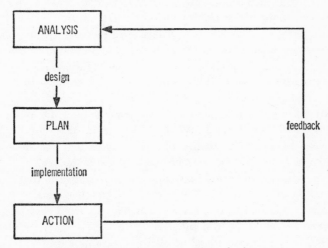

Figure 1. The blueprint model of planning.

1. General medium or long-range plans
2. General medium-term investment plans
3. Long-term financing plans
4. Annual plans (national budget)
5. Project plans

This concept of planning derives essentially from architecture and engineering, where planning refers primarily to the design of blueprints. The major difference of course, is that complex economic decisions cannot be carried out in precise detail, even if the government should resort to the massive application of force. There must be a regular process of *feedback* from the scene of action, so that both goals and programs may be periodically reassessed on the basis of new intelligence.

But the moment the notion of feedback is introduced, the blueprint ceases to be a stable set of goals and priorities for use as decision criteria. National economic blueprints, as a rule, are formally revised every few years. This is only a matter of convenience, however. In principle, reevaluation and reformulation of plan elements should be continuous, and that, more often than not, is precisely what happens. *But the continuously adjusting plan, the daily blueprint, is no longer a blueprint.*[11] Different from one moment to the next, it ceases to serve as an instrument of system guidance and becomes just one of a number of possible devices for recording decisions. The physical appearance of the continuously adjusting "blueprint" will be ephemeral—in the extreme instance, computer print-outs in a loose-leaf binding; conceptually, it will come close to being what Peter J. D. Wiles has called (and condemned as) *epiphenomenal planning.*[12] The time lag between the reality of performance and the blueprint will be compressed to a point of practical insignificance.

Experience with varied planning situations suggests that this is indeed the correct view. Not only is it in practice usually impossible to separate the process of plan making from that of plan implementation; a central planning agency may even be unable to produce a "current plan" to please a curious inquirer. There simply may not be a plan; the entire concept may be irrelevant to the specific planning operation.

Where, for instance, is the "general development plan" for the Tennessee Valley? Just out of the University of Chicago, I went to work for the Tennessee Valley Authority, which was then known the world over as engaged in one of the grandest experiments in regional planning. The shock was great, therefore, when I was unable to discover anywhere within the TVA at Knoxville even the semblance of a general plan for the region. Here then, I had to admit, was planning widely acknowledged as successful, yet without a plan. This finding was decisive for much of my subsequent thinking.

If this argument is accepted, the blueprint model of planning must be amended. Plan formulation and plan implementation tend to merge into a single process, synoptic documents are eschewed in favor of fragmented decisions, they are no longer an essential part of deciding and acting, the whole of planning becomes an extremely fluid, ambiguous, and indeterminate network of information flows. And the new model will read as shown in Figure 2. In this model, strategic information impinges directly on the stream of ongoing activities, providing signals that lead to incremental adjustments. The information consists, for the most part, of a systematic assessment of the future conditions and con-

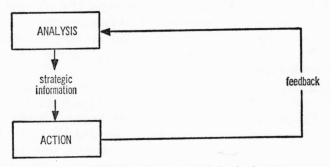

Figure 2. The informational model of planning.

sequences of action, of system-wide goals and objectives, and of the largest number of functional linkages among critical variables which are capable of being studied with the resources at hand. In this way, planning thought, understood as a form of seeking greater rationality, injects the inputs which allow a system to cope successfully with the future.

### Framework versus System

In the study of planning decisions, the viewpoint is decisive. One may regard planning decisions as constituting either a *framework for action* or a *system of action*. In the former sense, the technical, manifest functions of planning are emphasized; in the latter, its social functions. Though clearly not an absolute, this distinction is essential for understanding the influence of planning thought on the performance of the social system.

As a framework for action, planning provides information which acts as a constraint on decisions. In government, it provides essential criteria for implementing policy decisions, such as rules, instructions, and guidelines; it may also arrange for the exchange of information, periodic consultation, and review. To a large extent, this function requires specialized, trained competence. It is here, therefore, that the role of the technician in planning systems is most clearly apparent. It must also be recognized that wherever a planning process is formally initiated, it is done so usually to reap the benefits that are expected to result from the wider use of expertise: greater efficiency, coordination, and specific goal achievement. In its technical capacity, planning is supposed to work, to have a measurable and positive impact on the performance of the economy.

As a system of action, however, planning is merely an object of disinterested study for the social scientist. As such, it will be observed to carry out functions of an essentially social nature which stand in no necessary relation to its technical efficacy.[13] Depending on how they are organized, planning systems may strengthen the power of the chief executive, improve the political process, help create a new and more development-oriented mentality, assist in reducing social conflict, or aid in mobilizing external resources. Indeed, planning systems can also have significant dysfunctions, by contributing to the proliferation of an unwieldy bureaucratic apparatus, for instance, or by throttling individual initiative, or by reducing the ability of the system to respond effectively to change. Formal government planning, however, is frequently supported in practice precisely because it is thought to yield positive side effects, and for this, its technical accomplishments need not be high.

Although the study of the relationship between the technical and social functions of planning is an interesting subject, it does not concern me here. The immediate objective is to answer the question of how various institutional forms of planning are functionally related to action (the ongoing stream of activities). It specifically concerns the technical aspects of planning.

## A Model for Comparative Study

I referred earlier to the presumed existence of distinctive styles of national planning. My hypothesis was that these styles will be associated with differences in certain aspects of the decision environment and, further, that this environment will be structurally related to a smaller number of complex system variables as defined earlier. These relations may be set forth as shown in Figure 3. The model shows that planning decisions are expected to affect the system variables in two ways: directly (for instance, through helping to increase agricultural output) and indirectly (for instance, through substantial improvement in the performance of public administration as a part of the decision environment). The actual pattern of interaction is, of course, extremely

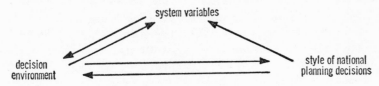

system variables

decision environment

style of national planning decisions

Figure 3. A model for comparative study.

complex: causality must be expressed as a series of feedback loops; some patterns are best treated as the result of stochastic processess; in short, there is no single valid explanation of a social phenomenon. We are still in search of promising hypotheses and possible correlations among the three elements in the model.

The style of national planning can also be studied in a single country, in full cognizance of its unique historical and geographical configurations. Studies so conducted not only may yield important insights into the national characteristics of planning but also suggest ideas of a more general nature. All this may be admitted. But it must also be recognized that such an approach will render cross-national comparisons immensely difficult. There are over one hundred nations in the world, and one would like to be able to make significant statements about the form of planning decisions in each one of them. The model set forth above has, in principle, predictive power: if the relationships I have suggested do, in fact, exist, the general style of planning can be predicted for any country on the basis of only a small number of system variables. In the second place, lack of prior agreement on the categories to be used in describing planning would be a serious obstacle to the transfer of knowledge from one national situation to another. A proper level of abstractions must be sought, close enough to reality to allow one to make significant distinctions in the study of social behavior, yet not so "earthy" as to preclude the possibility of information transfer to another social system.

The principal elements of a model for the cross-national study of planning decisions are given below. A number of caveats, however, must be entered at this point to prevent a possible misunderstanding. First, hypotheses linking the several elements of the model to each other are lacking, they must eventually be provided. Second, both the variables for classification and individual descriptive categories may be changed as a result of empirical study. They are not intended as a straitjacket. Third, each category, whether of the decision environment or of the form of planning decisions, needs to be exhaustively investigated in one or more countries for each class of social system identified. Only historical detail can bring the analysis to life. Fourth, in description, the categories will necessarily become blurred, just as system classifications, though seemingly discrete, in fact describe a continuity of characteristics. If these considerations are borne in mind, no difficulty should be experienced with the suggested approach.

### Major Elements of a Preliminary Model for Cross-national Research into the Institutional Forms of National Planning Decisions

1. *Criteria for classification of national systems*
    *a.* Level of economic-technological development
    *b.* Form of political organization
    *c.* Historical tradition (e.g., Latin-American, Soviet-type, former British colonies)

2. *Descriptive categories of aspects of the decision environment*
    a. Number and diversity of organized group interests; their influence on decisions in the "central guidance cluster" [14]
    b. Acceptance of, and catering to, political opposition
    c. Dependence of the economic system on private enterprise; characteristics of enterprise and entrepreneurial behavior
    d. Efficiency of the relevant information systems: capacity, load, reliability, promptness, secrecy, etc.
    e. Measures of bureaucratic status, professional competence, and reliability
    f. Predictability of change within the system and of external changes affecting its performance
3. *Aspects of the institutional form of national planning decisions*
    a. Distribution of capabilities for planning throughout the system
    b. Extent and forms of government involvement in total system activity
    c. Scope and comprehensiveness of planning activity
    d. Relevant time horizons used
    e. Degree of system-wide coordination of innovating activities
    f. Types and distribution of activators being used to obtain results: persuading, pressuring, promoting self-activation [15]
    g. Specificity of goal formulation

### Applying the Model to Latin America

In the foregoing model, system variables are used in the classification of countries as the initial step in the analysis. The first system variable is a measure of economic-technological development achieved. This suggests dividing countries into three broad classes: transitional (T), transitional with a strong modern sector (TM), and modern (M). The frequently used measure of income per capita is, in actuality, a rather poor indicator, especially for international comparisons. A more comprehensive measure has recently become available in the form of a factor analysis of development variables by Brian J. L. Berry.[16] The following "second values" on Berry's technological scale were selected for each of the categories: M, 106 to 215; TM, 216 to 302; and T, 303 to 471.

The second system variable is the form of political organization. Here a number of different classification schemes compete for attention.[17] The one I have used in this study has been proposed by David Apter, whose threefold classification includes what he calls reconciliation systems (R), modernizing autocracies (MA), and mobilization systems (MO).[18] Combining the economic with the political scale, a three-by-three matrix results, as shown in Figure 4. The countries listed serve as illustrations only.

Historical tradition was suggested as a third system variable. As a practical consideration, this may or may not be impor-

Political Organization

| | | R | MA | MO |
|---|---|---|---|---|
| Economic—Technological Development | T | Nigeria | Ethiopia | Mainland China |
| | TM | Venezuela | United Arab Republic | Yugoslavia |
| | M | United Kingdom | Japan | Union of Soviet Socialist Republics |

Figure 4. System types.

tant. Only research will show whether the suggested matrix has sufficient explanatory power to be useful. Soviet-type countries all fall under the MO systems of political organization in Apter's scheme. But a number of other "traditions" do seem capable of adding a third dimension to the matrix, for instance, former British colonies, Latin-American countries, Middle Eastern (Arab) countries. No systematic classification will be proposed.

The group of countries selected for a more detailed investigation of planning-decision behavior are *reconciliation systems of the transitional-modern type*. They will be referred to as TMR systems. The complete list of TMR systems includes Ireland, Mexico, Argentina, Venezuela, Chile, Uruguay, Malaysia, Israel, Brazil, Lebanon, Greece, Turkey, Colombia, Iceland and India.

The concept of reconciliation requires some clarification. According to Apter, political systems founded on the principle of reconciliation are characterized by the existence of many interest groups, voluntary organizations, and political parties; the responsiveness of system goals to public opinion; and severe restrictions on the use of government power.[19] Reconciliation systems are thus constrained by the necessity for compromise. Authority is pluralistic, ideologies are diffused, and loyalties are multiple. Except for the very lowest portion of the development spectrum (low T systems), the category appears to be independent of the level of economic achievement in a society. Both Nigeria and the United States may be called reconciliation systems. The class is rather a crude one; it has the distinct virtue, however, of not exceeding present inadequate knowledge of political systems.

Nearly one-half of the fifteen countries originally classified as TMR systems fall into the great Latin-American historical tradition (*Kulturraum*). I decided to focus my discussion on these in the hope of holding cultural variability approximately constant. Whether this separation is a useful distinction for further research into national planning remains to be proved.[20] The seven Latin-American TMR societies include Mexico, Argentina, Venezuela, Chile, Uruguay, Brazil, and Colombia.

## THE DECISION ENVIRONMENT IN LATIN-AMERICAN TMR SYSTEMS

The empirical materials to be presented derive chiefly from studies of national planning and government policy in two countries, Venezuela and Mexico.[21] They are backed up by personal but random observations of national planning in Brazil and Chile and by a wide survey of the literature on Latin-American social systems.[22] The conclusions should therefore be regarded as no more than hypotheses for future depth studies in any of the countries included in my classification. The brief summaries for each of the relevant categories of the decision environment and planning-decision behavior scarcely do justice to the richness of their historical realities. Their only purpose is to lead the investigator more deeply into his subject. I hope that they will provide him with some of the keys for unlocking the puzzling contradictions, complexities, and ambiguities he will encounter.

The environment for decision, then, comprises those aspects of the social system which must be taken into account as relevant by a prospective decider. In Latin TMR societies, the more important elements of this environment include the following:

## Number of Interests

Economic development, urbanization, and a generally tolerant political system have contributed to the emergence of the "middle sectors" as an important element in national planning. The middle sectors are by no means a homogeneous group; they include businessmen, industrialists, professionals, bureaucrats, and a burgeoning group of white-collar workers. But of all the social sectors, they are the most articulate and economically powerful in their respective national societies, and their diverse interests have come to be reflected in government policies. Their emergence has transformed a stark elite-mass dichotomy into a pluralistic system, in which several elites are competing with each other in the accommodation of a growing number of both organized and unorganized publics. A clear consequence of this situation is the loss of ability to obtain a quick consensus on any vital issue, and the necessity to admit the possible validity of many different points of view. *This* has entailed a shift to the techniques of bargaining, compromise, and building pragmatic agreements for collective action. Solutions decreed by a tightly interlocking elite of powerholders can no longer be imposed by fiat upon a docile populace.

## Tolerance and Acceptance

Latin TMR societies shun uniformities of any sort. Their politics and values are to a large extent particularistic, even personalistic. The abstract rule of law is rendered more humane by the web of deeply personal relations that pervade the social system, constituting its very essence. Contrary tendencies—an insistence on universalistic standards, for example—may be observed to exist here and there, but have not become dominant. Political opposition, though fierce and categorical at times, is widely tolerated; in fact, it is regarded as a national sport. Public life is almost wholly politicized: the process of politics is itself viewed as a major value. It is not the abstract issue that counts, but the person advocating or opposing it. Loyalties are polarized, and the resulting deadlock can be broken only by the President, whose position at the apex of the entire social system is exceedingly powerful. Commands and sanctions must be used within the structure of the law, and coercive power is severely limited. With the move and flux of economic affairs, unstable coalitions, and fresh perceptions of crisis, goals tend frequently to shift in emphasis. The society remains stable at the boundaries only. Seen in a time perspective, its internal structure appears kaleidoscopic, fluid, and elusive to both an outside observer and to the participants themselves. All attempts to cast the structure of society into a more inflexible mold are fiercely resisted.

## Private Management with Public Financing

Most economic transactions in Latin TMR systems are private, despite the fact that the majority of the largest firms are in the hands of the government. Development capital, on the other hand, is to a very great extent available only through official channels. Except for the largest privately owned enterprises, which may rely in part on their own sources of financing, this statement is true for both agriculture and manufacturing. Entrepreneurial expectations in the modern sector are for very high rates of return in the short run. Organized capital markets exist in only a rudimentary form. The rate of business failures is high. The concept of business management as a profession has only just begun to penetrate. On the other hand, the "free" peasants are poor, illiterate, and extremely conservative. Their culture is light-years removed from the urban businessman's world. Their ability to break with traditional subsistence habits, even if offered a chance to do so, is low. In short, most of what might be termed the "private sector" is, as a matter of historical record, very much dependent on government largesse. The potential government control over the private sector is therefore substantial. The use of these controls, however, is heavily constrained by other elements within the social system.

### Imperfect Information

The amount of reliable information on economic conditions that is readily available to planners in TMR systems of the Latin type is meager. The known record of the economy's performance is at best spotty, and ignorance of potential resource capabilities or the economic situation elsewhere in the world is remarkable. Existing statistics have a large degree of error; there are few usable time series extending over more than a decade on any major variable. Reporting systems have a high propensity to fall apart. There are in any event substantial time lags in the reporting, analysis, and dissemination of information. Independent checks on information are few; rather, there may simply be confusion because of multiplicity of sources reporting essentially the same information with contradictory, or at least diverging, results. Many public agencies hoard information more secretly than any intelligence agency would, and a synthetic overview of the economy has become possible only recently with the preparation of national plans. This synthesis of relevant information is having a salutory influence. It points to major gaps in knowledge, tends to improve the apparent accuracy of information (if only by suppressing or replacing other official sources of information), and contributes toward the standardization of statistical information gathering and processing.

The postal and long-distance telephone services are working rather imperfectly. Many parts of the country are difficult to reach by either means effectively, and even where regular connections have been established, as between major urban centers, the service is both unreliable and slow. In all really important matters, recourse is had to personal contact. This reliance on face-to-face communications reinforces the broad tolerance of the political system already referred to.

### Weak Administration

Bureaucracy in Latin-American TMR societies is a high-status, low-income affair. University graduates have traditionally sought entry into the bureaucracy, though of late competition is luring the very best of them into more lucrative fields. The high status of government bureaucracy is largely due to a paternalism-dependency syndrome in Latin culture. Government has *always* taken care of the public's needs, just as the feudal landlord regarded his subjects with a benevolent kindness. The resulting dependency relation has so raised the bureaucrat in the public's esteem that the sons of the elite understand public employment more as a right than a responsibility. A small group of dedicated officials is, of course, exempt from this description, but for the middle and lower rungs of the administrative hierarchy, it holds widely true. As a result, private-regarding are more prevalent than public-regarding ends among the bureaucracy, and particularistic approaches are favored over the unyielding application of universal standards. Few cases that come before the bureaucracy are treated in a routine way; the vast majority are handled as personal exceptions. The result is perhaps higher justice for those whose cases are resolved, but many more cases do not reach the attention of the bureaucrats in time to be of any help. The system is thus grossly inefficient and inegalitarian. Bribery and other forms of graft are flagrant. At the same time, strong and personal loyalties in superior-inferior relations allow for an exceptionally large measure of agency autonomy. Deliberate efforts at coordination are difficult to carry through.

The low professional quality of the majority of administrative personnel, the highest levels excepted, leads to extreme forms of administrative centralization. Key public officials are reluctant to delegate significant authority, and most issues for decision, even those of a minor or routine nature, are brought to their attention. Their effectiveness as policy makers is therefore seriously reduced, their overload with information is chronic, and filtering devices are difficult to apply. As a consequence, the bureaucratic style frequently has the appearance of spontaneous improvisation. This contributes to the uncertainty of programming and policy implementation and to the near-impossibility of arranging for exactly timed sequences of action.

## Vulnerability to External Conditions

The economies of Latin-American TMR systems are confronted by large uncertainties. Their level of investment is to a very great extent dependent on the behavior of export markets and windfall gains from foreign aid. Neither is capable of being much influenced by national planners. Their economies are consequently exceedingly prone to suffer crises externally induced.

At the same time, Latin TMR systems suffer from the fact that many of their new investments are unique and result in major structural changes, especially in the industrial field. Neither their economic nor their social structures provide much "slack," so that miscalculation or unanticipated consequences are difficult to absorb except by frantic reorganization efforts. This situation has, no doubt, contributed to the general instability of Latin-American political systems, though in view of the problems they face, a number of them seem to have managed their affairs rather well. Nevertheless, external and internal vulnerabilities have rendered predictions for even single years virtually worthless. Survival needs dictate that close attention be given to the very short run as the most critical, decisive period for decision making and adjustment. Latin-American TMR systems can scarcely be said to be masters of their own destinies. This is not to say that major guidance efforts have not been undertaken or that they have been uniformly unsuccessful. It only suggests that their eventual outcome was largely unpredictable and that the commitment to make them was an act of faith. Much of the planning appears like the charge of a Polish cavalry regiment, with colors flying. When they do, indeed, gain their objective, there is much surprise and celebration.

## INSTITUTIONAL ASPECTS OF PLANNING IN LATIN-AMERICAN TMR SYSTEMS

The foregoing pages describe some of the salient features of the decision environment in the countries selected. They give a picture of the conditions which their national planners normally encounter. Though the system is gradually changing, the basic characteristics of the decision environment remain as residues for a long time. In the short run, to act rationally means to adapt to the conditions as one knows them. A successful planner in Venezuela or Brazil must not depend too much on written rules, for instance; under a personalistic system of administration, he can fairly count on their being "overlooked." Nor can he expect to guide the economic system smoothly toward quantitatively precise targets for more than a few months ahead. While much of his effort will go toward expanding his base for rational action, current planning decisions will be shaped by the desire to prevail in an environment that, after all, is rather hostile to the practice, if not the idea, of national planning. The style of planning that results from this situation is described in more exact language below.

### High Government Involvement

The central government is injected into nearly every major economic transaction and especially into those which have developmental aspects. To start with, the central government has a majority interest in the largest corporations of the countries concerned.[23] They include monopolies, or near-monopolies, in electric energy, transportation, communications, heavy industry, and development banking. It is, therefore, impossible for any significant economic activity to occur without at least some form of government participation. A critical aspect of this situation is the extreme form of financial concentration in public hands. Private banks, though numerous, are for the most part ill equipped to enter the field of development financing. They lack the experience, the technical competence, and, above all, the will to engage in this admittedly risky operation. Their strong preference is for the garden variety of commerical loans. In the priority fields of investment, private initiative is not as strong as it might be, and in some sectors, especially agriculture, it is almost totally lacking. As a result, it is the government which must act the Schumpeterian innovator, forging ahead in fields that have failed to attract private enterpise capital in sufficient sums. Is it a failure to read opportunities correctly? That is part of the story, surely. Information on investment possibilities is usually unavailable to potential investors. Is it the lack of an organized capital market? That is another part of the explanation. Is it a tradition of centralization in government and the existence of a paternalism-dependency syndrome? That, also, contributes to an understanding of this failure of innovating entrepreneurs to arise in sufficient numbers. Is it the pursuit of politics as a sport? Is it the vast concentration of economic power in the government and the high development elan among the top officials? All these are partial explanations. But central government participation is not identical with planning; on the contrary. Yet, for the moment, it is the only feasible course of action for the achievement of national development objectives. The interjection of government into economic transactions is historical fact. It is the starting point for any constructive thinking about national planning. It is a fact heavily reinforced in the environment for decision encountered by government planners. The planners find it difficult seriously to entertain a radically different alternative in which the government's involvement would, for instance, be confined to a night watchman's job. The question is rather, given the present condition, how better decisions can be made in the national interest.

## Uneven Distribution of Planning Capabilities

As stated elsewhere in this volume, [24] five areas of planning activity may be identified:

1. *Aggregate* planning for general levels of output, income, employment, consumption, investment, balance of payments, etc.
2. *Cross-sectoral* planning for the supply and distribution of specific resources, such as manpower, goods, credit, or information
3. *Sectoral* planning for such areas of activity as manufacturing, transportation, education, health, or other specific sectors
4. *Enterprise* planning by or for private, public, or mixed enterprise
5. *Spatial* planning for the geographical distribution of activity and coordinated area development

Looking at these five areas in the Latin TMR situation, it is possible to assert that (1) aggregate planning is either nonexistent or purely informational; (2) cross-sectoral planning is just beginning to be tried and is still extremely weak in most countries; (3) sectoral planning exists, but is quite spotty; (4) enterprise planning is almost totally missing and, where present, is generally confounded with sectoral planning; and (5) spatial planning, especially as regional resources development, has been tried earnestly here and there but in the absence of any comprehensive public policy for the spatial distribution of activities.[25]

In short, some fairly effective planning is done in a rather incoherent manner. This confused incidence of planning behavior varies chiefly with the type of the activity concerned, the distribution of technical skills among administrative agencies, the disposition of individual ministers or agency heads to support planning or not, and the extent to which investment is dependent on foreign aid. As a general rule, planning for transportation, electric-energy development, irrigation, and housing will be more prevalent than for other activities. They are fields closely allied with architecture and engineering and consequently build on a certain tradition of physical planning. Admittedly, such planning tends to be overly simplistic; it is normally devoid of any but the crudest kinds of financial consideration. Somewhat greater sophistication may be found in regional planning where autonomous public corporations are usually in charge and foreign aid is heavily committed.[26]

This patchwork character of planning reflects the uneven distribution of planning capabilities in the administrative system, the large measure of existing institutional autonomy, and the poor quality of information and communication systems.

## Focused Planning

The uneven distribution of planning capabilities tells little about the relative emphasis in actual planning activity. Roughly speaking, two choices are possible: planning efforts can strive for the synoptic quality of comprehensiveness in the range of activities that ought to be "planned," or they can *focus*.[27] The focus may be on current *bottlenecks* (technical awareness) or *crises* (political awareness), or on those critical achievement variables which promise large payoffs for still tolerable risks. Focused planning is an attempt to use available resources for planning effectively. Large areas of decision making can accordingly be left to traditional ways of handling.

In focused planning, an oscillating path between crisis and

achievement orientation tends to be pursued.[28]   During Phase 1, economic growth creates non-self-correcting dislocations.   These are recognized either from a technical standpoint as obstacles to further growth or are projected to the political scene as crises. In both instances, immediate solutions are demanded to keep the economy viable.   Planning expertise will be focused on the specific issues posed.   With equilibrium restored in Phase 2, a return to achievement-oriented planning becomes possible.   This is likely to focus on leading industries, strategic transport networks, "growth poles," or technical education.   Intellectual, financial, and physical resources will be concentrated in planning for key sectors at the cost of relative neglect of other activities.   Where this policy is successful in stimulating growth, the cycle is repeated, with remedial planning moving once more into the center of attention.   In actuality, of course, the two phases tend to overlap a good deal, and present the rather confusing, seemingly irrational picture of public decision making to which we have become accustomed.

Appropriate illustrations are not difficult to find.   Rapid industrialization in Venezuela triggered an exceptionally large migration of rural people to the main urban centers.   This produced crises in the supply of basic urban services, especially housing, and created the new phenomenon of visible mass unemployment.   Emergency programs had to be devised to cope with both the housing and unemployment situations.   Once the crisis stage had been surmounted, thought could once again be given to the long-term strategy for development, especially to the intensive effort to create a new base of heavy, export-oriented industry in the Guayana region.

In the Northeast of Brazil, public policy has been oscillating for decades between immediate drought relief and constructive development planning, both efforts being focused on specific issues: emergency food distribution and irrigation programs in the former case, development banks, electrification, and road programs in the latter.

Focused planning appears to be adaptive to the virtual inability of the administrative system to sustain attention equally over a large number of variables spanning the entire economic system. Aside from purely administrative difficulties and low information inputs, there is the high cost of bargaining and of constantly shifting alliances in the absence of a wide consensus on goals and purposes. Some degree of comprehensiveness in the planning system may be reflected in a more or less nonoperational national planning document where the logic of the model artificially imposes a series of sectoral and intersectoral balances. But operational planning in Latin TMR societies will inevitably concentrate limited energies and capabilities for planning on a small number of high-priority issues, variously in accordance with political demands and strategic considerations.

### Short-range Emphasis

The short-run period had overwhelming priority in Latin TMR planning. This characteristic is of course adaptive to the vast amount of remedial planning that is going on.[29] From the point of view of harried administrators and overburdened politicians, the long run is an avoidable luxury. There is a great absence of talent and leisure to engage in speculations concerning the more distant future. And the payoffs are, in any event, thought to be slight.

In the Latin-American context, long-range planning might be said to refer to anything beyond the time span of the annual budget. In this sense, long-run planning considerations are subservient to political considerations, much as party platforms are in the United States. The only difference is that they are likely to be cast in a more technical language. The long-run also serves to inform the planners: it constitutes one of their bases for arriving at judgments about current issues. And, in this sense, it is also quite useful for project evaluation where some measures of costs and benefits must always be derived. But in every other respect, the image of planners is of a group of men desperately striving to prevent the worst of calamities from happening.

There are good reasons for this behavior, quite apart from the partial explanation already given. For choosing the short run is the most rational adaptation to the following conditions in the decision environment: vast uncertainties about the future, high time preference, and an unstable, shifting pattern of goals. Lucian W. Pye, in another context, has reminded us: [30]

> The profound social changes in the transitional process tend to compound uncertainty, depriving people of that sense of shared expectation which is the first prerequisite of representative government. The possible and the plausible, the likely and the impossible are so readily confused that both elation and resignation are repeatedly hitched to faulty predictions. Thus, in the political realm, where conscious choice and rational strategies should vie in promoting human values, it becomes difficult to discern what choices are possible and what are the truly held values of the people.

In Burma, to which this quotation refers, Pye finds the response in a drift away from realism. There are elements of this too in the Latin-American situation, but the main response is a determined grappling with real problems within a context of shifting purposes. In doing so, a large measure of flexibility is maintained, and future options are held open to the extent possible. The lessons of failure drawn from experience with long-run, irreversible commitments, such as Brasilia, are not easily forgotten.

It is difficult accurately to convey this propensity for short-run planning, since all decision making can, in a sense, be made to look like immediate "problem solving." Therefore, in concluding this discussion, I wish to draw attention to the amazing amount of advance planning done in the United States, where the decision environment is altogether different. We are not surprised, for instance, to find city planners gazing ahead to the year 2000, and the Corps of Engineers to a cool one hundred years. We are not surprised to speak of ten- and twenty-year plans in connection with lunar landings and highway programs. We have introduced the notion of contingency planning in connection with both defense and business recessions. Advance planning of this type is exceedingly rare in Latin-American TMR systems. In most of the countries it does not exist at all.

## Low Coordination

The urge for Cartesian clarity is great, but the opportunities for imposing an abstract rational pattern upon an apparently chaotic social existence are few. Deliberate coordination is, therefore, mild. In Venezuela, for instance, a fairly elaborate planning machinery has been established chiefly for the purpose of obtaining a higher degree of intergovernmental coordination of development programs. But in practice, coordination has been left to the voluntary option of individual ministers and agency heads. Had he wished, the President might have forced the issue, but he was unwilling to sacrifice political loyalties for a possible small gain in allocative or operational efficiency. At the same time, central planners regarded the establishment of competent sectoral planning as deserving first priority. They reasoned well that, in the absence of adequate sectoral planning, there might be little to coordinate on a cross-sectoral basis.[31]

Coordination, no less than other aspects of planning, tends to be focused. Only under conditions of focus is it possible to break the widespread resistance to coordination on the part of those whose lot it is to be coordinated for a higher purpose. This resistance draws its strength from a number of circumstances in the decision environment. To begin with, there is the pattern of personal loyalties and institutional autonomy to which reference has already been made. The varied distribution of planning capabilities poses a problem of a different sort. "Strong" ministries refuse to be coordinated with "weak" ministries, unless they themselves can do the coordinating. On the other hand, weak ministries experience coordination as a threat to their already tenuously occupied position. Personal rivalries compound the difficulties even further. Nor is it entirely clear whose purposes are to prevail. Agreement on any but vague generalities is not easy to obtain. It is far easier, therefore, to wait with explicit coordination until a concrete issue arises in which all participant agencies stand potentially to gain from coordination. In the absence of such concrete issues—for instance, regional planning in the Venezuelan Guayana or industrial investment planning in Mexico sufficiently concrete so that technical criteria can be applied—the cavalry style of planning is much more suited to the prevailing conditions.

### Lack of Coercion

National planning concerns the management of the economy. But the economy of Latin-American TMR societies is founded on private enterprise. Thus there arises the question of the relation between the private and the public sectors. The businessman views himself as completely at the mercy of the government. This is not because government has the means to coerce him but simply because he is unable to engage in any important transaction without in some way involving a part of government. The government intervenes frequently and directly in private business transactions. But it does so generally in a nonplanning, particularistic fashion. This practice has drawn sharp comment from Raymond Vernon in his brilliant essay on Mexico's political economy: [32]

> Most of the *técnicos* do not draw back from the implications of their particularistic approach to economic development. They do not flinch from the task of deciding in detail which investment should be made with public funds and which not, which product should be imported and which exported, which items should be relieved of taxes and which actually subsidized. For them the word *dirigiste* has none of the invidious connotation which it usually carries in the French tongue. The *economía mixta*, according to their view, is the swiftest way to growth and social justice in the Mexican setting.

But the problem of how national purposes are to be translated into programs for the economy's development is not resolved by a mere reference to the proclivity of bureaucrats to tamper with the economic machinery. Some of the ways that have been tried in attempts to come to grips with this issue may be listed:

1. Ignoring the private sector, restricting planning to the public sector only, and treating the expected performance of the former by assumption

2. Engaging in pseudoplanning, formulating purely symbolic, hortatory targets for the private sector
3. Placing major reliance on the indirect controls of fiscal monetary policy in the achievement of public purposes
4. Employing particularized incentive systems, such as subsidies, licenses, tariff controls, multiple exchange systems, and tax exemptions
5. Creating a favorable business climate through public investments in infrastructure
6. Expanding the public sector either through outright nationalization or through public participation in mixed investment ventures
7. Experimenting with various forms of participant planning, co-opting the private sector into the planning process

None of these methods is used exclusively; they are always present as a *mix* of widely divergent elements, from complete isolation of the private from the public economy to the total absorption of one by the other. In their effects, of course, these policies diverge. Indirect controls (3) and public investment in infrastructure (5), for instance, have a rather uncertain outcome on the private sector. The former is, therefore, employed quite experimentally and, for best effect, depends on the existence of an efficient information system which sends accurate, quick signals to the policy strategists. The latter, on the other hand, requires something bordering on act of faith. Building a road, it has been found, can open up new markets, but it can also lead to the quick removal of these markets into the old centers through accelerated migration. With regard to particularized incentive systems (4) it has already been observed that they display a strong affinity for corruption. Rather more effective in terms of the ability to influence choice is the approach which stresses mixed investment ventures (6), a method which is rapidly gaining popularity in Latin TMR systems. Participant planning (7), finally, is still to be attempted on a significant scale, though the French planning model is being studied with interest and overtures to initiate such planning have been made in Venezuela. In participant planning, however, with its emphasis on reciprocity and compromise, the precise outcome of planning decisions is uncertain.

### Vague and Diffused Goals

After what has been said, the character of national goals in Latin-American TMR systems is scarcely a surprise. Their diffuseness falls readily into the pattern of fragmented, focused, short-range, little-coordinated planning that has been described. This is true, however, only if one thinks of goals as technically precise descriptions of a desired future state which can serve as the basis of a decision process which reduces general goal statements to specific programs, projects, and budgets. This linearity is not present in TMR systems, and it is not clear how it might be introduced, even in principle, without altering major features of the decision environment.

But goals do find expression. Former President Kubitschek of Brazil announced a five-year goal plan at the beginning of his term of office; rousing goal declarations are made from time to time by highly placed political personalities; party platforms, party doctrines, are meant to be regarded as serious statements of intention. These are the "goals" of the system and consequently cannot be reduced into clearly operational language. Their function is political rather than technical. They are supposed to help in the creation of a broad consensus about purposes *on a national scale;* they serve as a national conscience, as a counter to self-seeking, localized ends that are still prevalent; they are intended to create a development spirit and an *élan* which, far from being general, has first to be induced.

All this is done quite deliberately. The study committee which prepared Mexico's second six-year plan declared: "Inasmuch as it is not a case of a detailed and rigid program enunciating all . . . of the activities to be undertaken, which would be *undesirable,* but of a true general guide. . . . The annual program of execution . . . must give details. . . ." [33] The "true general guide" might be safely ignored by the planners, so long as its spirit was not contravened. The plan was to be used for quite a different purpose, far more important than the task of deciding on efficient sequences of action. It was considered as a major tool in the remaking of Mexico. Robert J. Shafer has expressed this function beautifully in speaking of the first six-year plan: [34]

> Whatever the criticism of the immediate effects of Cardenas' economic policies, or the carping at his lack of interest in administration, or the real weight of corruption in those years, the fact remains that the national economy sprang from the material and spiritual accomplishments of his administration into a period of rapid and self-sustained growth. Although the succeeding administration had the advantage of wartime demand for Mexican products, the same leap could not have been made from the institutions and public temper of 1933. A part of the change both in institutions and public temper relates to confidence in the ability of Mexico to achieve growth; a part relates to the notion that government action, including at least a modicum of planning, was a serviceable instrument for the increase of the national product and for its more equitable distribution. Cardenas, in sum, performed that service of widening demand for change, which antique philosophers recognized as a prelude to change itself, and which a recent literature celebrates as operative in connection with the economies of underdeveloped countries as well as in relation to modifications in class structures and changing fashions in the content of higher education.

## IN SEARCH OF GREATER RATIONALITY

I have described some of the short-run institutional adaptations of planning-decision behavior to the prevailing environment for decision in Latin-American TMR societies; but clearly, the situation does not remain as it is. On the contrary, one of the major efforts of national planners is to extend the basis for rationality in decisions. This can be done, as my analysis suggests, by reducing the ignorance of the deciders, reducing the number of interests relevant to planning decisions, and increasing the ability of the planners to influence the actions of others.

By so portraying what it is they try to do, it is immediately clear that the extension of rationality is not a politically neutral

affair that can be safely left to planners, experts, and technicians.   Much of the political controversy is over the issue of
whether the existing reconciliation system should be reduced to
only one and controls backed up by the state's power to command and to coerce.   Democratic opponents, equally concerned
with enlarging the scope of rationality, argue that the area of
consensus can be expanded by other means and that a good part
of the control problem can be solved by adopting French-type
participant planning.   The struggle is joined, and the outcome is
by no means certain.   Much depends on the continued successful
performance of the economy.   Where this should disappoint for
an extended period, the principle of reconciliation will almost certainly be abandoned for a totalitarian mobilization of resources.   Reconciliation systems, it will be claimed, are too irrational.   Lack of adequate "planning" will be declared a major
reason for economic failure and the forms of reconciliation the
principal obstacles to better planning.   An increase in the capacity for rational choice is therefore one of the most urgent
objectives for those who are committed to reconciliation as a
basic ethical principle of social order.   This may lead to action in
the following areas:

## Building and Enlarging the Area of Stable Consensus

This is facilitated by the widespread acceptance of surrogate
goals, such as industrialization, modernization, or nationalism,
which have vague meanings but, perhaps just for that reason, are
capable of expressing the substance of a persuasive ideology.   In
this complex of ideas, planning is usually presented as part of the
modern instrumentation for achieving so-called "revolutionary
objectives."   The ideology fulfills an emotional need: it encom-
passes symbolic values in terms of which conservative and radical
alike can justify their claims to history.   It also is a source of
identity to nations, such as many Latin-American TMR types,
which lack a strong and positive self-image.   Without wide
agreement on the fundamental purposes of a development society, planning is likely to remain technically ineffectual.

But, as one dimension of the public interest, symbolic consensus is scarcely sufficient as a condition for expanded rationality

unless it is also accompanied by effective cross communication among diverse social groups and specialized interests. Internal dissension must be overcome.

## Arranging for Continuing Dialogue

This is done among groups whose accustomed mode of communication is a shouting exchange of doctrinaire positions, none of which can be compromised without some loss of face. Dialogue and reciprocity are needed as a basis for reaching limited agreements on immediate objectives, programs, and projects across the entire social spectrum. The national plan and the associated planning process can serve here as a catalyst in bringing together the principal interests concerned with any problem on the common ground where facts are task meters and dialogue replaces doctrine.[35]

## Improving Information Processes

This is a continuous and costly undertaking. Planning systems require higher accuracy and wide coverage of statistical data, the coordination of statistical work through appropriate institutions, the stepped-up use of sample surveys and special studies, the introduction of automatic data processing, better and more uniform reporting procedures, major investments to improve the general census of the country and increase its frequency, heavy investments in modernizing and expanding the basic communications facilities of the country, and, finally, the expansion and qualitative improvement of technical education, especially in engineering, economics, and statistics.

## Improving Administrative Structure and Practices

This is accomplished by working toward the establishment of a permanent, independent career civil service, expanding the use of impersonal standards, shifting the weight of bureaucratic effort from nonroutine handling, and reducing the number of separate elements with which planners must be concerned. The list is short and incomplete. However, any improvement in the direction of more ample, more reliable, faster, and wider distribution of information, and the adoption of functional, universalistic standards in administration must be understood as serious efforts to increase the scope of rationality within the system.

### Decreasing Vulnerability to External Change

This, of course, is one of the major reasons for undertaking national economic development and a major determinant of the principal policy features. Industrialization, import substitution, export diversification, and building an internal market each contribute to the eventual reduction in the external dependency of the economy. But to realize this objective within a politically acceptable time period, the economy's dependence on foreign aid increases. For Latin America, however, the giving of foreign aid through the Alliance for Progress has been made contingent on the preparation of a national plan.

### Creating Central Planning Bodies

In TMR societies of the Latin-American type this appears primarily as an instrument for enlarging the basis of rational action. Their purpose, in the majority of cases, has been to prepare a national plan for submission to the Nine Wise Men of the Alliance. Initially, they were useful primarily in mobilizing critically needed foreign capital.[36] In addition, they helped coordinate government investment projects, strengthen the Presidency by providing it with independent technical advice, or, as in Venezuela, arrange a common and objective meeting ground for diverse economic interests seeking mutual accommodation within the general frame of national objectives. The social functions of these planning bodies often appeared far more important than the technical work they did and were the true source of their political support in the beginning.

## CONCLUDING OBSERVATIONS

The results of this study must be regarded as only a temporary way station in the long course of research on national planning. Some elements of a style of national planning have been identified for a group of Latin-American countries. An attempt has been made to relate this style to a set of conditions identified as the environment for decision. It was also shown that planning, as a form of adaptive rationality, seeks ways of enlarging the basis for rational choice, and that this endeavor is not politically neutral but may involve a choice among competing political systems.

Referring once more to the Lindblom model of disjointed incrementalism, the observant student will note a certain superficial resemblance between the Latin TMR style of planning and Lindblom's descriptive terms for policy decisions. Lindblom speaks of decisions as remedial, serial, exploratory, incremental, and fragmented. The Latin TMR style of planning does not contradict this description. This raises the question of whether the hypothesis relating planning decisions to their social context is at all meaningful. Lindblom derived his categories from a study of decision making in the United States. Is it conceivable that the style of planning in the United States (an MR country) is the same as for Chile, Uruguay, and Mexico? That it should share some elements is scarcely surprising; that it should be identical in all respects would be a major discovery.

Two considerations arise in connection with this question: First, superficial similarity may relate to the level of descriptive generalization. The problem here is one of finding the proper level of descriptive language (and of analysis) which will permit one to grasp significant differences without washing out important similarities. It is a matter of the "grain" of analysis. It is therefore important that section headings not be confused with section contents; the latter is the relevant subject for comparison. Second, it is indeed possible that the amount of uncertainty, ignorance, impotency of power, and necessary reconciliation remain relatively constant as planners confront society at different periods in the course of its historical evolution. Thus, the means of information and communication are infinitely better in the United States than in Colombia; but the United States is also a much more complex and an infinitely bigger society, and when it comes to formulating planning decisions, United States planners may act in as large an area of ignorance, relatively speaking, as their Colombian counterparts. This possibility is not to be ignored and, if verified, would constitute a major conclusion of this line of research. For the moment, however, I incline to the view that they are measurable and important differences in the planning styles of both countries and that my basic working hypothesis regarding the variety of planning styles still stands.

Looking toward further research, what needs to be done next? In the first instance, the empirical findings of this study are inadequately supported. They suggest merely research hypotheses for depth studies of planning in all the countries identified. Second, parallel studies should be carried out in countries falling in other boxes of the matrix for the classification of national systems. This will contribute to the major working hypothesis that the institutional form of planning decisions is strongly correlated with different combinations of economic, political, and historical variables. How many clearly distinguishable styles of national planning may eventually be identified and serve as the basis for more penetrating research I do not pretend to know, but the number is likely to be smaller than nine and larger than two.

## NOTES

[1] I wish to thank all my colleagues at the July, 1964, International Research Seminar on "Action under Development Plans" (Minnowbrook Conference Center, Syracuse University) for their exceptionally stimulating critiques of an earlier version of this chapter. I am particularly indebted to Bertram M. Gross, Peter Wiles, Tariq Siddiqi, Robert Jones Shafer, and Irving Swerdlow for their many helpful comments and suggestions.

[2] James G. March and Herbert A. Simon, *Organizations*, John Wiley & Sons, Inc., New York, 1958, pp. 203–210.

[3] David Braybrooke and Charles E. Lindblom, *A Strategy for Decision: Policy Evaluation as a Social Process*, The Free Press of Glencoe, New York, 1963, chap. 3.

[4] Pierre Masse, *Optimal Investment Decisions: Rules for Action and Criteria for Choice*, Prentice-Hall, Inc., Englewood Cliffs, N.J., 1962.

[5] Jan Tinbergen, *On the Theory of Economic Policy*, North Holland Publishing Company, Amsterdam, 1952; Karl A. Fox, *Econometric Analysis for Public Policy*, Iowa State College Press, Ames, Iowa, 1958; *Programming Techniques for Economic Development*, United Nations Development Programming Techniques Series, no. 1, ECAFE, Bangkok, 1960.

[6] Braybrooke and Lindblom, *op. cit.*, pp. 48–57.

[7] From a legal standpoint and with reference to the development of city

planning in the United States, this problem is discussed in Charles M. Haar, "In Accordance with a Comprehensive Plan," *Harvard Law Review,* vol. 68, no. 7, pp. 1154–1175, May, 1955.

[8] This may be termed the "classical" form in which planning has been viewed. This particular statement comes from A. H. Hansen, *Public Enterprise and Economic Development,* Routledge & Kegan Paul, Ltd., London, 1959, p. 111.

[9] A typical example of such a plan is described by Enrique Tejera-Paris. See his discussion of the Chilean *Plan de desarrollo agricola y de transportes,* in *Dos Elementos de Gobierno,* no publisher, Caracas, 1960, pp. 72–73.

[10] "Progress in Planning in Latin America," *Economic Bulletin for Latin America,* vol. 8, no. 2, table 1, October, 1963.

[11] This possibility has apparently been recognized by the French planners who have been reluctant to initiate continuous or revolving planning because of the difficulty of explaining the results to the noninitiated. Cf. John Hackett and Anne-Marie Hackett, *Economic Planning in France.* Harvard University Press, Cambridge, Mass., 1963, p. 299.

[12] Peter J. D. Wiles, *The Political Economy of Communism,* Harvard University Press, Cambridge, Mass., 1962, pp. 72–75. According to Wiles, "real planning is, by definition, not to predict nor merely to react, but to produce a document and stand by it in the short period at least" (p. 75).

[13] For a more complete discussion of the latent functions of planning, see John Friedmann, *Venezuela: From Doctrine to Dialogue,* Syracuse University Press, Syracuse, N.Y., 1965.

[14] For the concept of a central guidance cluster I am indebted to Bertram M. Gross. See "The Managers of National Economic Change," in Roscoe Martin (ed.), *Public Administration and Democracy,* Syracuse University Press, Syracuse, N.Y., 1965.

[15] For a descriptive analysis of various types of activators, see Bertram M. Gross, "Activating National Plans," Chap. 7. Another comprehensive treatment of the subject will be found in Robert A. Dahl and Charles E. Lindblom, *Politics, Economics and Welfare,* Harper & Row, Publishers, Incorporated, New York, 1953.

[16] Brian J. L. Berry, "Basic Patterns of Economic Development," in Norton Ginsburg (ed.), *Atlas of Economic Development,* The University of Chicago Press, Chicago, 1961, part 8.

[17] David E. Apter, "System, Process, and Politics of Economic Development," in Bert F. Hoselitz and Wilbert E. Moore (eds.), *Industrialization and Society,* UNESCO, Mouton, 1963, pp. 135–158; Edward Shils, "Political Development in the New States," *Comparative Studies in Society and History,* vol. 2, no. 3, pp. 379–411, July, 1960; and Milton J. Esman, *The Politics of Development Administration,* CAG Occasional Papers, American Society for Public Administration, Comparative Administrative Group, International Development Research Center, Indiana University, Bloomington, Ind., August, 1963; and Fred R. von der Mehden, *Politics of the Developing Nations,* Prentice-Hall, Inc., Englewood Cliffs, N.J., 1964.

[18] David E. Apter, op. cit., passim.

[19] Ibid., pp. 148–149.

[20] The choice is reinforced by the existence of what Hirschman calls the "Latin American style." See Albert O. Hirschman, Journeys toward Progress: Studies of Economic Policy Making in Latin America, The Twentieth Century Fund, New York, 1963, chap. 4.

[21] On Mexico: Howard F. Cline, Mexico: Revolution to Evolution, 1940–1960, Oxford University Press, London, 1962; Robert J. Shafer, Mexico: Mutual Adjustment Planning, Syracuse University Press, Syracuse, N.Y., 1966; Miguel S. Wionczek, "Incomplete Formal Planning: Mexico," in Everett E. Hagen (ed.), Planning Economic Development, Richard D. Irwin, Inc., Homewood, Ill., 1963; Raymond Vernon, The Dilemma of Mexico's Development, Harvard University Press, Cambridge, Mass., 1963. On Venezuela: Friedmann, op. cit.; Edwin Lieuwen, Venezuela, Oxford University Press, London, 1961; Relations of Nation, States, and Municipalities in the Government of the Republic of Venezuela, Public Administration Service Survey, Chicago, 1959; Carl S. Shoup, The Fiscal System of Venezuela: A Report, Johns Hopkins Press, Baltimore, 1959.

[22] José Medina Echavarria, Consideraciones sociologicas sobre el desarrollo economico de America Latina, United Nations, Economic Commission for Latin America, Feb. 10, 1963 (mimeographed); John J. Johnson, Political Change in Latin America, Stanford University Press, Stanford, Calif., 1958; Luis Ratinoff, El desarollo social de America Latina en la postguerra, United Nations, Economic Commission for Latin America, May 11, 1963 (mimeographed); K. H. Silver, "National Values, Development and Leaders and Followers," International Social Science Journal, vol. 15, no. 4, pp. 560–570, 1963; Kalman H. Silvert, The Conflict Society: Reaction and Revolution in Latin America. The Hauser Press, New Orleans, 1961; United Nations, Economic Commission for Latin America, Toward a Dynamic Development Policy in Latin America, New York, 1964; Albert O. Hirschman (ed.), Latin American Issues, Essays and Comments, The Twentieth Century Fund, New York, 1961; Frank Brandenburg, The Development of Latin American Private Enterprise, National Planning Association Planning Pamphlet 121, Washington, D.C., 1964; John H. Kantsky (ed.), Political Change in Underdeveloped Countries, John Wiley & Sons, Inc., New York, 1962 (contributions by Merle Kind and George I. Blanksten).

[23] See Frank Brandenburg, op. cit., chap. 3, for detailed statistics on six Latin-American countries.

[24] See Chap. 9, "What Is National Planning?"

[25] For details, see United Nations, Economic Commission for Latin America, "Progress in Planning in Latin America," Economic Bulletin for Latin America, vol. 8, no. 2, October, 1963.

[26] Not all these corporations are intended to work, however. Some are established for purely political reasons, such as the Amazon Development Authority (SPVEA) in Brazil.

[27] The term is borrowed from G. L. S. Shackle, Decision, Order, and Time

*in Human Affairs,* Harvard University Press, Cambridge, Mass., 1961. By *focus element* Shackle means that element which "has some special and extraordinary power to command and concentrate upon itself the decision-maker's attention" (p. 122). Cf. also chap. 19.

[28] This process has been described, though somewhat differently from here, in Albert O. Hirschman and Charles E. Lindblom, "Economic Development, Research and Development, Policy Making: Some Converging Views," *Behavioral Science,* vol. 7, no. 2, pp. 211–222, April, 1962.

[29] For the concept of remedial planning, see the discussion in Braybrooke and Lindblom, *op. cit.,* pp. 102 ff., 120 ff., and elsewhere.

[30] Lucien W. Pye, *Politics, Personality, and Nation Building,* Yale University Press, New Haven, Conn., 1962, p. 23.

[31] This point has been much stressed by Enrique Tejera-Paris in his excellent comparative study of Latin American planning, *op. cit.,* part 2, "La administracion publica y la politica de desarollo," pp. 3–165.

[32] Raymond Vernon, *op. cit.,* pp. 148–149.

[33] Robert J. Shafer, *op. cit.,* p. 47.

[34] *Ibid.,* pp. 75–76.

[35] The catalyst role of planning has been of great importance both in Venezuelan and French experience. See especially Hackett and Hackett, *op. cit.,* p. 290 and chaps. 18–19.

[36] Of the six Latin-American countries included as TMR systems, new central planning organizations were established or major reorganizations of central planning functions occurred in 1961 in every case but Chile, Mexico, and Venezuela. Both Chile and Venezuela produced national plans for the first time that year—following appointment of the Committee of Nine of the Alliance for Progress for the review of national plans. All these countries, however, fall short on those aspects of planning which alone would render it effective: short-term planning guides, mechanisms for project formulation, program budgets, and planning information instruments. Cf. United Nations, Economic Commission for Latin America, "Progress in Planning in Latin America," *op. cit.,* tables 3 and 4.

# 3

# *The Cultural Context*

*Fred G. Burke*

Two world wars, in conjunction with the triumph throughout the world of what are essentially Western social and political values, have thrust equality—and its political handmaidens, national self-determination and popular sovereignty—to the fore. New nations have little or no choice: the principle of government of the people, by the people, and for the people now prevails. The time when the peoples of Africa or Asia could be treated as pawns to be moved, rearranged, or reorganized to serve the interests of an elite, domestic or foreign, no longer exists. The universal political myth of equality requires that the people be *involved,* be *consulted,* and be *informed,* or that they be manipulated to believe they are. Thus, the politics of planning—the process whereby power sources are identified, manipulated, and employed to help define the desired state of affairs and the steps taken to achieve that state of affairs—is of critical importance.

The success of national planning in the new states is not measured so much by the extent to which the projected state of affairs is reached, but rather by whether the people believe the system has performed and produced in the manner in which they were led to believe it would. The new polities are the product of dissatisfaction with an existing state of being. The new leaders, by their own admission, are charged with the responsibility of moving the nation from an undesirable state of affairs to a desirable one. Their success, therefore, is measured not in the validity of their procedures as judged by either traditional or modern criteria but in the substance produced by their rule. We need to know more about the exact nature of expectations, about the extent and manner in which they can be manipulated, about the forces—the power centers—which are most sensitive to gaps between expectations and fulfillment. Knowledge of this sort will help us to speculate intelligently as to the strategies that might enable the political system (1) to lower its expectations, (2) to increase the capacity of the system to produce that which it is expected to produce, or (3) to manipulate the citizenry into believing that the expectations are being met or that the system is meeting other expectations which take precedence. The expectations flowing from the politics of independence and modern nationalism in the African countries which have suffered a protracted period of racial subjugation and indignity are frequently contradictory. The elite are faced with the problem of tailoring their plans and plan implementation to coincide with the expectations for modernity on the one hand and expectations for racial equality on the other. The elite are expected (and are so judged) to improve, simultaneously and rapidly, the material well-being of the people as they replace experienced trained expatriates with inexperienced and untrained Africans.

The purpose of this chapter is to explore some dimensions of the relationship of culture to planning. A considerable amount has been written by anthropologists and others about culture and social change. In recent years political scientists, concerned over a predominately economic interpretation, have emphasized the administration and politics of development. This emphasis has proved particularly useful in the analysis of development of new nations where the ultimate goals can most often be best comprehended in political terms. Furthermore, the realization of these goals in new nations seems to be more affected by organizational skills and stratagems than by the availability and allocation of capital and labor. This chapter suggests that a predominately economic, political, and administrative interpretation of planning in new nations requires an analysis of selected aspects of the culture situation within which planned formulation and implementation of necessity must occur.    This is an exploratory chapter raising some new questions, rather than answering some already posed questions.    Hopefully, the questions are useful generally within the developing world, but as the author's experience is predominately in Eastern Africa, the illustrations surely, and possibly the generalizations, are correspondingly limited.

In an earlier study we have defined planning as the "description of a more desirable state of affairs projected to a given point in the future, supported by an outline of the steps thought to be required to achieve that state of affairs." [1]

Too often "culture" is perceived as static, an inflexible behavior and value system which modernity must circumscribe or destroy.    Culture analysis is predominantly descriptive, perceived in terms of artifacts, role interrelationships, and carefully dissected value patterns.    Culture does not lend itself easily to process analysis.    Culture diffusion is a more dynamic concept but rarely related to modern organizational change or political values.

An existing state of affairs, viewed in terms of its institutions, customs, values, and hardware, is essentially a culture.    National planning can therefore usefully be regarded as a deliberate attempt to alter culture.    The changes effected as the consequence of plan implementation in a material culture are not important in and of themselves, for it is the alterations in attitudes, in the way in which the inanimate elements in a culture are perceived, that is significant.    There is, then, a critical relationship between national planning and culture diffusion.[2]    The new-nation recipient culture is selective and borrows only aspects of Western culture.    One major function of nation building is the attempt to inject the diffused aspects of Western-donor culture into the host culture.    The success of diffusion is a product of the skill with which it is injected, its compatibility with existing and related elements of the indigenous culture, and the extent to which the exported behavior or ideas are thought likely to correspond to popular expectations.    The goal of nation building combines elements of ideological homogeneity (nationalism) and Western modernity. Thus, those elements of Western culture most in demand and most likely to be incorporated in a national plan are political institutions and concepts designed to alter behavior and identification away from parochial-kinship institutions characteristic of traditional culture and toward territorially defined nationality. Secondly, the culture-borrowing process is restrictive in that it selects out Western technology and related economic and educational institutions calculated to meet expectations for modernity. Thus, national planning and its operative administrative institutions are themselves aspects of Western culture currently being diffused throughout Africa.

## THE ROLE OF CULTURAL ELEMENTS

As Linton and others have noted, hardware and techniques are relatively easily diffused, whereas concepts, ideologies, and abstractions threaten the foundation of the recipient's culture system and are rarely accepted in their entirety. Consequently, the diffusion of modern technology and nation-state political institutions frequently come into conflict with the more resistant elements of traditional culture. Concepts of time and space, comprehension of authority, cognition, organizational and relationship mores, the aesthetics of design and structure, and fundamental indigenous ontologies are some of the more resistant elements of traditional cultures.

A requisite aspect of the process of culture diffusion is that clear-cut conflict between the borrowed elements of Western culture and the indigenous culture must exist. A people's conceptualization is, in essence, a definition and explanation of the reality of the social and physical environment. Alterations in conceptualization in a direction consistent with the demands of those elements of Western culture being diffused require a confrontation of culture bits, which itself is an alteration in the milieu. Such alterations, in turn, require reconceptualization. Unless attention is paid to the components of the indigenous culture(s) with particular respect to their accommodative capacity, a projected state of affairs perceived from the national capital will remain only that: projected. We need to identify and catalog those aspects of Western culture which are most sought after and, more important, the corollary cultural concepts which are requisite to their successful cultural grafting. At the same time, it will be necessary to identify and categorize those aspects of traditional and *transitional* culture which are antithetical to the successful diffusion of selected Western culture. For example, it would seem that "time" as an element of culture is difficult to diffuse and in much of Africa persists as an obstacle to the successful inculcation and operation of those elements of Western culture requisite to political and economic modernization.

It is interesting to note that in the African context two aspects of contemporary Western culture may be contradictory. Here we have reference to mass participation in the political process and economic modernization. Historically modernization in the West, including the U.S.S.R. and the United States, depended upon the power of a relatively unfettered elite to plan and to implement the plans. In Africa today, again because of the time variable, the elite, at the very inception of the modernization process, are faced with a mass polity to whom considerable energy and resources must be allocated. Thus, whereas the donor nation developed cultural elements sequentially and thereby complementarily, the recipient society is required to accept all elements simultaneously. It is this factor, among others, that contributes to the evolution of a new culture which is considerably more than a combination of the retained and the borrowed elements.[3]

## THE DYSFUNCTION OF TIME

Western culture is peculiarly time-oriented, and some philosophers feel we have sold the good life, our very birthright, to a technology we invented to serve us. Stanley Diamond demonstrates well the anthropologist's grasp of this phenomenon:[4]

> In machine based societies the machine has incorporated the demands of the civil power of the market, and the whole life of society, of all classes and grades, must adjust to its rhythms. Time becomes lineal, secularized, "pre-

cious"; it is reduced to an extension in space that must be
filled up. The collapse of time through an extension of
space . . . has bowdlerized our national and human
rhythms and helps disassociate us from ourselves. Even
now, we hardly love the earth or see with eyes or listen
any longer with our ears, and we scarcely feel our hearts
before they break in protest.

Diamond develops the thesis that the quest for the primitive,
the pristine society, is a part of Western culture, because civilization in its denial of humanity creates a need for constant redis-
covery or at least a harkening back to the fountainhead of primitive life. We will not here pursue the fascinating question as to
whether simple societies are therapeutically requisite to complex,
disjointed cultures. We will, however, draw attention to the
differences in the sense of time between the two cultures and
then speculate as to the significance of this difference.

Planning is the ideal illustration of what Diamond refers to as
the machine which persuades "us at every turn to fulfill our intentions which we have built into them. . . ." Planning requires a
conceptualization of an abstract state of being, frequently defined
in quantitative terms, which too often appears to have lost its
concrete reference. Sectors become detached from their moor-
ings and float in abstract space; targets become numbers, and
numbers emerge from machines demanding that depersonalized
Homo sapiens perform in a manner calculated to meet this abstract end. Planning implies linear time, and we therefore speak
naturally of linear programming.

Time is an absolute measurable quantity. This concept of
time, which lies at the heart of the scale of planning, is quite inconsistent with time as conceived by most rural Africans. Yet
given the unusual commitment to equalitarian mass participation,
that is, their being at place $x$ at time 1 and at place $y$ at time 2, it
is requisite to the success of national planning. As we shall note
below, a cyclic, as contrasted to a linear, conception of time structures communication in an indeterminate fashion, thereby rendering difficult indeed the relatively exact time and space predictions
so necessary to the implementation of scientific planning.

Rapidly developing societies require a sense of exact linear time with its inference of progression, of unique occurrences, to hurry them even further away from an undesirable point of departure. But to the peasant, history "is the recital of sacred meanings within a cyclic as opposed to a lineal perception of time. The merely pragmatic event, uninvolved with the sacred cycle, falls as it were, outside history, because it is of no importance in maintaining or revitalizing the traditional forms of society." [5] In much of Africa, the elite, educated in schools run by the clock, and persons heavily involved in a market cash crop economy requiring the performance of sequential activity if life is to be maintained, are already victims or, depending on one's point of view, benefactors of civilization. However, a more primitive sense of time persists in the conceptual frame of reference of the elite, despite the increasing tendency to think in terms of linear time, and, certainly, still dominates the lives of much of the peasantry.

The implications of this dichotomy on plan formulation and implementation are many and significant. As planning concepts and techniques are essentially borrowed from Western culture, the planning process is dependent upon an absolute linear, inflexible concept of time. To the extent to which timing is crucial to sequential decisions and the postulation of cumulative effects, planning in the Western sense might well require "adjustment" if it is to succeed in Africa. Considerable research is required to explore the operational significance of the differing concepts of time and to test alternative approaches to plan implementation which might profit from, rather than suffer from, an essentially cyclic time sense. Nor need we regard such an experiment as necessarily a reversion to the primitive, for in one sense the cyclic view of time is more consistent with nature and with recent thinking on the nature of the universe. The theory of spatial relativity renders the question "when" with respect to linear time quite meaningless, for it is necessary first to identify the system(s) wherein, or on which, time is being measured. Furthermore, the general relativity theory suggests that time may indeed be cyclic rather than linear.

The importance of variations in culturally derived conceptions of time can hardly be overemphasized. For example, our preoccupation with linear time and with the "timetable" rapidity of African independence and development inclines us to exaggerate the oft-noted gap between expectations and the capacity of the politicoeconomic system to produce. Employing our sense of linear time, we are inclined to conclude that the African masses have been led to believe that independence will bring immediate change in their standard of living and that once the system fails to deliver on *time*, the mass will rebel and topple the government. It is conceivable, however, that a less precise and linear concept of time will tolerate a greater divergence between inflated expectations and actual results than our culture-bound interpretation inclines us to believe. If this indeed be true, then some of our fundamental assumptions underlying foreign assistance and the dynamics of nation building will require critical rethinking. This variable conception of time is intricately related to the question of "progress," or cumulative linear change.[6]

## PROGRESS AND CHANGE

Primitive cosmology employs rational as well as nonrational techniques to cope with the problem of existence.[7] Malinowski has shown vividly how primitive peoples combine rationality (empirical means to achieve an empirical end) to gain their food but also employ magic to aid the process of agriculture. He makes the important distinction that there exists a clear-cut difference between knowledge about plants, climate, soil, etc., and magic, which is employed to cope with the domain of the unaccountable.[8] As much of the environment in a nondeveloped society lies within the domain of the unaccountable, the tendency to employ nonrational techniques is relatively greater. Thus magic and ritual are frequently employed to explain events which science accounts for in Western culture.[9]

Science is relatively predictable, and it is therefore possible, using the scientific method, to order events in a sequential fashion, or at least it is possible to calculate frequency and distribution. Primitive man, however, employs magic and religion to explain such events. This, in conjunction with a cyclic sense of time intimately related to a religion which emphasizes the generational relationships of the dead, living, and still-to-be-born, suggests, as Diamond notes, that "primitives have no *secular* sense of history, and no *lineal idea,* and hence no prophetic *ideal,* of social progress. Moreover, progress as an abstraction has no meaning for them." [10] If it is true that people who still reside within a primitive culture have little, if any, sense of linear progress, then there is a likelihood that planners and bureaucrats are communicating in a "language," or set of terms, with people from whom the required response is unlikely to materialize. Max Weber, when discussing "types of rationality," poses a similar question. He notes that differing types of social action depend on differing modes of rationality. Scientific planning is what Weber would term "Rational orientation to a system of discreet individual ends . . . that is, through expectations as to the behavior of objects in the external situation and of other human individuals, making use of these expectations as conditions or means for the successful attainment of the actor's own rationally chosen ends." [11] Weber adds that "action is rationally oriented to a system of discreet individual ends (Zweckrational) when the end, the means, and the secondary results are all rationally taken into account and weighed." To this he contrasts social action that is "traditionally oriented through the habituation of long practice." [12] Thus so long as two elements in the policy—the elite and the mass—are socially organized according to radically different cosmologies, the new behavior of the mass, even though consistent with the ends projected by the planners, from the individual's point of view will likely be either meaningless or not rationally related to the ends.

A number of hypotheses requiring field research emerge from this general observation. First, it would be necessary to determine to what extent and at what level people in a new nation do or do not possess a sense of linear progress. It is conceivable that interviewing by psychological methods would show that an older, illiterate generation thinks predominately in a cyclic time and does not conceive of sequential progress, whereas the younger generation, partially educated and involved in a cash economy, combines elements of linear and cyclic time by rational orientation and values sequential progress. The elite would most closely resemble Western culture. If this were found to be the case, then there would arise the question so critical to nation building or planning: how to educate simultaneously these two generations. Can Western educational technology be employed to design schemes capable of rapidly substituting one form of rationality for another, to import skills which are functional vis-à-vis nation building even though essentially meaningless in a total cosmological sense? Research designed to test sample categories of the population with respect to a sense of causation, time, progress, and rationality is possible, and some research has already been carried out in Africa among school children.[13]

## COGNITIVE RANGE

One's cognitive level can be spatially defined, and in primitive illiterate societies where parochialism is the rule, cognition rarely exceeds the cosmological or territorial limits of the subsistence community.

Nation building, for which national planning is a blueprint, is an international exercise with respect to sources of capital and technical assistance, and in the behavioral alterations the plans seek to make within the society. Therefore in one sense, the ends of nation building involve a radical extension of cognitive range. Extension of cognitive range is a requisite to modernization.[14] The term *community* implies a shared cognitive orientation, as does *nation*. Nation building is the extension of shared cognition over an area and a people territorially defined by the confines of the state. As Levy notes, "It is the empirically observable effects of a given type of cognition on the actions of those who hold it and/or on that of those with whom interaction takes place."[15] Nation building implies a rapid increase in interaction between persons with whom one does not share similar traditional cognitive orientations. In circumstances of this nature, the likelihood that suspicion, confusion, fear, and withdrawal will characterize the relationship is great. However, the extension of cognition is an instrumental aspect of national planning and might usefully be so perceived.

In the absence of an explicit recognition of the instrumental cruciality of cognition, the likelihood of success for programs requiring fundamental technological alterations in behavior is considerably reduced. Research is required to determine whether community development programs and cooperative society development do in fact extend cognitive range in the desired direction. Controlled experiments along these lines are possible.

Patterns of thought and knowledge are obviously related to expression and thus to the important relationship of the communication and translation of national plans, via implementation into empirical alterations in mass behavior and attitudes.

## LANGUAGE

To Levy, communications are a functional requisite of any society in a manner peculiarly relevant to planning as defined here. "The activity or process whereby one or more individuals infers from the behavior (whether language . . . gesture or posture) of another individual . . . an idea or feeling or *state of affairs* that the other individual(s) is trying to convey." [16]

We are primarily concerned here with the problem of the use of language by persons (expatriates as well as Africans) grounded in Western culture, to convey to the masses "an idea or feeling" quite different from an existing state of affairs. As the proposed state of affairs is essentially new and is not possessed of concrete—or, for that matter, even abstract—referents in the frame of reference of the mass peasantry, new language or new construction of old language is required. Thus it is not surprising that the terminology of planning, even when intended for a non-English-speaking peasantry, is usually expressed in English (written as well as oral). Nonetheless, the English expression, at least initially, must be defined in the vernacular, and therefore some words must be employed from a language not structured to cope with modern ideas or actions.

As nation building involves the diffusion of new and essentially Western culture elements, moreover, there tends to be semantic confusion. The cognition achieved, therefore, is extremely variable and often indeterminate: the perceived message is not always that which the planners hoped to convey. The author has had occasion to undertake a study of Tanzania socialism (termed *Ujamaa*) through the device of numerous interviews with persons from widely differing socioeconomic levels and regions. It was discovered that *Ujamaa* conveyed a wide variety of meanings, some of which closely resembled "socialism" in the Western, Marxist sense while other interpretations resembled more closely the literal Swahili meaning: "brotherhood" or "familyhood." More important, but more difficult to measure, is the attitude and behavior that the varying perception of the term activates. Nation building is more often translated *Kujenga-Nchi*. *Kujenga* means to build; but in the absence of a widely held analytical, abstract sense of institution or progress, does *building* convey to the Tanzanian peasant what it does to the planner or to the politician? *Nchi* refers not to *nation* as a cultural entity or as a language grouping but to *territory* and can be used to refer to districts or to regions as well. One sometimes hears the term *Nchi yetu* (literally "our country" or "fatherland") but, unlike its meaning in a Western culture, in a Tanzanian it more likely evokes feelings of attachment to parochial regions rather than to national territoriality.

Development is sometimes translated as *Maendeleo*, which might best be translated as "the carrying on." Absent here is the ideal of progress—the employment of organization to systematically reorder the system. The word used to connote organization (*matengenezo*) can be translated as a "body" or "thing for fixing."

## ORGANIZATIONAL STRUCTURE

Most African traditional social systems are small-scale and characterized by diffuse organization. There are, of course, exceptions, the most notable being the Hausa Emirates in Northern Nigeria, and the interlacustrine kingdoms of East Africa. Most African tribes are either remarkably small or diffusely organized into essentially autonomous clans, lineages, or age groups. Consequently, the nature of social organization is relatively unspecialized, with authority tending to cluster about the elders, while leadership tends to be situational rather than general.

There exist few full-time, specialized organizational roles, and the social system usually is remarkably egalitarian. Interpersonal relations tend to be of a face-to-face variety and intimate, though highly structured and ritualized with little room for initiation. Rules regulating role interaction are memorized and inviolate. Obligations are owed and authority is exercised primarily on the basis of *who* one is, e.g., kin, blood brother, in-law, rather than *where* one happens to be. Collective decisions binding on the members of the parochial society generally must elicit the consent, or at least the concurrence, of all. Membership in the decisional assembly or council, though differing among the many societies, is not rigidly defined.

It is not our intent here to describe small-scale African polities in any detail; this has been done at length elsewhere.[17] What we are suggesting here is that the nature of traditional social and political organization tended to endow the emerging national society with a number of attributes which have affected national planning. Such attributes, for example, as a tendency toward informality of organization, bifurcation of organization, inclination toward proliferation of local organizations, and "Quaker meeting" consensus are indicative.

The relationship between the structure of society and organizational attitudes is well recognized:[18]

> Society was not merely a model from which classificatory thought took its departure; its very framework was used as a framework of the system. The first logical categories were social categories; the first classes of things were classes of men into which these things were integrated. It is because men lived in groups and thought of themselves as groups that they have abstractly grouped everything else, and the two types of groups began by being so fused as to be inseparable.

Durkheim's insight into this important relationship cuts to the very heart of the matter. He, more than any other scholar, has drawn our attention to the fact that organizational conceptualization is subjective and that the way in which men structure, categorize, and interrelate phenomena is, in large part, a reflection of the way in which their own society is organized. "This is why the nature of things changes in a way from one society to

another; they affect the feelings of different groups differently.
. . . [Important concepts as time and space are] at each moment of the history in close relationship with their corresponding social organization." [19]

If we are to gain the requisite insights into planning in the new states of Africa, it will be necessary to explore this question of organizational theory as affected by culture. Research to identify the key cultural characteristics and then to relate them to the organization of the planning process will be required.

Organizational skills—a readiness for, and ease of coping with, multiple variables and their interrelationships in sequential fashion so as systematically to maintain postulated goals—are essentially culturally acquired. Western culture generally, and probably American culture in particular, emphasizes the acquisition of organizational skills very early in life. From the moment the Western child enters school, he is faced with organizational responsibilities, some simulated and others quite real. Thus, for the mature American the association of variables, the management of feedback, the choice of alternative paths, and the choice of a priority of sequence in order to move from one state of affairs to another is "traditional," or habitual. If an African has had the advantages of formal school experience, he acquired his education in a highly structured, relatively authoritarian European colonial system. Thus, organizational skills in modern Africa are rare and alien, and consequently the task of implementing an idea or a plan requires an expenditure of relatively enormous energy, for there is no learned, habitual behavior pattern to ease the burdens of interrelating multiple variables.

Western culture teaches its citizens early in life to think in abstract, "model" terms. Children play with miniature replicas of real objects and are quick to develop a sense of representation and fantasy—but with concrete referents. A boy who has worked with model and scaled airplanes and automobiles is quick to grasp the use of symbols to represent reality. Planning, particularly as it emphasizes quantitative projection and formula determination of alternatives, requires a highly developed sense of abstraction, an aspect of culture particularly lacking in most underdeveloped societies. We have noted on numerous occasions the sharp contrast between the capacity of East African planners to imagine and postulate a desired state of affairs with precision and great deftness but then to be frustrated by the task of blocking out the steps required to move to that state of affairs.

The process of plan implementation as related to organizational skills reflected in a given culture has been too little studied; yet it lies at the very heart of successful planning. It is necessary to test the observations made above and then to explore the possibility of rapidly inculcating requisite organizational skills or study the feasibility of altering the planning process to coincide more closely with the existing organizational culture.

Traditional African small-scale diffuse sociopolitical organization is but one aspect of a more general approach to structure and order. It is necessary, if we are to cope with problems of plan implementation as affected by local institutions, to be aware of this element of traditional culture. The Western planner is inclined to think in linear terms and project his thoughts conceptually and symbolically in terms of right angles, straight lines, and tables of organization. Traditional culture is not attuned to accept concepts in this manner, but rather conforms more to the irregularities dictated by the physical environment. To the African peasant, the environment is a force to which one must conform, not something to be straightened, mastered, or manipulated. The frustration of the expatriate administrator or the AID economist because of what often seems to be a lack of organization, an *ad hoc* system of decision and action, or a failure to follow channels can be explained largely by this divergence between cultures. Successful planning requires that this phenomenon be explored in order to propose alternative forms and techniques more consistent with the traditional organizational apparatus often depended upon in the last analysis to implement plans.

In the above discussion of culture as a major variable affecting national planning we have sought to demonstrate the significance of disjointed cultural diffusion. Such factors as cognition, language, form, and time are as critical to the planning process as such more orthodox variables as manpower, national resources, transportation, or infrastructure. A purpose of the chapter is to draw attention to the need for bold and innovative research in this neglected area.

## NOTES

[1] Fred G. Burke, *Tanganyika: Preplanning,* Syracuse University Press, Syracuse, N.Y., 1965, p. 4.

[2] Culture diffusion as used here is merely consistent with Linton's usage: "The transfer of culture elements from one society to another." See Ralph Linton, *The Study of Man: Introduction,* Appleton-Century-Crofts, Inc., New York, 1936, p. 324.

[3] This point is developed at some length by Martin Kilson in "Political Change and Modernization," *Journal of Modern African Studies,* vol. 1, no. 4.

[4] Stanley Diamond (ed.), *Primitive Views of the World,* Columbia University Press, New York, 1964, pp. viii–ix.

[5] *Ibid.,* p. v.

[6] "Independence now," heard so often in East Africa, is indicative. It did not mean "independence now" but was meant to indicate that a desire for independence had reached an intensive level of expression.

[7] The debate which used to rage over whether or not primitive societies were capable of abstract reasoning is little heard these days. There is little question but that the thought processes and action consequences of primitive man are of the same time as those of so-called "civilized" man.

[8] Bronislaw Malinowski, "Rational Mastery of the Environment," in Talcott Parsons et al. (eds.), *Theories of Society,* The Free Press of Glencoe, New York, 1961, vol. 2, p. 1056.

[9] There is reason to speculate whether the employment of econometrics and other highly sophisticated devices in some developing countries, where the data capable of rendering such techniques useful are absent, is not, in effect, a form of magic and ritual employed to explain the inexplicable.

[10] *Op. cit.,* p. v.

[11] Max Weber, "Types of Rationality," in Parsons et al., *op. cit.,* vol. 2, p. 1063.

[12] *Ibid.*

[13] See Chap. 11, "Attitudes and Beliefs on National Planning."

[14] We prefer Levy's definition of cognition: "knowledge or understanding of a situation or phenomenon." See Marion J. Levy, Jr., *Structure of Society,* Princeton University Press, Princeton, N.J., 1952, p. 168.

[15] *Ibid.*

[16] *Ibid.,* p. 56. (Italics are ours.)

[17] See for example Lucy Mair, *Primitive Government,* Penguin Books, Inc., Baltimore, 1962; John Middleton and David Tait (eds.), *Tribes without Rulers,* Routledge & Kegan Paul, Ltd., London, 1962; and Fred G. Burke, *Local Government and Politics in Uganda,* Syracuse University Press, Syracuse, N.Y., 1964.

[18] Emile Durkheim and Marcel Mauss, "Social Structure and Structure of Thought," in Parsons et al., *op. cit.,* vol. 2, p. 1065.

[19] *Ibid.,* pp. 1067–1068.

# 4

# *The Biophysical Environment*
## *Lynton K. Caldwell*

The Twelfth International Congress of Entomology warns land-use planning agencies against the dangers of indiscriminate methods of insect control.

The First International Conference on Estuaries (Jekyll Island, Georgia, 1964) finds our fundamental knowledge of estuarine and coastal environments inadequate to guide wisely their growing development for food, recreation, commercial, and waste-disposal purposes.

The Surgeon General of the United States reports findings of surprising concentrations of DDT in deep-sea fish.

The government of the Netherlands calls for strict international controls to end pollution of the downstream waters of the river Rhine.

The government of Pakistan seeks aid in restoring some 6½ million acres of once arable land ruined by faulty methods of irrigation.

The General Conference of UNESCO (Paris, 1962) recommends action by member states to safeguard or restore threatened or impaired landscapes and urban and natural areas of cultural and aesthetic interest which often are important factors in national economic and social life and affect human mental and physical well-being.

The United Nations Conference on Science and Technology (Geneva, 1963) observes that man's combustion of fuels annually adds some 6,000 tons of carbon dioxide to the atmosphere with a resulting raising of the earth's surface temperature entailing presently unforeseeable consequences for climate and health.

## THE ENVIRONMENTAL CHALLENGE

Statements comparable to those just cited could be extended almost indefinitely. They can be found these days in any issue of leading newspapers in nearly any country. Their common theme is the dangers that man is incurring through injudicious manipulation of his biophysical environment.

Hazards resulting from damage to the biophysical environment are not new. Deforestation, soil erosion, siltation, endemic disease have, since ancient times, rendered once prosperous or populous areas impoverished or uninhabitable. Indeed some of the great monuments of ancient and classical civilization are also monuments to man's misuse of his natural environment. Peoples survived these past catastrophies usually by moving away, often preëmpting the unspoiled lands of others. Today it is becoming increasingly less feasible to find new lands to exploit. But science and technology, it may be optimistically argued, are now freeing man from dependence on natural environments. Auspicious forecasts are being made for the establishment of artificial environments for human living, even, perhaps, on other planets.

### The Urge to Dominate

This optimism is consistent with certain pervasive attitudes that evidence deep-seated psychological drives. The first of these attitudes is the urge to dominate. There is a tendency in the human animal to impress its will upon its surroundings, both human and, in the broader sense, environmental. Since prescientific times the conquest of nature has been one of man's more common epic themes. The ruthless destruction of nature has been the darker consequence of this attitude. Its brighter aspects include spectacular achievements in science, engineering, and medicine. With the growth of knowledge the primitive urge to dominate has in some measure, and among some men, given way to respect for the complex order of nature. In the light of scientific understanding, the urge to willful dominance over nature leads to unnecessary risk and irrational innovation. The man of science knows that he manipulates his biophysical environment only to the extent that the rules by which the universe operates permit him to do so. Acting within the rules he can make an atom bomb, but no amount of will power can prevent destruction if the natural forces of the bomb are unleashed. Scientific man may harness, yet cannot arrest, the tides of the seas, but man guided by prescientific attitudes and undisciplined emotions may be unwilling to brook subordination to natural laws. He may thus thoughtlessly shape his environment to his own ultimate disadvantage and may do so under the illusion of "progress" and "development."

### The Myth of Endless Abundance

A second attitude that encourages exploitation of the biophysical environment is a belief in the endless abundance of the earth. This is the myth of "mother nature," the eternal cow that gives milk without limit and never runs dry. The modern sophisticated version of this attitude is found in reassurance from natural-resources economists to a Malthus-worried world: overpopulation and resource depletion are fears of the faint-hearted, the foolish, and the uninformed—the vast wealth of the earth is scarcely touched; beneath the oceans, in sea water, and in the laboratory are answers in abundance to all of man's material needs; and, in the editorial language of *The Wall Street Journal*, "technology, as always, can serve them." [1]

It is true that science and technology may unlock vast new storehouses of material wealth; it is true that man, if need be, may find ways to live in highly inhospitable environments. But the world is finite, and there are severe and inflexible limits for the natural environments that human experience and biological science have found to be most favorable for man's welfare. The danger of uncritical optimism regarding man's capacity to meet his resource needs through technological innovation is that it fails to discriminate between those areas in which confidence is justified and those areas in which the biophysical environment presents challenges that we are not yet prepared to meet.

## The Need for Understanding Environmental Relations

While these attitudes of domination and endless abundance can be shown to be inconsistent in principle with our growing knowledge of the biophysical universe, they persist—indeed, prevail—in modern industrial society. They are rooted deep in human needs for self-expression and security, and they are reinforced by traditional values, by literature, and by religious scripture. Though other views of the relationship between man and nature may be cited, in the traditional philosophies of China and India, in certain primitive cultures, and in Western and industrial society as well, the need to dominate and the right to exploit have been implicit, unvoiced assumptions underlying much of man's handling of his biophysical environment. More importantly these same uncritical attitudes are built into much present-day thinking about the goals and processes of national development. If these attitudes or assumptions are in fact contrary to biophysical realities, then large-scale planning and development can easily involve mankind in serious trouble.[2]

It is apparent that many of our failures at environmental management have followed from insufficient, faulty, or misguided planning. As science reveals the interrelatedness of things, the need for environmental planning becomes evident if we are to avoid untoward, inadvertent consequences of human action. Before science and technology so greatly extended and accelerated man's capacity to shape his environments, trial and error could be risked. Mistakes, even when disastrous to those involved, were localized. Today when whole nations, continents, or the globe itself may be affected, the risks of error may be prodigious. It is questionable whether the old attitudes that served practical man for centuries are safe to guide the use of the powers available through contemporary scientific technology.

To state the problem briefly: our capacity to effect swift and massive changes in the biophysical environment has outrun our understanding of ecological relationships. Environment-shaping measures in development planning are all too frequently projected without adequate consideration to their possible consequences. The problem, therefore, is to bring our understanding of the biophysical environment and our own role in it into line with our capacity to alter it irreversibly, possibly for the worse. Until this problem is understood, there is real danger that development efforts may do more harm than good. In the opinion of many of our most reputable scientists, we risk disaster through well-intentioned but ill-informed efforts at large-scale manipulation of the biophysical environment.

## ANALYSIS OF ENVIRONMENTAL PROBLEMS

The problem of bringing man's comprehension of his biophysical environment into line with his capacity to manipulate it may be analyzed at three different but interrelating levels: first, there is the level of *perception,* the way man sees his relation to the external world; second, there is the level of *information,* the nature and extent of knowledge of ecological or environmental relationships; and, third, there is the level of *operation,* the methods by which this knowledge may guide decisions about the biophysical environment. At each of these levels subproblems are encountered that must be resolved, if anything constructive is to be done about the larger problem.

### Perception

It is not easy for us to perceive our relations with the external world in the terms in which science now describes it. The complex matrix of interdependent relationships that comprise the human environment is not the picture of reality found in our folkways, our literature, or our theology. There is a wide gap between what is known or can be known about the biophysical environment and the way we reason or act in relation to it. We have already noted the discrepancy between certain common attitudes toward the biophysical environment and the reality that science discloses. A brief examination of the concept of "environment" as a totality is necessary to clarify why it is that this seemingly simple concept may be difficult to understand.

The simplicity of the concept is deceptive. Like many fundamental ideas, its essential propositions are so elemental as to be axiomatic, yet their implications are so far-reaching and complex as to appear incomprehensible. It follows, therefore, that one can be led into either of two wrong conclusions: (1) that the environment as a general concept is so obvious as to be trivial or (2) that the environment is so complex as to be unmanageable as a concept in other than highly abstract terms. In either case the concept could be dismissed as of no practical value. But neither conclusion is correct, and both follow from the failure to distinguish between the theoretical basis of the environmental concept and the ways in which the concept is applied to practical situations.

The basic proposition of the environmental concept is that everything in the universe is interrelated. Nothing exists of itself alone. As a general concept environment implies systematic situational relationships. It refers to the relationships between a thing environed and the sum total of the surrounding things or forces interacting with it. These things and forces constitute an environment only when considered in relation to a thing environed. Environment has no meaning if applied indiscriminately to things-in-general without regard to their interrelationships. Interrelationship is the essential element in the environmental concept. From this point of departure a number of relevant propositions follow.

Environments or environmental relationships are always *relative*. They are relative to whatever is environed, and in an everchanging world these complex relationships are always *variable*, never really constant. Specific aspects of man's biophysical environmental relationships may hold relatively constant; e.g., he must breath oxygen to survive. But he has a range of tolerance within which this environmental need may be satisfied: the quantity of oxygen and the quality of the air that he breathes can vary, within limits. Finally, because environmental relationships are neither rigid nor permanent but in constant flux, the direction of their changes may to some extent be influenced if their critical elements can be controlled. Thus, while it is necessary for man to adapt his behavior to certain environmental conditions over which he has no control, there are other dimensions of his environment which he can manipulate and shape to suit his purposes.

It is with respect to this malleability of the environment that an understanding of the true nature of environmental and ecological relationships becomes important. These relationships are rarely, if ever, 1-to-1 interactions. Instead, a complex matrix of multiple relationships is always involved. Change in any one factor in an environmental complex may affect relationships among some of or all the other elements in the matrix. These effects may be localized or minimal, or they may ramify widely with reverberations of increasing magnitude. It therefore follows that in effecting environmental change it is needful to anticipate the consequences. If there is a significant possibility that results will be other than those intended, reappraisal of the projected action will be wise. At the least, measures to keep the consequences under control may be indicated.

The practical connotations should now become clear. It will make a difference in development planning whether the "planners" perceive the environmental matrix within which action is to occur as being composed of discrete elements or of interconnected elements. But the total environmental matrix of any object, individual or national, is so complex that it must be broken down conceptually into groups of more closely interrelating aspects in order to deal with this environment in any practical way. Thus the environment—any environment—can in practice be dealt with only through its parts and not directly as a whole. However, in order to deal knowledgeably with the parts, the whole and the relationship of the parts to the whole must be kept in mind. Unless this is done, any action in relation to the environment is shortsighted or blind, with all of the hazards that accompany a combination of ignorance and imperfect vision.

### Information

To deal with environmental factors in practical terms, it becomes necessary to focus upon some definable group of environmental relationships. In dealing with the process of development planning in this chapter attention will be confined to the biophysical aspects of the environment: the land, water, air, living organisms, and astrophysical radiations that comprise the natural world. This selectivity does not diminish the importance of other aspects of man's total environment, especially the psychosocial, but the biophysical aspects have been selected for treatment here for two reasons: first, they are basic to life itself and, hence, to all aspects of human endeavor; second, they have been neglected, because they largely fall into the areas between the great divisions into which contemporary man has organized his knowledge.

Environmental questions tend to be residual and interstitial. They are leftovers in the division of knowledge among the biophysical sciences, the social sciences, and the humanities. This has happened because man has tended to organize his knowledge first around things (objects or phenomena), subsequently around processes, and only latterly around relationships. Understanding of the biophysical environment is difficult in part because it must cut across all the major divisions of knowledge—physical, biological, and social. Man's biophysical environment cannot be studied with man left out. Where the attempt has been made to include him, too often it is only the biophysical elements *in* the human environment that have been studied—climate, topography, or natural resources. The environment itself as an interrelating complex totality has frequently escaped attention.

Man, being a culture-bearing animal, cannot be understood solely in physiological terms. His beliefs, his values, and his traditions, as we have noted, are of critical importance to the way in which he relates to his biophysical environment. Environmental knowledge is, therefore, multidisciplinary in character and, in addition, constitutes an area of synthesis among the sciences that is as yet very inadequately developed.

Another way of understanding the informational facet of the environmental problem is to recognize that the environmental whole is more than, and different from, the environmental parts, as a forest is more than the sum total of its individual trees. There are many things about forests that cannot be learned from a study concentrated exclusively upon trees. In like manner, full knowledge of man's biophysical environment cannot in practice be obtained merely by cumulating in some systematic manner all existing knowledge relating to its parts. Two kinds of knowledge are contrasted here: knowledge of the substance of things and knowledge of relationships among things. The subject matter may in either case be the same—a forest, for example. Knowledge of the components of the forest, however, is of a different order from knowledge of the ways in which these components form a forest, of how forests evolve, and of the relationships between forests and men.

Information about any environment, therefore, has primarily to do with the relation of the whole to parts and of parts to the whole. Information concerning any specific aspect or intrinsic component of a biophysical environment may, for example, be classified as geology, biochemistry, oceanography, meteorology, or microbiology. Both kinds of information or knowledge, the relational and the intrinsic, are needed in the solution of many human problems, including those of development, but only the intrinsic has been generally translated into operational concepts through such applied disciplines as agriculture, engineering, and medicine. Holistic knowledge, partly because of its volume and complexity, is difficult to codify; moreover, its contribution to understanding of the internal interrelationships of complex systems is frequently inadequately developed and, hence, has a low predictive or manipulative value.

Thus, in the development process, the agronomist, the civil engineer, and the public health technician apply their special knowledge and skills to specific bits and pieces of the total biophysical environment. The consequences of their actions may interrelate and will surely make changes in the total environmental complex. Yet neither they nor anyone else is usually in a position to know what the inadvertent outcomes of this interaction and change may be. Their specialties do not extend to comprehensive environmental analysis, and modern society has scarcely begun to recognize the need for this function, let alone to consider how it might be effected. We are beginning to see that the environmental concept may hold great meaning for development planning, but we have not yet moved very far toward making the concept operational.

## Operations—Expressive and Normative

A first step toward making environmental concepts operational is to rule out the absurdities to which environmental analysis might be carried. In so doing it is necessary to be clear about the several ways in which the concept of environment may be used. In order of increasing relevance for development planning these uses may be described as (1) expressive, (2) normative, and (3) instrumental.

Environment as an *expressive* concept has significance for the development planner insofar as images of the nation can be evoked in environmental terms. Such images may be conjured on behalf of national planning, and they may also be used to reinforce opposition to change. A nation's physical domain and its characteristic features expressed in environmental imagery have commonly provided a symbolic reference by which artists, poets, and politicians emphasize the national identity. Patriotic oratory is replete with these geophysical references: the black soil of the Ukraine; the island fortress of England; the continental sweep of America "From sea to shining sea." Such allusions symbolize distinguishing elements in the complex matrix of historical and environmental circumstance that make up the life of a nation.

National emblems—badges, flags, coats of arms, and postage stamps—draw extensively upon the natural environment for expressive imagery. Familiar examples are the maple leaf of Canada, the cedar of Lebanon, the palm of Haiti, and the Southern Cross of Brazil. By way of contrast, economic development of the physical environment is implicit in the sheaves of grain and the hammer and sickle of Soviet and Eastern European republics and is most explicit in the national coat of arms of North Korea depicting a hydroelectric dam and power plant.

National development plans, however, characteristically have been phrased in the language of economics and have dealt with environmental factors only as discrete material resources. They have seldom utilized environmental imagery, or even simple description, to enable people to see more clearly what life may be like when development plans are realized. To persons versed in econometrics, statistical projections may hold meaning, but for the less sophisticated mass of humanity it is probably true that one image-forming picture is worth a thousand abstract indices.

The abstract statistical language of development plans and the resulting difficulty of relating them meaningfully to real-life conditions would seem to offer one possible explanation for apparent popular indifference to them in many countries. It may be useful to the future course of development planning to examine the extent to which economic considerations separated from their cultural and biophysical implications can inspire popular cooperation and support. This is not to suggest more power plants on national coats of arms but rather that more concrete imagery picturing what a nation is to become may be a useful tool in mobilizing a national development effort.

This proposition leads directly into the *normative* uses of environmental concepts. Development planning implies the conscious articulation of social goals and may envisage the systematic application of science and technology to their attainment. In the development process the total environment of people—psychosocial, cultural, biophysical—is changed, and the consequences and implications of these changes influence the possibilities within which people may shape their lives in the future.

The close interrelationship between the biophysical environment and social behavior has increasingly been demonstrated by researchers in animal behavior.[3] The extent to which this evidence has relevance for human societies is still uncertain; nevertheless, environmental factors have been identified as causal in certain behavioral syndromes and in physiological changes frequently associated with disease.[4] Biometeorology has become an active focus for biophysical research, particularly in relation to man's need to contrive a microenvironment to surround him in his exploration of outer space. Yet notwithstanding this evidence of relevance, the influence of environmental concepts in the social sciences and in development theory and planning has been relatively slight.

Past efforts to postulate an environmental influence on human affairs have frequently outrun empirical evidence. Some of the "environmentalist" geographers early in this century appear to have fallen into this error. In the negative reaction to environmentalism, the whole environmental concept was discredited, and a generation of scholars has been largely diverted from certain lines of research that might hold much promise for the development process. Similarly in sociology, undemonstrable assumptions about the effects of environment upon social behavior—in slums, for example—caused many social scientists to associate environmental concepts with subjective impressions and unmeasurable values. In consequence, the tendency of contemporary social science has been to leave the biophysical environment to the biophysical sciences and to treat its presence in human affairs as if it were neutral. Unfortunately for the advancement of knowledge, biophysical scientists have, for the most part, been slow to bring the implications of their findings for human institutions and behavior to the social and behavioral scientists. Where social scientists have been concerned with problems growing out of new scientific knowledge, in genetics, for example, they have often experienced great difficulty in dealing with these implications within their own methodologies.

The normative value of environmental concepts is therefore widely discounted among social scientists and development planners. A partial but significant exception, however, is found among certain theorists of Soviet and Eastern European Socialist planning who perceive an indivisible relationship between the objectives of Socialist society and the biophysical environment in which that society is built. The idealist city of Socialist man is seen by Soviet planners as the physical expression of Socialist society, and from the same perspective slums, congestion, pollution, and uncontrolled urban sprawl are described as the physical expression of free-enterprise democracy.[5]

Among an influential number of Western planners such idealist concepts of the urban environment are written off as utopian, which generally means that they cannot or should not be realized. There is a tendency among some planners to regard *comprehensive* physical planning as expressing the aesthetic or moral prejudices of particular planners and social classes and as of doubtful consistency with democratic values or with the dynamism of modern technology. Thus a seeker for some set of environmental norms or standards by which to guide or evaluate the course of development may feel that he has been turned away empty-handed, that his search is naïve, and that the "experts" (ecologists, planners, and economists) have offered conflicting advice.

An environmental norm is not necessarily a derivative of scientific evidence. Norms in any case reflect preferences or values that may or may not depend upon a valid interpretation of the natural world. Where scientific evidence is lacking, skepticism regarding the value of environmental norms is justifiable. The ethical or aesthetic content of a norm may be defended on its own philosophical grounds, independently of environmental theory, but the case for these important nonscientific considerations would be strengthened if supported by findings in the sciences of psychology and physiology. It is conceivable that such support may in time be discovered.

Meanwhile, environmental standards of operational value are only now beginning to emerge out of research in the biophysical and behavioral sciences, in engineering and in public health. In the growing evidence concerning the effects of pollution of air and water, in the biochemistry of the soil and of human nutrition, in the psychological manifestations of crowding, isolation, and other environmental states, some verifiable environmental relationships are being established. From these relationships it may become possible to formulate operational standards of environmental safety, quality, or satisfaction. As biophysical environmental factors can be empirically demonstrated to have a causal relationship to human welfare, the receptivity of both "natural" and "social" scientists to the concept of environmental norms for human society seems certain to grow. But acceptance or confirmation of these norms are acts of public policy and the particular concern of politicians. If science is to play an informing and guiding role in development planning, effective communication among scientists, planners, and politicians would appear to be essential.[6]

Biophysical science already provides much more "hard" knowledge than the economic and social architects of new nations (or old) seem ready to employ. How this knowledge may be better utilized and expanded was the theme and purpose of the 1963

United Nations Conference on the Application of Science and Technology for the Benefit of the Less Developed Areas. The data accumulated in more than two thousand technical papers illustrates the range, complexity, and interdependence of the biophysical aspects of the development process.[7] But these papers also demonstrate the highly specialized, compartmentalized character of this knowledge and of the great difficulty and urgent need of its organization into coherent standards or guidelines of practical relevance to development plans and action. At this point, the holistic concept of total environment becomes clearly relevant to the development task, and the need for more ways to give this concept operational utility becomes evident.

## Implications for National Planning

The relevance of a general or holistic concept of environment to the practical operations of development programs is best illustrated by the *instrumental* applications of environmental knowledge. Even though environmental concepts have been widely neglected and misinterpreted, the biophysical environment itself has not escaped practical attention. In one form or another it has been a major focus for development planning. Man has been manipulating his environment and developing his surroundings ever since he invented clothing and agriculture. Environments have been altered on a large scale by deliberate choice as well as by inadvertence. Forests have been felled, grasslands burned, marshes drained, wild land cultivated, and rivers canalized. The ancient "hydaulic civilizations" of China, Mesopotamia, and Egypt were based essentially on environmental administration.[8] In a sharply contrasting way, the Mongols' destruction of urban centers were not wholly acts of war but were also deliberate efforts to reshape the environment from one suitable for city dwellers and cultivators to a pastoral condition suitable for the nomad's flocks and herds.[9] Conversely, American legislation on homesteading and irrigation favored, in effect, the supplanting of open grasslands by a pattern of enclosed family-cultivated farms. The development plans of modern nations characteristically involve drainage, irrigation or clearing of lands, engineering of river systems, road building, mining, relocation of populations, massive environmental health controls (as in the antimalaria effort), changes in agricultural land tenure and technology, and, almost universally, industrialization. Seldom, however, is consideration given to the composite effects of these changes upon the total environment of a nation or its neighbors. Indeed, the evidence of miscarried projects and of environmental impairment that has resulted from all too many development efforts suggests insufficient attention to even the most direct and foreseeable environmental consequences.

The 1963 United Nations Conference on Science and Technology for the Benefit of the Less Developed Areas was given sobering examples of disastrous environmental mismanagement. In the report of the conference, Roger Revelle of the United States cited the loss through faulty irrigation practices of $6\frac{1}{2}$ million acres of once-arable land in West Pakistan. "The soil affected is in the Indus Valley, where the population is increasing at the rate of ten more mouths to be fed every five minutes and where, every five minutes, an acre of land is being lost through water-logging and salinity." [10] Soviet academicians U. P. Gerasimov and E. K. Fedorov pointed out the irreparable damage to soils resulting from improvident agricultural practices leading to severe erosion in "almost half of the total cultivated area of the world." [11] Zacarias Papovici of Peru described the urgent problem of contamination of sea and air resulting from the improper disposal of the residue of fisheries. [12] The conference report concluded that "Ecology, that branch of science which is concerned with living things . . . their habits, their relationship to each other in the global community, and to the surroundings which they share, has become, belatedly, an essential study in the evaluation and development of natural resources." [13]

Nevertheless, evidence does not support the optimistic belief that, past errors recognized, future mistakes will be avoided in the planned development of new areas. As Jean-Paul Harroy of Belgium observed at the conference, ". . . when planning programmes for the economic development of these areas are being organized (based in the vast majority of cases on renewable natural resources), the power and the decision are all too often left in the hands of the economists, engineers, financiers, political leaders and members of government departments, whilst the specialists on these resources—the naturalists, ecologists and geographical surveyors are not included in the exercise." [14] Although the ultimate social, economic, and physiological consequences of environmental deterioration have been extensively documented, Harroy expressed a misgiving shared increasingly by ecologists and students of public health in his observation that "it is strange to find how little public opinion and national or international authorities seem to be aware of, or even worried about, this." [15]

On the contrary there is an optimistic belief that science and technology can offset whatever errors or profligate miscalculations that man makes in reshaping his biophysical environment. The exponential expansion of scientific technology places new instruments of environmental change in human hands at a rate that far exceeds our present inclination to subject the effects of these methods and devices to careful study. Research and development applied to the solution of specific problems, for example insect depredations, have often come up with answers that have created new difficulties replacing those purported to be solved. The fault lies not in scientific technology, but in a technology that is insufficiently scientific, one that is based upon a very partial reading of the environmental situation, in thinking that has never been schooled to search out the more probable and predictable consequences of action or to develop criteria of search that may discover the hidden, unknown factors that would otherwise be missed.

The primarily instrumental value of the environmental concept for development planning is, therefore, its usefulness in forcing a comprehensive search for the factors relevant to contemplated action. But it is apparent that something more tangible is needed than an exhortation to view environmental issues comprehensively. The translation of environmental knowledge and concepts into operational terms is a major task for research. Need for practical systems or methods of environmental analysis is only now beginning to be recognized. Standards or guidelines that define or describe desirable environmental conditions are being established for particular aspects of life, but we are still far from a knowledge of optimal conditions regarding most areas of biophysical environmental relationships. Nevertheless, avoidance of demonstrably harmful environmental consequences is sufficient justification for more frequent recourse to comprehensive environmental analysis.

In addition to a frame of reference for comprehensive search for the probable consequences of biophysical changes, the environmental concept provides another instrumental utility. In a recent study of city and regional planning in Poland, Wojciech Morawski has cited the value of examining changes in the physical environment for verification of the effects of national economic planning.[16] The ultimate purpose of a large part of economic planning is improvement in specific aspects of the biophysical environment—in agriculture, transportation, housing, and urban conditions, for example. The ultimate test of the efficacy of this planning is in its actual accomplishments.

Inconsistencies and contradictions that may be rationalized in the planning process may become glaringly apparent when translated into action. In any event, the physical changes attributable to development planning afford some measure of the desirability and effectiveness of the plans. Thus not only may the extent to which plan objectives are realized be verified by reference to tangible results, but the very objectives of the planning may, at least in part, be evaluated by reference to results. In short, outcomes may be found to be consistent with planned objectives, but these objectives, when tested by results, may sometimes be found to be undesirable, often in ways that were not foreseen.

## THE NEED FOR RESEARCH

The foregoing paragraphs have developed a case for a more valid perception of man's biophysical environment in his efforts to adapt that environment to his purposes through development planning. The thesis has been that man's technical capacity to influence environmental change has moved forward much faster than has his understanding of the complex interrelationships upon which his health, happiness, and survival depend. This hiatus between comprehensive knowledge and specialized technique is widely recognized and deplored, but not easily bridged. Experience has shown that it is much easier to discover how to manipulate the environment than to explain the cause-effect relationships that are thereby brought into play. Primitive man first learned to use fire without understanding its physical causes or potentialities. In the aggregate, trial and error have hitherto served men well, primarily because the magnitude of error has been restricted by man's limited technology, but this safety factor is rapidly being effaced by technological growth.

Nuclear physics has given man the power of sudden and possibly universal destruction; the biological sciences are discovering slower but no less lethal counterparts. These are the more obvious evidences of the risks inherent in man's capacity to effect rapid and even irreversible environmental changes. There is also in this knowledge the power to improve the human condition. The powers made available by science and technology are neutral; it is their utilization on behalf of human purposes that gives them significance in human affairs. In lesser, less evident ways, this capacity to effect change is being enlarged in almost every direction. The development process is a deliberate effort to apply this accelerating capacity to effect change to the multiform, varied, and often urgent problems of mid-twentieth-century man. In this process, particularly in the so-called "less developed areas," an eagerness, even anxiety, to catch up with the more technologically advanced nations makes the prospect of shortcuts to development goals attractive. There is danger that impatient and inadequately tested action may impinge upon man's biophysical environment in a manner recalling the fable of the sorcerer's apprentice.

There is widespread agreement with this thesis but much less agreement as to what can or should be done about it, and not all observers would agree as to the extent of urgency involved. There appear to be deep-seated factors in the human personality that make it difficult for men to adjust their thought and action to the picture of the real world that science is revealing. The human urge to dominate and exploit is rooted deeply in instincts that made for survival in the Stone Age. But their utility in an age of science is less certain, and the creation of perceptions and values appropriate to man's new condition is a profoundly difficult task.

To give a greater practical utility to the environmental or ecological knowledge now available is an obvious first step toward a more rational development of the biophysical environment. The formulating of criteria for weighing environment-affecting decisions would be one way of reducing scientific knowledge to administrative practice. Even as homely a tool as a checklist of environmental or ecological considerations properly safeguarded as to purpose and use might prevent many inadvertent errors in development planning and might serve to condition the minds of its users toward a new perception of environmental relationships. Scientific considerations are not the only factors entering into environment-affecting decisions, but their clearer delineation should also help to clarify the actual basis for environmental decision making.

The process by which societies and governments make decisions that shape the biophysical environment needs more than the cursory attention it has thus far received. Research in depth and in detail is needed to get at the mainsprings of man's attitudes and action toward the biophysical world. Until more is known about why men make the type of environmental decisions that they do, it will be difficult to say what means must be taken to obtain better decisions. Case studies of issues and motives involved in environmental change could contribute greatly to this knowledge.

Ironically our very backwardness in making environmental concepts operational has been a major obstacle to accomplishing this task. Recognition within governments, universities, and research foundations of the importance of environmental relationships has been qualified by skepticism regarding the utility of environmental concepts in practical affairs. We have, therefore, been more willing to pay the high costs of trial and error in actual environmental change than to hazard lesser funds for research into environmental relationships and their management in human affairs. Where the issue has been specifically defined, as in certain aspects of public health or urban development, research support has been forthcoming. But the larger and more fundamental aspects of man's environmental relationships are harder to conceptualize, and support for research to bring these concepts closer to application in practical affairs is not easily obtained. Thus our shortcomings in the reduction of environmental knowledge to usable, down-to-earth terms tend to be self-perpetuating.

It is possible that a broadening and intensifying of research into environmental factors in development must await some massive, man-made miscalculation that will arouse public demand for measures to prevent recurrence. There are scientists in considerable number who fear that disastrous eventualities are near-certainties. The greatest danger is perhaps less in such dramatic and obvious disasters as nuclear holocaust than in harmful trends that are hidden, subtle, and irreversible and, in the absence of research, may not be discovered until it is too late for remedies.

The so-called "developed" and "developing" nations share a common global environment. The people of the earth are in effect fellow passengers on the same planetary spaceship, which is also their only base. The lessons of interdependence in our biophysical universe have long been taught but never fully learned. Today as never before it is necessary for men to bring their learning up to where it will meet the challenge of the situation into which they have worked themselves. There is no foreseeable end to the process of development. Its continuing task is the shaping of present conditions that will influence, if not determine, possiblities to be realized in the future. If the implications of this process are fully grasped, there can be no question of the need for more attention to the environmental consequences of development efforts.

## THE ROLE OF NATIONAL PLANNING AGENCIES

The foregoing argument implies several considerations in the organization and functions of national planning bodies. It implies that the scope and focus of their activities be broadly conceived. The concept of national development planning as primarily *economic* is inadequate even to provide an appropriate allocation of economic values. Economics may afford the substance of the greater part of planning activities, but its role should be subordinate to the full range of human values. Health, public safety, social development, cultural growth, and aesthetic and ethical values are some of the ends of development efforts that do not necessarily follow from economic "progress," although favorable economic conditions are obviously important supporting factors.

The primacy of economic values reflects needs and circumstances prevailing in a predominantly commercial and industrial society. The politization of economics, as in Soviet-type states, does not appear to offer a real opportunity for other distributions of values in public planning, perhaps because Marxist ideology is based upon an assumption of the primacy of economics as the determining force in society. The assumptions upon which current development planning tend to be based reflect more often the conditions of the nineteenth century than those brought about through science and technology in our times. A second implication for national planning agencies is therefore to lay down a basis for national development that is broadly based and more appropriate to the full spectrum of mid-twentieth-century human needs than one derived from the assumptions of Adam Smith and Karl Marx.

One obvious reason for the overworked approach to national planning through economic criteria is the advantage afforded by use of quantification. Economic criteria are more readily reduced to arithmetic terms than are the criteria of health, ethics, aesthetics, or justice. The relatively advanced state of economic accounting offers a measure of clarity and precision that is difficult to approximate in most other areas of social concern. One major advance in public planning would be the development of national systems of social accounting that would extend some of the methods of economic accounting to other areas of value without simultaneously imposing the assumptions and logics of economic thinking.[17] It is not economics, as such, but its misapplication that is at fault. Economic thinking embraces many diverse viewpoints, and the criticism advanced here should be interpreted as an objection to an overly narrow and intolerant overemphasis on specific economic assumptions. The importance of economic analysis in planning needs no defense.

A third implication of this chapter is the need for national planning agencies to build research into their activities as perhaps the most important ingredient. Some planning agencies, such as the former National Resources Planning Board in the United States, have had more of the nature of research agencies than planning bodies. This represents an overbalance in the research direction as opposed to action. All national planning agencies are in some measure dependent upon research and in some measure engaged in it through their own personnel, or indirectly through research institutes or universities. But the accumulating testimony from planners and scientists points up the inadequacy of knowledge for the guidance of many of our most fundamental planning decisions. In no area is this need for knowledge more evident than in man's relationship with his biophysical environment.

Overreliance upon economic criteria in planning decisions is too often a consequence of lack (or neglect) of hard knowledge about the biophysical implications of the proposed action. In matters affecting medicine and public health, for example, the potentialities of science for human welfare have been severely restricted by the inadequacy of our knowledge regarding "the effects of the total environment upon the human condition." [18] Research for national development therefore implies support of a much wider range of research effort than has customarily been considered relevant to development planning. A national planning agency is ideally an "information switchboard" or clearinghouse for the great diversity of research pertaining to national development, not only that which is available in the home country but also that relevant research which is undertaken abroad. A valuable service of national planning agencies could be not only to identify and locate the sources of data necessary to wise planning decisions but equally to identify the areas of dangerous ignorance and to seek out ways to stimulate and assist research where it is needed.

Not all planning research can or should be undertaken in all the countries to which it might apply. It would be impossible for even the largest and wealthiest states to marshal the resources of men and money to cover all aspects of environmental relationships in which research is needed. International organizations clearly must play a greater role in research for environmental planning than they have done hitherto. There is an obvious economy in centralization of research relating to very similar types of problems. There is also a research advantage in the comparative study of various instances of comparable relationships. Thus a sound basis in knowledge for environmental planning may be obtained through research in individual countries organized and coordinated through international agencies.[19] In addition, direct communication, cooperation, and collaboration among planning agencies and planners should be greatly increased, just as increased interdisciplinary relationships among the relevant fields of biophysical and social sciences and the public service professions are necessary to enlarge and strengthen the base of knowledge upon which wise planning rests.

The conclusion of this chapter is therefore that analysis and evaluation of the biophysical consequences of development planning are as important to its purposes as are the means by which the plans are put into action. Successful implementation of ill-conceived plans is not the kind of action that serves the ultimate purposes and goals of planning. Action under development planning should therefore imply much more than plan implementation. It should imply research, testing, and consultation among a wide range of competencies. Implementation is the final phase of action, but its antecedent phases are, or should be, an integral part of the action process. It is in this analytic and evaluative phase that science can make its greatest contribution to planning, but it is also in this phase that political impatience and disregard for objectivity are most pronounced.

Development planning cannot improve man's condition if it fails to respect the fundamental unity of the biophysical world. The unity of science is merely the evidence of the unity of reality. Technology, however, is disparate, and its employment unguided by any unifying concept of the goals of development, has often led to action at cross purposes and to destructive fractionalizing of the total fabric of a nation's cultural life.[20] Perhaps the most important single task, of the many that make up development planning, is to establish the mastery of man over technique in the service of goals that are consistent with our best verified understandings of man's environmental needs.

## NOTES

[1] Oct. 17, 1963, p. 10.

[2] Two basic surveys of man's impact on his biophysical environment are the essay and references by Paul B. Sears in "Changing Man's Habitat: Physical and Biological Phenomena," in William L. Thomas, Jr. (ed.), *Current Anthropology*, The University of Chicago Press, Chicago, 1955, and the comprehensive volume also edited by Thomas, *Man's Role in Changing the Face of the Earth*, The University of Chicago Press, Chicago, 1956.

[3] Cf. "Behavior and the Environment," in John Paul Scott, *Animal Behavior*, The University of Chicago Press, Chicago, 1958, pp. 206–234. For example, experimental studies on the effects of population growth have been undertaken with numerous species of animals: "Each species that has been investigated presents a new and fascinating series of problems, and their study has many practical as well as theoretical considerations for man's control of his biological environment" (p. 224). Also cf. W. C. Allee et al., *Principles of Animal Ecology*, W. B. Saunders Company, Philadelphia, 1949, and Vincent Dethier and Elliot Steller, *Animal Behavior: Its Evolutionary and Neurological Basis*, 2d ed., Prentice-Hall, Inc., Englewood Cliffs, N.J., 1964.

[4] For example, observations of Rene Dubos in *The Dreams of Reason: Science and Utopias*, Columbia University Press, New York, 1961, pp. 84 ff., and "Environmental Biology," *Bio Science*, vol. 14, p. 12, January, 1964. Also "Man—His Environment and Health," Supplement to January, 1964, *American Journal of Public Health*, part 2; Luther L. Terry, "The Complex World of Modern Public Health," Third Annual Bronfman Lecture, *American Journal of Public Health Association, Third General Session, Kansas City*, vol. 54, pp. 189–195, January, 1964; and Paul M. Gross, "The Fifth Estate in the Seventh Decade," *Science*, 143, p. 19, Jan. 3, 1964. In *The Dreams of Reason*, p. 84, Dubos summarizes the health-environment relationships as follows:

> Health is an expression of ability to cope with the various factors of the total environment, and fitness is achieved through countless genotypic and phenotypic adaptations to these factors. Any change in the environment demands new adaptive reactions, and disease is the consequence of inadequacies in these adaptive responses. The more rapid and profound the environmental changes, the larger the number of individuals who cannot adapt to them

rapidly enough to maintain an adequate state of fitness and who therefore develop some type of organic or psychotic disease.

[5] Jack C. Fisher, "Planning the City of Socialist Man," *Journal of the American Institute of Planners*, vol. 28, pp. 251–265, November, 1962; B. Michael Frolic, "The Soviet City," *The Town Planning Review*, vol. 34, pp. 285, 306, January, 1964. But see the comment of Dimitri B. Shimkin on Soviet neglect of environmental factors in "Resource Development and Utilization in the Soviet Economy," in Marion Clawson (ed.), *Natural Resources and International Development*, The Johns Hopkins Press, Baltimore, 1964, p. 185.

[6] Cf. Lynton K. Caldwell, "Biopolitics: Science, Ethics, and Public Policy," *The Yale Review*, vol. 54, pp. 1–16, October, 1964.

[7] Cf. *Report on the 1963 United Nations Conference on the Application of Science and Technology for the Benefit of the Less Developed Areas*, vols. I–VIII, United Nations, New York, 1963. Note particularly the numerous examples cited in vol. I, chap. 1, of man's misuse of his biophysical environment. Of special relevance are vol. II, *Natural Resources*, vol. III, *Agriculture*, and vol. VII, *Science and Planning*, and the "List of Papers" in vol. VIII, pp. 152–209.

[8] Cf. Karl A. Wittfogel, *Oriental Despotism*, Yale University Press, New Haven, Conn., 1957.

[9] Cf. Otto Franke, *Geschichte des chinesischen Reiches*, Verlag von Walter de Gruyter, Berlin, 1948, vol. IV, p. 279: "*Am liebsten würde Dschingis Khan alle Städte in Nordchina zerstört und das ganze in Weideland umgewandelt haben.*" (Genghis Khan would have wished to have all cities of North China demolished and turned into pastureland.)

[10] *Report on the 1963 United Nations Conference on the Application of Science and Technology for the Benefit of the Less Developed Areas*, vol. I, p. 5.

[11] *Ibid.*, p. 4.

[12] *Ibid.*, p. 8.

[13] *Ibid.*, p. 9.

[14] *Ibid.*, vol. III, p. 7.

[15] *Ibid.*

[16] Jack C. Fisher (ed.), *City and Regional Planning in Poland*, Cornell University Press, Ithaca, N.Y., 1966.

[17] Cf. the paper by Bertram M. Gross, "State of the Nation: Social System Accounting," in Raymond A. Bauer (ed.), *Social Indicators*, The M.I.T. Press, Cambridge, Mass., 1966.

[18] Cf. Rene Dubos, "Environmental Biology," *op. cit.*, p. 11.

[19] Cf. Egbert de Vries, "International Transfers of Knowledge and Capital," in Clawson, *op. cit.*, pp. 434–435.

[20] Cf. Jacques Ellul, *The Technological Society*, Alfred A. Knopf, Inc., New York, 1964.

# 5

## The Limitations of "Perfect Planning"

### Zygmunt Bauman

The "perfect planning" model may be thought of as the alternative of the "perfect market" model widely described by the economists. Perfect planning may be defined initially as the second pole of a continuum which has the perfect-market situation as its first pole. The opposition between the two poles consists of (1) the opposition between an aggregate of individual and group actions diffusively motivated and a macrosocial process as a system of coordinated partial actions; (2) the opposition between social process determined genetically and social process determined teleologically, that is, between the kind of social process in which the goal is an outcome of action and another kind in which the action is prefigured by the goal, and (3) the opposition between a situation in which the mechanism determining the global "behavior" of the social whole is sharply different from the mechanism determining the behavior of its individual units and a situation in which the two mechanisms are identical. The idea of perfect planning has been to fit the total social process to the model of individual human behavior derived from the human being's inherent capacity of rational thinking and action. Although the perfect-planning situation has not yet been achieved in any social system, it remains the conscious or unconscious goal of any big organization and also of government organizations seated at the highest level of societal integration.

It is not our task to evaluate the virtues and vices of perfect planning as an aim of social thinkers or practitioners. We are not inclined to decide whether perfect planning is desirable or even what is the proper frame of reference suitable for estimating its eventual merits and shortcomings. The sole end of this chapter is to enumerate some important obstacles which, at least at the present stage of social development, counteract achievement of a perfect-planning situation and thus are responsible for maintaining the gap between planning ideals and the reality of action. It is our contention that these obstacles are to be found in some salient contradictions between functional requisites of the perfect-planning model and important parameters of the social structure of modern society.

We want to elaborate this statement by (1) formulating the functional requisites of perfect planning, (2) describing some experiences of the planning process derived predominantly from Polish examples, and (3) trying to formulate in general terms those structural characteristics of the planning societies which are responsible for the fact that the functional requisites of perfect planning have not been met.

## FUNCTIONAL REQUISITES OF PERFECT PLANNING

Any planning activity obviously requires some decision-making and planning agent that makes the plan and thus plays the role of at least one of the factors influencing social action. Perfect planning, however, requires something more: it requires that agent to be the only and unchallenged factor determining the totality of social action. Not every social situation makes such a role possible, although any executive of a big organization wants to achieve it. The basic requirements listed below must be met if this situation is to exist.

## Resource Self-sufficiency

The social system must be self-sufficient and isolated in the sphere of those activities which are subjected to planning (in this context of terms *self-sufficient* and *isolated* are for all practical purposes synonymous. This means that all conceivable resources —physical, human, mental—necessary to perform activities subjected to plan should be (1) available inside this given system and (2) freely manipulative, that is, circulated according to decisions made by the planning agent. This means also that no agent from outside the system (*outside* has a meaning which is not confined to the physical space only) or, to put it in different words, that no agent which itself is not manipulated directly or indirectly by the decision-making center of the system should interfere with the circulation of resources now under discussion. Whenever this condition is not met, coordinated action is replaced by the clash of diffusively planned competitive actions, and so events genetically determined are substituted for those which were expected to be teleological.

## Perfect Information

*Resources* is a broad term, and it may be defined in such a way as to include also information as a foremost resource in itself in any systemic process. At the same time the processing of information has peculiar qualities which distinguish it from the process of resource supply. That is why, perhaps, cyberneticists view any system as a cluster of two intertwining though separate channels, one of energy circulation and one of information circulation. We prefer also to confine the term *resources* to that class of phenomena which is dealt with in cybernetics under the rubric of "energy." Thus we should repeat in respect to information what was stated above on resources: the perfect-planning model requires all possible information important and valid from the point of view of the activities subjected to plan to be in possession of the planning agent. This refers first of all to information concerning availability and possible uses of resources as well as the technology of manipulating them. Failure to meet this requirement does not lead necessarily, as in the case of resources, to the very process of planning being undermined. Nevertheless, it does lead to planning which is not "perfect," this time in the sense of not being rational enough and not being a match for the actual opportunities rooted potentially in the given social situation.

### Perfect Rationality by Planners

The perfect-planning model requires further that the planning agent be capable of making decisions which are not only realistic but also most effective in terms of the overall systemic goals. This, in turn, requires that (1) the planning agent should be "depersonalized," free of any motivations which are not identical with the preestablished goals of the system as a whole, acting as a kind of fleshless and soulless embodiment of the "interest of the system" alone; (2) the planning agent should be competent in the sense of being able to choose among many alternatives how to use available resources to achieve the best solution, which implies both reliable knowledge and skill and necessary executive power; (3) the alternatives among which selection is to be made must be reducible to a common denominator, commensurable, exhaustible by a simple and universal quantifying and quantifiable measure. To be subjected to any selection, alternatives must be compared; to be compared, they must be comparable; to be comparable, they should possess common dimension, just to be located in the same frame of reference for the sake of comparison. They should differ from each other only in terms of *more* and *less*, in their quantities, not qualities. If this is not so, then criteria of rationality cease to be sufficient tools of decision making, and no longer is any single-dimensional frame of reference suitable to judge the planned as "the best" or "not the best" without stating from what point of view. This is the case with all human systems which are concerned not only with producing one or several simple goods but also with satisfying the needs of their component human beings.

### Social Homogeneity

Perfect planning implies also that the social system is homogeneous in the sense that there are no events which are beneficial to one part of the system and harmful to another at the same time, in other words, that the system does not consist of parts which have mutually conflicting interests. The interest of the system as a whole, which is the necessary reference pattern for systemic planning, cannot be just a kind of ideological projection of interests of one part of the system, nor can it be reduced to alleviation of conflicts and prevention of their overt manifestations. To play its role as a reference pattern, it must be something more: it must be not only the interest of the system but also the common interest of the parts of the system, whatever criteria are applied to distinguish them (these two quite different notions are often and misleadingly dealt with interchangeably). Only then may the systemic goals retain their priority over any other goals, which is the premise of perfect planning as it was defined initially. Conflicts of interests bring into the planning process unpredictable and basically unmanageable influences which can seriously disturb the demands of pure systemic rationality.

## Perfect Hierarchic Control

Closely connected with social homogeneity is the further requirement that there be nothing in between the planning agent and elementary units of behavior which does not derive its decision-making and executive power merely from delegation by the planning agent. In other words, there should be no place for any autonomous sources of power or influence. Of course, in no complex system may all decisions be made directly by the planning agent itself; on the contrary, several hierarchized levels of systemic integration are necessary; but agents responsible for the intermediary levels must make sure that, when choosing, they select the alternative which best of all fits the demands of the planning agent. Now, if there are conflicting interests within the system, they are always a basis for interest groups, and if there are interest groups, then it is a rule that no decisions taken at the systemic level are able to motivate all parts of the system to react in the desired manner. Stimulating the positive behavior of some groups, each decision is likely to stimulate resistance of some other. It seems that some form of interest conflict may be traced whenever the functional requirement now under discussion is not being met. Also, the presence of conflicting interests within the social system seriously impedes the meeting of the second of our requirements, that concerning availability of all information on the level of the planning agent. In a system divided into conflicting parts, all data are incomplete because they are relative; seen from positions of conflicting interests, the same social reality is a source of conflicting information. Placed in uncoordinated frames of reference, facts cease to be neutral and thus can, and indeed are, mentally organized into many different and mutually conflicting systems. No single agent is able, therefore, to collect all information circulating inside the system.

We are not sure that the foregoing inventory of functional requirements of the perfect-planning model is complete. It seems, however, to account for the foremost reasons why in no known social system has perfect planning so far been achieved. Following is an attempt to trace contradictions which appear when efforts to meet requirements of perfect planning are made in a social system which does not fully conform to the model.

## INITIAL LIMITATIONS OF SOCIALIST PLANNING

The scope of decision taken on the enterprise level is determined by the scope of power possessed by the planning agents (in regard to realistic and potentially effective decisions only). The scope of power is, in turn, determined by the limits of ownership. Management is able to manipulate the volume of resources and raw materials which are actually in its possession or may be acquired with available funds. Thus the whole producing and marketing activity in the private ownership system is divided into a multitude of parts, each of which is submitted to another planning agency. As each agent submits its planning to the goal of profit maximization, there is always a danger of economic disequilibrium on the societal level. To avoid this danger some noneconomic institutions must interfere. On the societal level, the notion of "economic rationality," which on the enterprise level has been identified with profit gain, must be broadened, and additional criteria, not always reducible to monetary measurement, must be introduced into the process of planning.

The primary function of society has always been and still remains the need satisfaction of its members. Not all profit is "rational" from this point of view, but only that kind of profit which is operative for harmonious need satisfaction. The nineteenth-century free-market ideologies made the mistake of neglecting the autonomy of the societal-level need-oriented goals and of considering it exhausted and solved by the profit goal operating at the middle level of an economic system.

The manager of a prosperous enterprise does not have to be bothered by where and how his employees will obtain the goods necessary to satisfy their needs, provided he has paid them relevant wages and salaries. The commodity actually manufactured by this particular enterprise has nothing to do with the variety of goods which are needed and wanted by the employees in their consumer capacity. The full coverage of the totality of needs by the totality of varied products is not a problem which the manager of a single enterprise is expected to solve or even with which he is expected to bother himself. But the situation is different when we move to the level of society as a whole.

As far as the scope of planning is concerned, planning in Socialist countries may be viewed as the simple extension of the scope of enterprise planning: the planning state may be viewed simply as a gigantic factory management. The extension of scope is here a direct consequence of unifying the economic power heretofore divided and accumulating all available resources under single ownership. To extend our analogy, we can compare citizens of a Socialist country with the shareholders of a company; their participation in the state-scale enterprise profits may be dealt with in terms of dividends. The issues involved in their access to control of the process of production are not basically distinct from the problems we confront whenever we try to understand relationships between management and rank-and-file shareholders in an average company.

Besides, in the sphere of foreign trade, which is still based on free-market exchange, the gigantic "national enterprise" does act as if it were a single, though formidably big, firm concerning itself almost exclusively with the opportunities of possibly good profit.

### Foreign Trade

We have passed here from enterprise planning to state planning, having modified the value of one variable only, the scope of planning, which is in its turn the direct function of the scope of ownership. This procedure depicts the Socialist type of planning as a quantitative rather than qualitative change in what is rather an old and well-known practice. Also, this extension of scope has never been complete and in all known cases is still very far from reaching its theoretical limits. The extension of the international market exchange proceeds at a much higher speed; as a result, no state society is able to satisfy the totality of its members' needs with its own products. Therefore in its need-satisfying functions it is dependent on the international exchange of goods, which remains beyond its power to control. That is why the spontaneous and unexpected modifications in terms of trade interfere also in the intrastate economic system and heavily restrict the effectiveness of planning (perfect planning always requires the availability of all relevant information and the capability of manipulating all variables involved in the planning equation). *The planned activity of economic units outside the boundaries of the planning state is the first limitation of effective planning on the societal level,* just as the plans of other companies limit the effectiveness of factory-level planning in the free-market economy.

### The Household Frame of Reference

This kind of abstract model would not, however, lead us very far unless we introduced additional variables to characterize not only the quantitative but also the qualitative peculiarity of planning at the societal level. The planning state society differs from the planning enterprise in that it is not only a producing but also a consuming unit and thus is responsible for satisfying the needs of its members and for the reliable redistribution of adequate goods. From this point on, the one-sided analysis of state planning in terms of company planning becomes completely misleading. The reason is that a planning state is not only a gigantic enterprise but also a gigantic (extended) family household; in its planning activity, it is concerned not only with rational selection of means relevant to a predetermined goal, but also—and in the first place—with selection of hierarchization of goals; the whole diversified totality of variable needs must be met somehow inside its boundaries. The analytical model we look for may thus emerge only as a result of combining tools applied usually to analysis of factory planning, on the one hand, and concepts used to describe a type of social unit which performs both production and consumption functions (for example, the peasant household), on the other.

That means that two frames of reference should be employed when society-level planning is analyzed: that of a commercial organization and that of the family household.

A rather long list of analogies between the planning state and the peasant household could be drawn up. In both units "household" (i.e., an institution serving consumption ends) comprises and subordinates "enterprise," in this case an institution which acquires goods through market exchange. "Enterprising" plays a supplementary role to "householding." In householding part of the total production is consumed inside the unit, and there always exists strong pressure to increase the ratio of the total consumed fund which is being made "at home," hence phenomena called *anti-import* production and crude, primitive, but money-free substitutive production in the peasant family. The volume of product destined to be sold on the market is determined not so much by the current terms of trade (and thus by profit expectancies) as by the market price of goods which cannot be made at home and hence have to be bought. That is why the market behavior of both the planning state and the peasant household is at times "nonrational": it consists of selling less when terms of trade are favorable and selling more when terms of trade become less favorable. These are merely a few examples taken at random from a rather large number of possible analogies.

The conclusion we thus have come to is very simple indeed: planning on the societal level (at any rate, when it is based on state ownership) is subordinated primarily to direct need satisfaction. The role of profit as a goal is limited to the sphere of marketing framed by lacunae in economic self-sufficiency and even in this domain is seriously modified by the priority of consumption goals. Thus state planning in a Socialist society may be viewed as reintroducing, this time on the macrosocial level, the old idea of the totality and all-inclusiveness of the community functions, challenged some dozens of years ago by free-market ideology and practice.

## HETEROGENEITY OF INTERESTS IN GOAL FORMULATION

The supreme task of state planning in a Socialist country is the maximization of need satisfaction of its members. Cultural, ecological, occupational, and educational differentiation of needs and their dynamics in a rapidly developing economy preclude, however, the possibility of selecting one single goal serving as a unique and exhaustive measure of appropriateness and equity of plan. This also distinguishes Socialist state planning from enterprise planning, where the goal of maximizing profit is taken for granted and criteria for plan estimating are lucid and indisputable.

An inventory of needs is not, however, a sufficient guide for planning. The important feature of all planning in Socialist states (vividly different from primitive subsistence economies) is a permanent lack of equilibrium between needs and the means of their satisfaction and an undiminishing, if not increasing, gap between global demand and global supply. That is why economic decisions neutral from the point of view of diversified interests of various groups simply do not exist. Virtually every decision is beneficial to one group and harmful to another. All decisions are loci of conflicting interests and are subjected to controversial attitudes and pressures. The domain of conflicting interests and of the struggle of antagonistic social forces articulated on their basis is the sphere of politics. Hence, economic decision making in a Socialist country is not separated from the political decision making process, and the goal-formulating process steps far beyond the boundaries of the realm we are accustomed to identify with the "economic proper" sphere of social functions. Available goods are scarce, and their distribution is always the resultant of fighting by countervailing forces. That is why the traditional tools of economic analysis appear insufficient if a system of macrosocial planning is to be investigated. Political and economic patterns of societal organization and process permeate each other; at the goal-formulating stage, at any rate, they are simply indistinguishable.

Hence the problem of the political check-and-balance system in a Socialist country is important also from the point of view of effective economic planning. *Allocation of goods consistent with the actual differentiation of needs may be achieved only on condition that the articulation of interests is unhampered and effective enough to bring the pattern of organized pressures into accord with the current pattern of interests.* Only thus can the danger of neglecting some important interests be avoided without violent and extralegal corrections.

There are, however, some remarkable contradictions in the process of macrosocial planning which restrict the free interplay of pressure-interest groups or effectiveness of planning or both (even if we eliminate transitional, incidental and extraneous impediments to this interplay).

### Investment versus Consumption

We have said above that the maximization of need satisfaction is the supreme and permanent goal of state planning. It is obvious, however, that the degree of need satisfaction is closely related to the level of output and that modern society knows no other ways to increase the standard of living but to increase the rate of investment savings, the only foundation for future economic growth. It is a well-known fact, also, that during the initial stages of economic growth the capital coefficient is particularly high. The rate of savings necessary if the national income is to be augmented by one unit is twice or even three times as much as in "after takeoff" periods. This means, in practical terms, that the higher and more rapid the expected future rise in the standard of living, the less fully can the already accumulated sum of goods be exploited to implement well-being here and now. The free interplay of pressure-interest groups would, however, result inevitably in lowering the rate of savings and, thus, in making the process of economic growth much slower than is ideologically and morally desirable (and perhaps possible) in a world subject to the constant pressure of the values of an industrial society. That is why at least a certain residuum of political restrictions can hardly be avoided if development planning is to be possible at all. Enthusiastic acceptance of industrial values and the great importance ascribed to economic growth is not tantamount to a disposition for thrift and the renunciation of present opportunities to get richer. We ought not to expect spontaneous and voluntary adherence to Puritan ethics in a century known for its lavish supply of refined consumer goods.

### Collective versus Individual Consumption

The incompatibility of immediate-need-satisfaction demand with the investment savings required by economic growth is not the only inherent contradiction which hampers the free interplay of interests. There is also the problem of so-called "collective needs," or "needs of the state." As a leading Polish economist, Bobrowski, put it, "There is the problem of choice between collective needs of the state (e.g., defense) on the one hand and the needs of economic growth and current consumption on the other. In this realm economic criteria do not exist and cannot exist and until the happy times of general disarmament not only economic accounts but also political decisions are necessary." [1] But still more important is the impact of another contradiction, the one between "collective consumption" and "individual consumption." According to common opinion, it seems that in no highly developed country has this problem been solved satisfactorily. Investments in the insurance system, public education, health, and other forms of collective consumption lag far behind the already achieved level of general growth. The problem is much more painful in the relatively underdeveloped Socialist countries, as heavy investments in collective consumption sufficient to provide for a minimum of social security must be made before desirable levels of individual consumption are achieved. This contradiction cannot be dealt with by the free interplay of articulated interests. The benefits resulting from collective consumption are much less tangible, although socially more important, than the immediate and "my own" advantages derived from raising the individual consumption fund.

## Income Leveling versus Income Differentiation

As far as individual consumption is concerned, there is also a sharp contradiction between two opposite trends, one leading, in accordance with general Socialist goals, to the leveling of incomes and general equality of living conditions, the second to highly differentiated incomes as crucial economic incentives for securing basic consistency of individual behavior with long-term economic policy. If the planned hierarchy of goals is to express itself in the necessary hierarchy of efforts, the structure of wages and salaries ought to correspond with the relative importance ascribed to diverse jobs by the plan and not with the current political strength of corresponding groupings. The logic of balanced economic growth is one thing, and the logic of balancing political participation with numerical strength and degree of militancy is something quite different. There will always remain a certain number of solutions which will have to be superimposed for economic reasons even if they are not backed by the current pattern of political forces.

## Goal Formulation versus Goal Attainment

Thus it is not difficult to explain why some restrictions of free interplay of pressure-interest groups cannot be avoided if planning endeavors in developing countries are to be effective. But that is only the beginning of our problem. The basic contradiction will be fully understood only if we confront our conclusion with the crucial requirement of the goal-formulating process: the efficiency of planned growth demands that free political struggle be somewhat restricted, but an adequate check-and-balance system, articulation of interests, and institutionalized channels through which pressure can be effectively exerted are necessary preconditions to the proper choice of goals, which is the initial and decisive stage of the planning process. We find ourselves in something like a vicious circle; the alternatives of "just good" or "just bad" solutions of this inconsistency simply do not exist. The weakening of the feedback mechanism is always the price to be paid for the increasing efficiency of planning, but, on the other hand, unlimited perfecting of this mechanism results in slackening the growth rate and making ambitious development programs simply inefficient. Thus *the contradiction between the requirements of goal formulating and the conditions of efficient goal attainment is the source of the second limitation of effectiveness of macrosocial planning.*

## THE PROCESS OF GOAL ATTAINMENT

These means-selecting decisions are, however, taken on three levels.[2] The highest is the level of macroeconomic decisions, which require a macrosocial frame of reference and should take into account the totality of social interests; these are decisions concerning the rate of increase of national income, division of this income into accumulation and consumption funds, the volume of investments and general pattern of their allocation, dividing the consumption fund into "collective" and "individual," and distribution of this fund among various classes and strata. At the other pole we find decisions taken on the "lowest level," namely, problems faced and decided by the individual in his productive and consumptive roles and concerning selection of goods to be bought on the market and the selection of a job (where to apply and sell one's labor). In between these two polar levels lies a broad and highly diversified sphere of decisions which (as we do not know any better term) we will call somewhat euphemistically *current economic decisions.* This heterogeneous sphere embraces such decisions as those concerning the global volume and structure of production, division of labor and cooperation, management and technology, and the volume and structure of employment in various branches. This type of decision concerns most directly the middle level of the economic system: the level of enterprise (firm).

### The "Middle Level" Problem

Giving the central planning agencies responsibility for the decisions of the first level and leaving the lowest level to the individuals are beyond discussion in a Socialist society unless one wants to give up the planned character of the Socialist economy and/or introduce the semifeudal "job ascription." Responsibility for the middle-level decisions is, however, not so obvious a problem. There is nothing in the nature of the Socialist society which restricts the number of possible answers to this rather ambiguous question. From the institutional point of view at least two answers are equally possible: (1) current economic decisions are taken directly by the central planning agency, with the role of the obedient and rather passive executor left to firm management, or (2) these decisions are left to the management of enterprises and influenced only indirectly by the central agency through a complex system of stimuli and establishment of some basic conditions which must be observed no matter what decision is made. Brus calls the first model "centralized" (this kind of solution prevailed until 1956) and the second "decentralized with extended market operation."

Sociologically we can, however, divide permissible answers into two different groups. In both cases the central agency exerts influence on the firm management; the two groups differ from each other solely in the means by which this influence is exercised. The general model of influencing may be characterized as follows: (1) $A$ faces alternative $X$ or $Y$; (2) $B$ wants $A$ to choose $X$; (3) $B$ enhances attractiveness of $X$ and/or makes $Y$ unattractive; (4) $A$ chooses $X$ and rejects $Y$. In other words, the statement "$B$ influences $A$'s behavior" means that $B$ manipulates the situation for $A$ and thus changes the balance between alternative choices. Now, this can be achieved by various means: $B$ can threaten $A$ with negative sanctions if $Y$ is chosen, but $B$ can also stimulate $A$ to choose $X$ by associating with this choice access to certain desirable goods. Thus we have a dichotomy between what might be called *manipulation by punishment* and *manipulation by reward*, respectively. We can now allocate all possible and practiced solutions of our problem on a continuum linking the two polar situations: one in which only manipulation by punishment is applied and the second in which the desired behavior is stimulated only by the reward system. In the process of planning, such rewards appeal first of all to the gain motive. Thus the incentive system is the most usual tool applied to influence decisions made on the level of the firm. When the incentive system predominates, the goals that the enterprise must achieve are determined by the central agency in the most general terms only. What is nevertheless much more important is that it is hoped that the compulsory character of this administrative command will be backed by the willing support of those to whom the command was addressed. In turn it is hoped that this support will be secured by the incentive system, which is designed so that the higher the fulfillment of the imposed tasks, the higher the profit of both the management and the rest of the staff. The incentive system operates exactly as expected if the firm tries to do its best to select the most efficient means of performing received tasks.

There are adherents in Poland of both polar solutions, although the vast majority of theoreticians and practitioners praise the virtues of a "middle way" which would combine the advantages of both poles and be free of their vices. The subject of most fervent discussion is often expressed in this way: how high a rung of the economic system might the laws of the market be allowed to reach? Or, are the operation of the profit motive, a fairly liberal interplay of demand and supply, and the domain of free choice of the *Homo economicus* type to be limited to the level of the individual producer-consumer or lifted to the level of the enterprise or even higher?

As we are now analyzing the stage of goal attainment and taking the general economic goals as given, the relevant criteria for answering these questions should be sought somewhere in the degree of approximation with which the economic results of a given solution approach the preestablished goal. That means that from the purely economic point of view the accepted solutions must be estimated according to the level of conformity with the planned goals to which they lead.

Thus from this point of view (if we set aside the political, social, and cultural concomitants of the respective solutions) influencing current economic decisions by an incentive system is "good" (only if the decisions thus made profitable for the firm and its staff do in fact lead to the attainment of macrosocial planned goals). There is nothing peculiar to planning in this conception. On the contrary, the proper functioning of each social institution depends directly on the degree in which individuals are stimulated by their own interest to behave in exactly the way which is necessary from the point of view of the "interests of society" and which is eufunctional for societal equilibrium and survival. The family is a good example. The perseverance and stability of family units are necessary conditions of the biological survival and cultural continuity of human society. But these macrosocial needs seldom function as the motivations of the individual behavior of would-be family members. To stimulate individuals to marry, to procreate, and to maintain family ties, there must be something in marriage and child rearing which satisfies certain purely individual needs of human beings. Moreover, in each epoch and culture this "something," though changing, must be available in family life only and be sought by individuals with the same degree of intensity. If this is not so, there appear immediately statistically significant dysfunctions in the working of the family institution, and we are induced to speak of "a crisis of the family." In the case of planning, the only difference is that someone wants individual motives and the interests of society to conform in a planned and conscious manner. If, for example, the central planning agency raises the salaries of engineers employed in elaborating technological implementations and firm managers shift to these jobs the most skilled and experienced personnel, the working of this particular incentive proves to be "good." Or, if because of the special bonus paid for export production many firms win new foreign markets by perfecting their products, the desired conformity is again achieved. These examples are, however, too simple to reflect the extreme complexity of the problem.

### The Qualitative Heterogeneity of Human Needs

This complexity is a direct result of the need orientation, rather than profit orientation, of the central planning goal. We have already discussed sufficiently the heterogeneity of need satisfaction as the goal of economic planning. Profit, which may function as an adequate guide in management decisions, is by no means relevant as the unifying measure in societal planning. It is doubtful whether any single measure consistent with subsistence goals can be found at all. There is no intrinsic harmony among the diverse elements in the cluster of human needs, and success achieved in the attainment of one chosen goal may very easily become failure when seen from the angle of other goals. Unavoidable troubles are involved in each attempt to construct intrinsically harmonious and proportionately built incentive systems safeguarding the hierarchy of efforts consistent with the hierarchy of goals. That is why no incentive system free of unexpected and even harmful by-products has so far been devised. On the contrary, the history of macrosocial planning may be described as an uninterrupted chain of enforced modifications of incentive systems induced by their successively demonstrated or disclosed inconsistencies. Thus, in 1960, the prices of raw materials in Poland were modified: prices of scarce materials were sharply raised to stimulate their replacement by cheaper ones—that is, those more easily available. The principle of determination of the wage and salary fund by the value of total output (dependent partly on the prices of raw products) was maintained. The inevitable, although unfortunately not anticipated, result was an increase and not a reduction in the consumption of scarce materials.

Ascribing the kinds of troubles just discussed to insufficient theoretical elaboration and inadequate information alone would be misleading. Even if available information were exhaustive and the theory of economic behavior perfect and unmistakable, there would still remain a residual problem which would not be likely to be solved by technical means alone. This problem is how to translate demands formulated in the qualitative, descriptive language of diversified needs into the quantitative and abstract language of profit. The profit yardstick, when applied to an enterprise, measures sources of gain in a way that cannot be applied to human needs. Moreover, these differences in evaluations cannot be expressed in terms of "more" and "less"; if they could, the expression would be merely metaphorical, and any attempt to find numerical, additive, and multipliable indices to make it really quantitative would be sheer misunderstanding. Thus we come across another inherent contradiction involved in macrosocial planning and seriously disturbing its effectiveness. This contradiction is found at the stage of plan implementation.

Activation by administrative command alone (manipulation by punishment) implies that many advantageous solutions will be overlooked and many opportunities unexploited and lost. It means also the loss of the rich resources of "from below" initiative. But the manipulation-by-reward system, which rests upon the expectation of rational choice, is also deficient, as it is rather doubtful if a system of incentives appealing to the profit motive but at the same time fully in accord with the pattern of needs can be constructed at all. Thus *the third major obstacle to plan implementation is rooted in the basic untranslatability of the need-oriented and profit goals and the difficulty of expressing the qualitative heterogeneity of human needs in the quantitative parameters of the profit-incentive system.*

Trying to minimize the undesired consequences of this contradiction, the Polish planning system oscillated in the past twenty years between two extremes. In 1949–1955, virtually all the economic activity of firms was regulated by administrative command through obligatory indices guarded by administrative sanctions. The total number of these indices was very great indeed; when gathered together they formed a rather stout volume.[3] In 1956 the number of indices determined on the level of the central planning agency was drastically restricted to a total of eight: (1) the total volume of output measured in wholesale prices, (2) the volume of output of most important goods measured in material units, (3) the global wage and salary fund, (4) the global gain (or loss), (5) the total sum which must be transferred to the state budget, (6) the total value of investments subsidized from the budgetary funds, (7) amortization funds, and (8) the total financial turnover. Since 1956, however, the number of indices imposed by command has systemically grown. In 1958, five further indices were added: (9) the value of export production, (10) distribution of the wage and salary fund among specific groups of employees, (11) the total amount of staff, (12) the ratio of self-expenditure in the value of global output, and (13) the limits of the development fund. By 1963 the total number of indices in various branches had reached twenty-three to thirty-five. The introduction of each new index was in all cases some-how imposed by discovering certain undesired by-products of the heretofore existing incentive system in some domain where the given stimuli were thought not to have any influence. Thus in the present Polish planning system obligatory indices are to some extent substitutes introduced to replace incentives which failed to push economic decisions in the desired direction and proved to be insufficient tools of submitting economic activity to need goals. But, as we mentioned before, although with the higher global number of indices the actual economic action more closely approximates the planned model, the opportunity to select the most rational solutions and utilize available resources fully is rather smaller than it was before. That is how the third contradiction expresses itself practically in plan execution.

### The Special Problem of the Present

The problem of incentive systems and their efficiency becomes particularly important in the case of those means of production which are not owned by the state and hence cannot be submitted to the direct supervision of the central planning agencies. That is the case of the Polish peasantry; so long as the private-ownership rights of peasants are unconditionally respected by the state, agricultural production may be included in the planned growth process only when influenced indirectly.

The problem of the peasant household enterprise cannot, however, be identified with the question of private ownership in general. There is one crucial difference between the traditional European peasant farm and private enterprise of the urban industrial-market type: an urban enterprise is almost by definition producing for the market only, and the total volume of its output is subjected to the "estimation by market" and thus to market pressures,[4] whereas a peasant family consumes at least part of its products itself; we may even imagine a model farm which is completely independent from the market and satisfies all the needs of the family with no mediation of money or even barter exchange. Few indeed are the items which are absolutely necessary for the life of a peasant family and which cannot be produced by the family itself and/or replaced by another good the family is able to produce, and in the countries with no industrial background the number of such items is virtually negligible. In extreme cases the peasant family is something like a closed whole, cut off from the rest of society, economically self-sufficient and excluded from the macrosocial division of labor. Where this is so, the peasant farm may be totally indifferent to market pressures and influences and may not react at all to profit incentives, as the category of "gain" is not contained by its need-oriented rationality. Unless this kind of self-sufficiency is destroyed or at least undermined, there is no possibility of influencing the economic behavior of the peasant.

Two factors helped to maintain the self-sufficiency of the peasant farm in prewar Poland. The first was the small capacity of the market for agricultural goods. This resulted in a price relation between grain and industrial goods totally unfavorable for increasing peasant production. The second was the negligible absorptive ability of the labor market. Stagnant, undeveloping industry was responsible for both factors. As there was no industrial development, the labor force of peasants had no market price and could not be sold. (During 1918–1939 the rural population in Poland increased by 5 million, but only 800,000 left the village for town. The overpopulation of the village was estimated by prewar economists as 3 million to 5 million, and according to Western European standards of efficiency employment per capita in agriculture was even more than 8 million.) Thus, contrary to the principles of market rationality, the peasant could not estimate his productive activity in terms of "efficiency." This term has no meaning when laborsaving is meaningless, and it is meaningless indeed when labor has no market price and thus must be "employed" in the household or lost. Because of the lack of contiguous points between the market and the domain of the peasant household, the two types of rationality, market and peasant, were simply untranslatable and mutually uncommunicative. Even the most labor-consuming way of performing a given productive task, although totally absurd when measured by market yardsticks, was still quite rational from the peasant point of view, as certain need satisfaction could be attained by it which could not be achieved by other means.

We can conclude that the primary condition for making peasant production responsive to the action of planners and hence manageable is to remove both factors which perpetuate the self-sufficiency of a peasant family household. This can be achieved by two measures: (1) providing a broad, capacious market for agricultural goods with a price structure sufficiently advantageous to stimulate peasants to increase their output and (2) providing a similarly broad market demand for labor, sufficiently strong to stimulate the replacement of inefficient human labor by modern technique and to effect a shift to "efficiency" thinking. These two measures have a common denominator: rapid industrialization. Developing industry sucks out the surplus labor force; by involving new masses of population in monetary exchange, it creates at the same time ever-increasing demand for agricultural products. Thus the higher the rate of industrial growth, the higher the responsiveness of the peasant farm to profit opportunities in general and to planned manipulation in particular.

There are two links in the economic cycle of the peasant farm where plan-supporting incentives can be effective. The first is situated between the expenditure of labor force and the act of consumption: the greater the portion of total products sold and the greater the portion of consumed goods bought, the broader the opportunity to influence peasant economic activity by manipulation in this area. The second link exists before the problem of how to utilize one's labor is decided: if the increase of agricultural crop per person employed in agriculture is considered a desired goal of planning, then the higher the wage a peasant would be able to get in a factory, the easier it would be to influence the peasant's economic behavior to this end.

As we have just seen, there exist two basic means to influence the agricultural production of independent peasant farms by planners. One consists of manipulating the structure of agricultural prices and the balance between the prices of agricultural and industrial goods. The second consists of manipulating the market price of labor and the availability of industrial (or, more generally, urban) jobs. The effectiveness of both means depends, we repeat, on the general rate of industrial growth.

The activation of market influences creates the general conditions for bringing the structure of agricultural production in line with planned goals. But this kind of intervention does not suffice as the agricultural output is permanently scarce and the market for virtually all kinds of peasant products is always unsatiated (and this has been the situation in Poland for years). In such a case the state planning agency has to apply supplementary and nonmarket measures, such as differentiation of taxation according to the structure of farm production and subsidizing certain scarce labor-consuming or capital-consuming areas. Stimulating the peasant's investment savings presents particular problems. In Poland this has been partly, though not perfectly, solved by the so-called "Agriculture Development Fund" (FRR according to Polish initials). Peasants are obliged to sell part of their crop to the state; the prices paid by the state are somewhat lower than on the free market, but this difference is duly transferred to the FRR, and from this fund the peasant's productive investments are rather lavishly subsidized. Thus investment savings were made compulsory and investment expenditures strongly stimulated. This measure, administrative to some extent, is enforced by the market situation; the easy availability of high profits, caused by the permanent overtaking of the supply by effective demand, makes investment efforts unnecessary and, for a rural population unaccustomed to investing, also unattractive.

Thus, in the domain where private ownership has been maintained, only incentive methods of influencing economic behavior are applicable, although the market is not the sole medium by which manipulating is performed. Administrative command is here excluded by the very nature of ownership relations. If applied, it can result only in curbing agricultural production and thus will act against the planned goals. Applying the incentive method to the whole domain of agriculture is, however, a rather costly undertaking and therefore accessible only in case of a state which has at its disposal very ample resources and funds drawn presumably from strong state initiative in the industrial sphere.

## INHERENT CONTRADICTIONS AS LIMITATIONS

So far, in tracing the experience of Polish planning, we have found some important factors which effectively limit both goal-formulation and plan-implementation processes and which are caused not so much by the technical reasons given above (e.g., insufficent skill of the people employed in planning) as by resistant contradictions between functional requirements of the perfect-planning model and important parameters of the social structure. These factors, or categories of obstacles, are listed in the paragraphs that follow.

### Institutional

In this category belong all obstacles resulting from lack of adequate power or lack of means sufficient to influence and stimulate, or both. This category may be divided into two subcategories, external and internal.

*External.* This type of obstacle is felt by all macrosocial planning agencies, with no exceptions. The power of each planning agency is limited, even in the most favorable conditions, to the territory of a single nation-state. It does not extend to foreign markets, where the endeavors of the planning agencies meet independent and often irresistible economic forces not submissive to planning. Even the most technically sophisticated and instrumentally perfect planning inside national borders is supplemented by nothing more than sheer forecast so far as external variables of internal economic balance are concerned. It can be assumed generally that the restrictive force of this circumstance is greater (1) the bigger the share of foreign-market exchange in achieving internal equilibrium between needs and supply, and (2) the smaller the international economic weight of a given nation, and thus the smaller the influence of its economic behavior on the terms of trade in the world market. This works against the developing countries; their economic position is the least favorable for effective planning.

*Internal.* The power of the planning agency is limited also inside the borders of a given society. Not all means of production are subject to direct regulation, and there always remain certain parts of the economy protected from planned interference by the unencroachable rights of private ownership. If these parts are too great, even indirect influence becomes more and more difficult because of the meagerness of resources available to back costly incentive systems. A sufficiently broad share of national product and income must be accumulated by the central planning agency to make its decisions sufficiently persuasive. The technical ability of planners is not a sufficient guarantee of efficient planning; the force of brains must be supported by the force of money and economic power in general. If not, the planning efforts turn out to be mere forecasts, powerless to modify the actual sequence of events.

### Political

To this category belong all kinds of impediments lying outside the sphere of economic life and bound up with the political expressions of conflicting interests. If available goods are scarce —and they are scarce indeed in most developing societies—there is no economic decision maker totally indifferent to all existing interests, impinging on no group rights and disappointing no expectations. It is not the pure and abstract rationality of the experts which actually functions as the moving factor in the decision-making, estimating, and accepting processes. The possibility of rationality lies in the sphere of means, not goals, and common agreement on some particular version of rationality may be reached only inside the group sharing the same goal. But goal selection is ruled by group interests or at any rate by what a group thinks its interests are. That is why the pragmatic utility of a given decision for economic growth does not suffice to make it acceptable for all groups and to eliminate possible stubbornness in resisting its execution. Economic planning has its extensions outside the sphere supervised by the planning agencies and not subject to manipulation by economic means. This is another variable unknown from the point of view of the economic equation. *When economic growth is the sole guide in the decision-making process, the planners are likely very soon to be lost and to find themselves helpless in front of difficulties incomprehensible and even indescribable in purely economic terms.*

### Instrumental

This is the third category of obstacles connected primarily with the problems of how to harmonize individual behavior motivations with common goals. As noted earlier, if a mass effort is to promote planned tasks, behavior consistent with the common goals must satisfy certain important needs and desires of individuals. As also mentioned, this is a tremendously intricate problem. The goals of planning on the macrosocial level are notoriously heterogeneous. Moreover, their structure must be easily changeable if planning is to be operative and adaptable to changing circumstances. It is easier to change planned goals than to adjust the structure of individual motivations and to modify behavioral customs fabricated by the former pattern of incentives. Because of this "behavioral lag" planners have to cope with a permanent tension between new tasks and the customary, less elastic, and obsolete models of individual behavior. The behavioral-lag factor always acts against the desired running of plan execution even if the technically complicated task of projecting the structure of goals into the structure of the incentive system is accomplished successfully.

### Technical

These are factors that are manageable, at least theoretically, by perfecting the organization of the planning process and that result solely from the insufficient experience and skill of the planning staff. Among them the following seem to be of great importance: (1) problems connected with communication, or, more precisely, with information flow, including problems of data gathering, organization of statistics, and elimination of the organizational impediments to truthful information; (2) the skill and flexibility of planning agents, particularly the ability to forecast probable results of action and to modify promptly previous decisions if results achieved appear to be inconsistent with expectancies; this subcategory includes the general scientific equipment of the planning agencies drawn from organization theory; (3) possession of a reliable and workable theoretical model of economic action and knowledge of actual correlations between various stages and fields of such action; this requisite may be called the need for *sociological imagination* by planners; and (4) the possession of adequate knowledge of the uniformities of individual behavior, knowledge that is essential if one wants to induce concrete reactions by applying reliable stimuli.

It is our view that only the fourth category of obstacles—the technical—can be removed by scientific investigation and an increase in expertise. The other three categories have a much more permanent character, and there is little chance of overcoming them merely by more highly skilled economic action. Some important obstacles are intrinsic in macrosocial planning; others are connected with supraeconomic reasons and will last until the institutional and political framework of planning is substantially modified. This is why the problems of effective planning cannot be solved within the purely economic sphere and by economic means alone.

## SUMMARY

Clearly, the perfect-planning model is an abstraction at the same level as the model of the perfect market. This does not undermine its heuristic utility or its practical usefulness for measuring the degree of approximation with which a given society reaches the ideal limit of planning coordination. The model also allows a deeper understanding of why so many planned goals are not attained and why no one planning agent has yet achieved a full rationality of macrosocial processes. Nevertheless, to be useful in this way, the perfect-planning model has to be treated as an ideal type and not as an empirical generalization. Comparing actual social structures with the perfect-planning model, we can more fully answer the question of why the actual planning did not rise to the level of expectation.

What, then, can be said, after analyzing one example of a planning society, about the possibility of meeting the functional requirements of the ideal model?

To begin with, the first requirement—that the social system must be self-sufficient and isolated in the sphere of those activities which are subjected to planning—is not met, no more in other societies than in Poland. It will be met less and less as international trade grows along with regional specialization of goods production. This has two important consequences, seriously diminishing the "perfection" of planning: (1) many unknown and nonmanipulative variables in each planning equation and (2) continuous contradictions between need-oriented criteria of "inside planning" and the profit-oriented criteria of rationality in "outside planning."

Secondly, as the actual life of a society is centered around concrete interests and as these interests in any modern society are continuously diversified, then the necessity to collect all information about the system is also not met, even as far as information concerning "international affairs" is concerned. To make up for the missing channels of information, the free interplay of interest groups becomes necessary. This, however, in turn contradicts the necessity to secure the neutrality of the decision-making center.

Thirdly, as there are conflicting group interests within any society, the planning agent inevitably faces two alternatives: (1) to neglect some group interests and to submit decisions solely to criteria of economic rationality; (2) to permit the free clash of competitive interests, thus submitting decisions to the balance of social forces and not to the balance of available resources or terms of trade. Both solutions are poor, as the first leads to increasing resistance against plan implementation and the second actually to renouncing the planned social process. However, there is no third solution apart from maneuvering between these two extremes.

Fourthly, the full comparability of alternative goals and means is not achieved if planning activity is need-oriented, and it is need-oriented if it is macrosocial. Needs are qualities and thus are inherently incommensurable. This restricts the applicability of the efficiency criteria for measuring the degree of rationality of alternative courses of action.

Lastly, each social system subjected to planning is heterogeneous in the sense that mechanisms determining social action on the higher levels of social organization differ from those which determine social behavior on the individual producer-consumer level. The two mechanisms demand different kinds of stimuli; the inevitable result is permanent tension between them and continuous search for the proper balance.

This chapter is offered as a contribution to a fuller understanding of the notorious difficulties in plan implementation and also, it is hoped, of the general ways of overcoming them. These difficulties, in our opinion, are located not so much in the planning process itself as in the social structures which do not meet at all or fully enough the functional requirements of the perfect-planning model.

## NOTES

[1] Czestaw Bobrowski, "General Problems of Economic Policy," in *Economic Policy of People's Poland*, vol. 1, Warsaw, 1962.

[2] W. Brus, *The General Problems of the Functioning of the Socialist Economy*, Warsaw, 1961.

[3] Z. Madej, "Functioning of the National Economy," in *Economic Policy of People's Poland*, vol. II, Warsaw, 1962.

[4] B. Galeski, *Peasantry as an Occupation*, Warsaw, 1964.

# 6

# Economic Activation, Planning, and the Social Order

*Peter J. D. Wiles*

## THE ECONOMIST'S RESIDUAL BENTHAMISM

This chapter tries to get away from economic Benthamism, or utilitarianism applied to the marketplace, and its corollary Taylorism, or Urwickism, which is utilitarianism applied to administration. People seek profit and obey the law: this is the be-all and end-all of the psychology underlying orthodox economics. It is time to set up a typology of all the other activators and relate them to the various institutional models of an economy.

Yet in seeking thus to widen our horizons I have been more and more impressed by the simple utilitarian point of view. It is not simply that profit maximization is a really rather adequate account of *enterprises* (not people) in markets. It is also that obedience to the law is a rather good account of a command economy. Moreover, where the law is disobeyed, it is normally for the sake of profit, and where profit is not sought, it is normally because the law forbids it. Discussing these matters with non-economists, I find an unwillingness to accept this amounting almost to obsession.   It is as if simplicity were per se unscientific or as if the status of one's own discipline would be threatened if it could not be shown to undermine that of economics.

My own bias is entirely toward undermining the status of my own discipline, not other people's.   I would have eagerly welcomed any evidence that I alone among economists was right, but this is not, apparently, how the chips have fallen.   Utilitarianism is in fact a *rather* adequate description of *most* existing economic motivation.   It applies much less to primitive and even ordinarily traditional societies, which are excluded from what follows.   Moreover, the very definition of the Marxist utopia at the end of all things, here referred to as *full communism,* is that people become very responsive to the moral activators and so may dispense with profit and law. Thus, I follow up to a certain point the orthodox Marxian scheme in this matter.   The two great utilitarian activators are seen as gaining importance in the course of history and as being supreme both under capitalism and under "socialism."   Whether they will in fact ever die out I dare not prophesy.[1]

The resistance to such reactionary views arises, I think, from the different interests of the social sciences.   The sociologist or management expert asks why the economic organization sticks together, who joins it, how they all behave toward each other. The economist asks what the organization produces, and why.[2] The motives that govern the whole organization vis-à-vis society, whether it faces a market or a planner's blueprint, are likely to be quite different from those that govern individuals within the organization reacting to each other.   If we look carefully at careful economists, we are struck with how little they dare to say about the running of an enterprise or trade union.   Similarly, sociologists dare to say almost nothing about the government management of the economy or about enterprises in markets.

To put it another way, the *motives* of human beings are very various, but very many of them can be satisfied with money. Money activates us, whatever our motives.   Moreover, organizations are still simpler, still more immune to such nonmonetary motives as the need to be loved or respected. Bentham will do very well for them.

## ECONOMIC MODELS AND ACTIVATORS

There are, then, innumerable ways of inducing economic activity, or *activators*. For our purposes I neglect labor activators, commonly called *incentives,* altogether, as well as the complexity of intraenterprise personal relations, and set forth various economic models and the kinds of enterprise activators that are most relevant to each:

### Free Market (FM)

There is no public motivation; all economic activity is conducted for private ends. The main such end is profit, but there are, of course, many others. So FM in this chapter is a broad category, including both nonprofit activators like loss-avoidance, the instinct of workmanship and mere habit, and such "diseases" of the free market as monopoly, advertising, speculation, ignorance, and error.

### Regulated Market (RM)

The initiative remains with private persons and bodies, activated as above, but the "public interest" tries in various ways to encourage, discourage, or stop certain things. The many direct private activators remain, and we now add to them innumerable *negative, or indirect, public activators.* The more important are:

1. *Moral:* ecclesiastical propaganda against usury, low wages, prostitution, or what not; governmental propaganda against smoking, discrimination in hiring, etc.
2. *Administrative-monetary:* taxes, tariffs, subsidies, qualitative banking controls
3. *Administrative-physical:* licensing, rationing, prohibition of drugs, safety regulations, antismoke ordinances, etc.
4. *Government open-market operations:* where the government is a contracting party with the private sector, buying or selling anything whatsoever, such as civil servants' labor, ICBMs, treasury bills (i.e., quantitative banking controls), wheat, gold, highway construction

Activators 2 and 3 are backed by legal penalties.

## Central Initiative (CI)

In some fields, at least, initiative passes to the government, which no longer limits itself to discouraging or stopping. Among positive public activators are:

1. *Legal commands* such as a Soviet enterprise receives, whether monetary or physical, in its output plan, or such as a United States public school gets from its school board; also conscription. These commands are backed by legal penalties.
2. *Monetary:* plan-fulfillment bonuses, plan-under-fulfillment fines. Note that these are not at all the same as profit and loss. They appeal, of course, to the same instincts of *Homo economicus*, but they can reward quite different services and on quite different occasions. They need not even be paid out of or into enterprise funds but may be directly administered by the central treasury.
3. *Moral:* the government persuades economic agents by various means that involve neither force nor reward to do what it wants. Such means are listed by Gross [3] and include individual demonstration, general propaganda, individual publicity, medals. A good instance in the U.S.S.R. is the propaganda used to get labor out into the virgin lands. In the United States and also the U.S.S.R. the government issues technical advice to farmers; in the United Kingdom the Building Research Station, a government body, organizes practical demonstrations; and everywhere there are model farms.

Public activators 1 and 2 are the so-called "command economy." They form a distinct whole, much more important than public activator 3.

## Joint Initiative (JI)

Here government and enterprise both freely take a hand in drawing up a blueprint for the future performance of the economy.

1. JI/FM, in which the only activators that subsequently operate to make enterprises follow the blueprint are those of the free market, as above. In this case, the blueprint has solely acted

upon their expectations: under government auspices, each has talked the other into playing his allotted part, because it would be, say, profitable to do so if everyone else would.

2. JI/RM, in which the government uses negative public activators to enforce the blueprint freely agreed upon.

3. JI/command, which speaks, then, for itself.

Thus under JI/FM the government helps, by moral means, to arrange a contract, or gentlemen's agreement, between private parties. In this case the parties do less what the government wants than what they come to want themselves. For example, the United States government provides a conciliation commission or an arbitrator [4] in a labor dispute. Under JI/command the Soviet government supervises a contract between a producing enterprise and the enterprise taking delivery and then enforces it as if it were part of the plan. The most interesting and important case, however, is JI/RM, in which the French government presides over the formation, by trade associations and other bodies, of the national plan. This is the so-called "concerted economy." It is enforced, if necessary, by banking controls and taxes.

### The Limitations of All Activators

All public activators are assumed in this chapter to include, by definition, the means of enforcing them: public auditors, tax inspectors, the Soviet control commission, etc. Enforcement is a very large and important subject, which I do not touch upon. The ways in which a large capitalist firm activates its branches are extremely similar to the activators the government uses on the firm, but discussion of this too is prevented by space limitations.

CI normally does not even try to cover the whole of economic life. The two great exceptions to this have been war communism in the U.S.S.R. (June, 1918 to March, 1921) and the Great Leap Forward in China (autumn, 1958), when a single, all-embracing authority—or in China many such authorities—tried to govern the whole of production and in addition the purchases of the consumer and the worker's choice of workplace, without the intervention of money at any point. Normally the authorities stop very far short of this point. Stalin and Khrushchev abandoned consumer purchases, most job choices, and nearly all agriculture to RM, even to FM. In particular, the procurement of industrial labor in the U.S.S.R. is an open-market operation.

Again, India and Pakistan confine CI to a huge public investment program. It might seem at first glance that this program is an open-market operation to which we should deny the name of CI. The logic of this is that the government's offer to buy labor and raw materials is freely either accepted or rejected. So, attempting to buy labor and materials to complete its capital projects, the government conducts an "open-market operation" as surely as if it were merely a central bank buying treasury bills.[5] But once in possession of its resources, the government orders them about at will. The actual choice of projects is very much an act of central initiative. It is true that the plants thus created operate on a free market, maybe even to the extent (as in Pakistan) of being privately owned. The fact remains that their creation was an act of state command. This model is important to us because it is the one most favored in underdeveloped countries.

Nor, of course, is FM ever pure. Every economy, what with its tariffs and the powers of central banks, operates RM at least in part. Taxation is necessarily a matter of command, and so are conscription and some social services. Weapon acquisition, on the other hand, is, of course, an open-market operation, however monopolistic.

Note that the broad classification here is logically exhaustive: FM means no government, RM means government without initiative, CI means that government has all the initiative, JI means that it shares it. There can be nothing else. The individual types of government intervention have not, however, been exhaustively listed; that would be tedious and unprofitable. Even those mentioned might, by another student, be differently allocated between CI and RM. It is indeed characteristic of really useful classifications that they are frayed at the edges. When, for instance, Stanley Baldwin "asked" a steel company not to leave South Wales, or when John F. Kennedy "expressed indignation" at a rise in steel prices, was this negative or positive public activation? It is and should be entirely a matter of definition.

In each economic transaction, then, there must be *either* FM *or*

RM *or* CI *or* JI, though in the whole economy there may be any conceivable mixture. Transactions are more or less pure, since our schema has been precisely designed to be logically exhaustive and cover them all. Systems of transactions, i.e., institutional models of the economy, are impure. We can only discuss a few of the possible mixtures.

*Activators are not criteria for making decisions; they are stimuli for carrying them out.* Profit happens to be both activator and criterion, as indeed is any goal we spontaneously set ourselves; but under CI divorce is easily possible. Thus we might say, "Produce as much as possible and damn the cost [criterion], or I will put you behind bars [activator]." But it would also be possible for the government to say to the manager, "Make profits for me [criterion], and I shall give you a cut of them [activator]" or "Make profits for me, or I'll put you behind bars."

*Every activator is inefficient.* Profit, the main activator under FM and RM, is, as is well known, no great spur to activity. Innumerable human beings of all ranks are quite idle in a profit-oriented system. Besides, the nature of these market systems is that you can choose your own activator, which may not be profit at all but something even more static, like following in your father's footsteps. Nevertheless, activation under the command economy is quite exceptionally difficult; it has to be artificially devised by the government and attains a baroque multiplicity unknown in the simpler models. Normally a government using this system will use more than one of the activators listed above: (1) it will issue legal commands, backed by legal penalties; (2) it will promise bonuses and threaten fines; (3) it will put flesh upon the bare bones of its orders by instructing the lower organs to make detailed contracts with each other in the spirit of those orders, and once these are valid, they serve, of course, as additional activators. It is the command economy as a whole, not coordinated blueprints in particular, that raises the activation problem in this acute form. Whether the government has a blueprint or not is in this context a small matter. The point is that it has taken over initiative.

The same activator varies in efficiency according to the circumstances in which it is used. In a very traditional society most of the activation is moral, but a market usually exists, and more or

less profit can be made in it.   Profit has, however, little drawing
power.   In any society public activation is more efficient in wartime.   Still more simple and important, persuasive taxation will
not raise much money.   It is again far more difficult to "concert"
a short-run income policy than a medium-run investment blueprint; the perception of this has been perhaps the principal secret
weapon of French planning.   The persuasive short-run income
policies of Britain and France have both been mainly epiphenomenal.   The British error was to suppose that the same applied in
other fields.   Dutch planning, mainly concerned with short-run
income policy, has folded up.   French planning, concerned with
everything else, has gone from strength to strength.   British
planning is now rising like a phoenix from its ashes, but in French
guise.   It is noteworthy that Communist command economies
also have a great deal of trouble with short-run income policy.

Unfulfillable orders induce more economic effort mainly in two
cases: *planner's tension* under CI and *unbalanced growth* in market systems.   This is almost a distinction without a difference.
In the former case the planner's order requires more output, or
less input, than is technically possible; in the latter, profits are
very high at some point.[6]   So there is more striving for output.
Either way the activator, be it profit or a government order, is
overloaded, but the result is not necessarily mere waste of effort;
it is often the discovery of unused resources and potentialities,
unsuspected by the enterprise thus activated.   This is what Communist planners mean when they answer complaints about the
plan with the cry, "Mobilize your internal reserves."

Holland Hunter [7] reports that Polish economists believe there
are diminishing returns in planner's tension.   Above a certain
level it simply causes corruption, chaos, and a catastrophic decline in quality.   This seems plausible, though extremely difficult to prove.   In much the same way, excess demand is generally thought to lose its stimulus as it increases over a certain
point.

But since activators are variously effective, the *choice of activator determines in part the choice of economic activity.*   Complicated products, miscellaneous products, fashion products,
prototypes, things requiring artistry and care, repair work of all
kinds—these are not done to simple order.   In each case, the

product is unique, and therefore its specification is unknown before it has been finished. But a positive public activator, such as CI by definition requires, is nothing at all if not a specification of the product. The notorious failure of CI in this field, or, if we prefer, the indispensability of decentralization, is almost an a priori necessity: where the enterprise does not know what or how to produce until it has begun producing, initiative has to be devolved to it. *Any* decentralized activator will, of course, set it going, but, even more clearly than in other cases, profit is here the best. For where individual inputs and outputs cannot be specified, clearly the only thing to do is to specify the ratio between all outputs and all inputs, which is what profit is.[8]

This is a useful proposition with many consequences. It shows that whether or not CI in general is a good idea, it is certainly bad in such agricultural tasks as livestock raising, viticulture, and horticulture, where the method of production is complicated and crises arise unpredictably, requiring individual attention. These are the "right-wing crops," as opposed to such "left-wing crops" as grain, potatoes, cotton. It is likely that more sophisticated agricultural machinery will in the course of time turn nearly all agricultural products into "left-wing crops." For instance, milk and chickens have recently changed their political color. Our proposition also shows that CI is much more likely to produce new machines and houses than to repair existing ones [9] and that art and literature cannot be blueprinted. Perhaps above all, it shows that *CI is bad where technical progress is quick.* For, of course, the quicker it is, the larger the percentage of things, that is, prototypes, and the larger, too, the number of types in serial production.[10] Hence we should not be surprised that Khrushchev had trouble with a system that, rightly or wrongly, satisfied Stalin. If the government wishes to enhance technical progress, it must operate through RM, e.g., by contracting for research.[11]

## THE NATURE OF PLANNING

A plan is something different again. Note, first, that the verb *to plan* is both transitive and intransitive. In the latter usage it means to look forward rationally, to take a long view, to prepare alternative courses of action, for oneself or one's organization. In this sense a capitalist or a general plans. Transitively, one draws up the same sort of plan and imposes it on others. A government plans in both ways; a private enterprise, only intransitively. Again, one normally plans the means to an end, but it is legitimate to speak of a plan of ends if there are more than one and they are deliberately coordinated. On the other hand, many people say *planning* when they mean government intervention in the market, even if uncoordinated and contradictory. Or, again, some use *plan* for any thought-out government strategy, even the strategy of promoting the free market, or for general "nation building" activities in underdeveloped countries. Indeed, for some people *planning* means government. No one word can bear such a load, and I eschew it. This chapter is concerned with *coordinated economic blueprints*, which are only a part of economic planning, which in turn is only a part of planning.

## Epiphenomenal Planning

Such blueprints can be related to economic activation as follows: the government can draw up a coordinated blueprint without doing anything to enforce it. I used to think that this was basically a waste of time, but am not now so sure. To quote my book: [12]

> The "merely predictive" plan is commoner. It is fatally easy for the government of some market economy to say in some detail what ought to be done, and publish it under the name of a plan; but provide no enforcement mechanism. We may examine a few instances. The first is the "control figures" (kontrol'niye tsifri, better translated "check figures") published by the Gosplan during the NEP. These were books of figures for the most important outputs and activities during the coming year. Trotsky said they were or ought to be orders, but there was no enforcement mechanism and enterprises were guided by the market instead. Unwilling to admit their futility on the one hand, or to exaggerate their importance on the other, the Gosplan described them as "orientation" (ori-

entirovka). This sort of equivocation is precisely what we mean by "epiphenomenal planning." There is, incidentally, direct continuity between the "control figures" and the annual plan of Stalin's command economy. The control figures of 1929 were his annual plan, but they were no longer mere orientirovka. The transition to a command economy *consisted* in giving the "control figures" legal force.

To the development under Stalin that under Attlee presents a sharp contrast. The "Economic Survey for 1947" (H.M.S.O., Cmd. 7046, para. 128), published in February, 1947, had many of the stigmata of a real plan (including of course its arrival after the period to be planned had already begun!). Yet the whole document rested on a basic confusion, as the following passage shows: "The Government has no direct control over the way in which man power moves; it can seek to influence the movement in a number of ways, but the ideal distribution of man power would involve changes of such magnitude that it would be impossible to bring them about by any means short of complete wartime direction. Even if direction were used, the transfer of labour would be limited by lack of accommodation. The following table sets out a distribution of man power at end-1947. This is neither an ideal distribution nor a forecast of what will happen; it represents the approximate distribution which is needed to carry out the objectives in paragraph 118 and which the Government considers can be achieved if the nation as a whole sets itself to achieve them."

Needless to reproduce here the table of man-power targets. Enough that at the end of 1947 right-wing economists were making fun of the extreme under- and over-fulfilment of the various targets; a thing far from unnatural since no enforcement mechanisms had been provided. Yet the "Economic Survey for 1948" (H.M.S.O., Cmd. 7344, para. 186) continued in the same almost self-contradictory strain: "Labour is not at present, and is unlikely to be in 1948, the limiting factor in economic activity as a whole. Any projected distribution such as is given in Table XXI is therefore largely a forecast of the results of other factors, and if some figures turn out differently it is not necessarily in every case a matter of regret.   But the labour forces proposed for coal, agriculture and textiles are *targets in the full sense.*   They are numbers believed to be required to reach specific objectives in the set of output and export targets decided for 1948.   The attainment of these man-power targets is among the first *necessities* in 1948." (my italics)

Note the apologetic tone induced by the failures of the previous year.   Note also the ludicrously undefined phrases in italics.   In subsequent years the "Economic Survey for 194(x)" has said more and more about 194(x-1) and less and less about 194(x) itself, until in March, 1954, the word "for" was dropped from the title, so that now in effect "Economic Survey 1959" merely means the economic survey *of* 1958, published *in* 1959.   After March, 1960, the whole series of documents was discontinued.   This, then, is the history of the Soviet "control figures" in reverse. Both started as "epiphenomenal planning"; the one de-veloped into the operative planning of a command econ-omy, the other withered away into mere undisguised pre-diction and then ceased to be even that.

The Yugoslav example is intermediate.   Since 1950 the Yugoslavs have continued to publish an annual plan and to cast material balances (500 of them in 1960).   In 1957 they returned to FYPs, which they had abandoned in 1950. (The formal date of expiry of the first FYP was 1952.   On present planning techniques cf. Branko Kubovic et al., "Economic Planning in Yugoslavia," *Jugoslavia,* Belgrade 1959.)   Yet the enterprise remains bound to the market, and there is no direct enforcement mechanism.   True, it sets up its own "plan," i.e. expression of intentions.   But in the harmonization of state and enterprise plans the latter have primacy.   Moreover, the enterprise may diverge from its own plan in the direction of the market, and so *a fortiori* from the state plan.   Asked about this, a Yugoslav plan-ning official said to me, "Contradictions between enterprise performance and the plan?   But the planner has monthly situation reports coming in, so he knows how to plan ac-cording to realities."   I pressed him for a more adequate reply: what happens when enterprises don't fulfil the plan? "You can't argue with an enterprise."

Thus epiphenomenal planning is FM plus a blueprint. Whether the blueprint is properly coordinated is irrelevant, since it is never carried out. Nevertheless, the mere existence of the blueprint has many effects. First, an initial period of epiphenomenal planning is necessary so that the blueprint makers may have a dry run and improve their statistics, working methods, etc. Secondly, such planning often starts people thinking and talking practically, instead of shouting ideologies at each other in the newspapers.[13] This should make politics more rational and emphasize national over sectional interests. Thirdly, it helps the government to manage rationally whatever sectors it can command or regulate, for it now has a better notion, even if purely predictive, of how the rest of the economy will react to its own actions. In this way a government managing directly a large sector might under certain circumstances regulate everything while not having any direct means of doing so. Fourthly, it simply emboldens the government to do more or restrains it from doing too much. Thus, the resurgence of epiphenomenal planning in the United Kingdom since 1961 has surely emboldened the government by showing that 4 percent growth is compatible with balance in foreign payments. Lastly and more cynically, an epiphenomenal plan enhances a government's status abroad and makes it more eligible for foreign aid; it is a "company prospectus" issued to the "investing public."

### Nonepiphenomenal Planning

Nonepiphenomenal planning is less subtle and may be more briefly dealt with. Then, if the previous section represents the first kind of blueprint, the following examples of nonepiphenomenal planning represent alternative strategies or methods:

1. The activators of RM may be used to enforce the blueprint. This, to be fair, is what the Yugoslavs also do. Only, of course, the blueprint cannot be very detailed or the enforcement very effective.[14]

2. We may use RM without any specific blueprint or perhaps even any overall strategy. Thus all taxes might be imposed to satisfy a number of uncoordinated lobbyists, or at random, or in accordance with past history.[15]

3. We may use the command activators to enforce the blueprint.
   (This is our main subject and is discussed later in the chapter.)
4. We may use command without a blueprint or, at least, without
   a properly coordinated one. That this too is a possibility
   needs to be shown. Two versions are possible:

   *a.* The prime exhibit of the first is the Soviet economy under
   war communism (1918–1921), but nearly any war economy
   shows elements of the same thing: the government simply
   takes hold of the economy and gives the instructions that
   currently seem best. Since it is running the whole or
   nearly the whole economy, its decisions are interdependent,
   and its actions react on each other. A practical notion of
   these reactions and constraints, and the ability to take account of them, is exactly what is meant by a coordinated
   blueprint. Therefore planless command causes the utmost
   chaos: mutually incompatible orders are withdrawn and
   replaced by yet other mutually incompatible orders, each
   link in the economy lurching from crisis to crisis.[16] The
   Soviet first Five-Year Plan (1928–1931) was also in effect
   planless command, since not even the "method of balances"
   was in use.

   > The "method of balances" consists in making a budget
   > of, say, coke production, stocks at the beginning of the
   > period, and imports: and seeing that it coincides with con-
   > sumption (ascertained by applying technical input/output
   > ratios to the outputs ordered for coke-using industries),
   > exports and stocks at the end of the period. It differs *toto
   > caelo* from rational choice in a command economy.[17]

   But the method of balances at least ensures that all orders
   are consistent with each other. If they are not, we cannot say there is a coordinated blueprint. The input/
   output analysis is in essence only the consolidated presentation of many balances in one matrix and the more
   rapid discovery of the general consequences of a change
   in any of the balances. It is merely an improved method
   of consistency planning, and so also has little to do
   with rational choice, which consists of ordering the in-

numerable possible coherent blueprints according to some scale of values.

*b.* The second version of planless command is deliberate and crisis-free: [18]

> Of the free choice of the planners, profit remains the sole indicator. This model we called the centralized market system. In it the government understands the scarcity problem as in a Western textbook, and the same economic theories underlie its actions. Only it centralizes all firms under what is basically one management, so that, for instance, profits and amortization quotas automatically revert to the centre, being only retained by the firm as a privilege; and no major decision may be taken without reference to the centre, indeed otherwise than at the centre. Essentially, then, these firms are also mere establishments as under CI, branches of the single nation-wide socialist firm. However, labour, land and capital are still hired on a free market, and consumer goods and services are still sold on one. Rent and interest, therefore, remain operative categories, as do wages. Thus the ultimate factors of production and the ultimate outputs are subject to the same pressures as before, only whereas previously all intermediate products were also freely bought and sold, not all are centrally allocated on the profit principle. The government endeavours to make the same rate of profit on all commodities, to respect absolutely the changing desires of the consumer, to allocate capital only in accordance with profitability, etc., etc. Then the government is really only a very large public monopoly of the same kind as a firm in one of the pure market models. So long as its internal accounting procedures are strict, and obey the rules of the free market game, it is simply reproducing the free market results at great administrative cost. The same price, output and location decisions are taken at the centre as would have been taken at the circumference without delay and correspondence. This is approximately the model recommended by Oskar Lange in his *On the Economic Theory of Socialism* (Minneapolis 1948), except that here he recommends "centralized market" for prices only and would leave outputs to be decided by the managers on the profit principle.

5. A more or less detailed blueprint might be concerted *à la Française*, i.e., under the system of joint initiative. There seems to be no enforcement mechanism, but in fact there is: the prior, voluntary agreement of all concerned, the government's direct management of its own sector, and its use of RM elsewhere.

6. The concerted blueprint might be enforced by command. This was the theory of the Czechoslovak reforms of 1958.

7. At least in theory, and the theory is very important for Communist ideology, the enforcement mechanism might be moral alone, even though the blueprint was very detailed indeed and drawn up not by concertation but by central fiat. This is the case of full communism,[19] in which the "state," i.e., the coercive organs of society, will have withered away, and the only remaining activators are moral. Realistic or not, this is the daily strived-for goal of some Communist countries.

Are not all plans really epiphenomenal? A Soviet planner in an off moment once compared the Gosplan to "a whorehouse, on a Saturday night, on fire." Boris Kidrić, who supervised the liquidation of Soviet-type planning in Yugoslavia, was once asked what his principal planning instrument had been; he replied, "The telephone." Yet I am strongly convinced that it is easy to be too cynical, or to exaggerate trifling deviations, or to fall prey to a prejudiced, indeed to an ontological, faith in market spontaneity, administrative rationality, etc. Soviet-type planning (item 3, page 151) is what it seems to be and is hardly more ragged at the edges than Soviet sources admit.

The crucial question is, do we adjust our actions to the blueprint, or vice versa? However many times a Soviet manager telephones Moscow, however often the blueprint is changed in response, and whatever the extent of his violations, the fact remains that *ceteris paribus* he follows the blueprint; it does not follow him. The essential criteria of not being epiphenomenal are that (1) the blueprint is altered only at discrete intervals, (2) it is altered more to suit local conditions than simply because the planners have changed their minds, (3) it is, in any case, enforced, where it is materially possible to do so.

### Lower-organ Participation: Communist

The less detailed the blueprint, the smaller the danger of contradictions and the more effective the activators. Even the indirect activators of RM may suffice. Or, vice versa, the smaller the enforcement apparatus, the fewer details the plan can carry. Then, too, *if the lower organs participate in drawing up the blueprint*, it will surely be much more easily enforced, and there are important gains of a political and psychological character. But cutting in the lower organs has immense costs in economic rationality, and this subject merits extended treatment.

Take, first, the command economy. We know extremely little about the process of drawing up a Communist blueprint, since it has seldom been described and never investigated. I believe, however, that I have factual warrant for what follows. Without the lower organs' participation, the center will make intolerable errors of every kind: they must participate a little. Yet they do not come to the process with clean hands, and it is vital that the center be able to override them. The principal biases they bring to the conference table are:

1. They want an easy plan,[20] not at all necessarily low outputs, but low output/input ratios.
2. They want a loosening up of the bonus system.
3. They want, subject to bias 1 above, large outputs; i.e., each subordinate organ wants to capture for itself whatever expansion, whatever investment funds are going, irrespective of the national interest. Everyone's promotion, and in Communist countries specifically every local Party official's promotion, depends on this. It is these political pressures during the drawing up of the plan that mainly determine, in Communist countries, the location of industry. But the vice is universal: as chairman of a university department I have myself been guilty in this way. Such squabbling is one of the many causes of *investment scatter* (see pages 167–168).
4. They resist their own amalgamation or suppression to the last ditch.

5. Similarly they oppose the foundation of new enterprises, pre-ferring the expansion of their own.
6. Apart from bias 3, they want a quiet life. They will conspire to obstruct the introduction of new techniques; they will support each other's restrictive practices. The famous words of Adam Smith, "People of the same trade seldom meet together, even for merriment and diversion, but the conversation ends in a conspiracy against the public, or in some contrivance to raise prices . . ." no doubt apply fully to the drawing up of blue-prints with enterprise participation.[21]

*For if the execution of a blueprint in a command economy is a nonmarket process, its drawing up is exceedingly like an event in the marketplace.* The economic literature of planning pays far too little attention to this point. Bargaining is not exorcized by command; very far from it. It is shifted from enterprise level to the center, and the counters used are now not so much promises of economic benefits as political considerations (good or bad) and nepotic pull. In part, of course, marketlike procedures are used: two enterprises, or organizations, or localities "bid" against each other by claims to suitability. But the bidding is not, at least in Soviet-type economies, open and formalized, and many far murkier methods of persuasion are also used.

In centralized market where, to repeat, the government retains all initiative but uses it merely to enforce the consumer's sover-eignty; there is no blueprint and therefore no process of drawing it up. Yet most of what has been said remains applicable. There remain strong counterpressures to government orders, only there is no single formal moment at which they are mainly exer-cised.

So much, then, for that low degree of enterprise participation that characterizes the true command economy. Turning now to JI/command, there have been to my knowledge at least three serious attempts to engage the lower organs more fully in the drawing up of a command blueprint. The first was in Czech-oslovakia, 1958–1962.[22] I am unfamiliar with the details, but essentially central planning was reduced to a long-term contract between government and enterprise, with profit as the main criterion and activator. The idea was (1) to decentralize, (2) to get the enterprise to make honest suggestions as to planning, (3) to enable it to think ahead over several years. The system ended in mid-1962, in chaos and catastrophe, mainly because of investment scatter (page 167) but also because of features of the Czechoslovak economy unconnected with the scheme. In the literature I have read, decentralization has been regularly and rightly blamed for investment scatter, but no one has suggested that the scheme failed to make the planning process more honest.

A similar attempt was made in Poland in 1959 and abandoned. The third is the early Soviet experiment of counterplans, already mentioned. Taking place in the high Stalin period, this was mainly a hortatory device.

Then there is the scheme of Liberman in the U.S.S.R.[23] This much-touted scheme bears a strong family resemblance to the one that failed in Czechoslovakia, even down to the danger of investment scatter pointed out by some of its opponents. As Liberman's scheme has not yet been fully implemented, we need hardly consider it. One feature, however, is worth mentioning, as it was not in the Czechoslovak scheme: Liberman so arranges his bonuses as to make the proposal of an honest but progressive plan more profitable than the overfulfillment of any plan; i.e., if you propose a plan that brings in a high rate of return on your fixed capital, you have only to achieve it to get a high bonus. The marginal rate of bonus on overfulfillment is smaller, so it would have paid you better to propose a larger output in the first place. Indeed, it is this that is the nub of Liberman's scheme; it was his conviction that good planning should be better rewarded than overfulfillment that was the seed of his plan.

Liberman's essential insight, then, is that blueprint-fulfillment activators necessarily cast their shadows before them, over blueprint drawing-up. If the lower organs are to participate effectively, they must be specially activated to do so. There is very likely a conflict between the two sets of activators; e.g., in Liberman's own proposals overfulfillment is less valued than ambition in drawing-up, and this necessarily leads to slackening off when the manager finds that after all his plan was easy.

**Lower-organ Participation: French**

Such participation plays an absolutely different role in France (JI/RM). In France planning rests on the basis of government *mediation* between enterprise proposals which are therefore *ipso facto* serious. Indeed, these proposals, as amended and agreed upon, *are* the blueprint. Of the modernization committees, who draw up the plans for each branch of the economy, only one-fifth are civil servants, and the General Commissariat for Planning, almost entirely composed of civil servants, is responsible mainly for the synthesis. A further incentive to honesty in proposals is that since there is little detail in the blueprint and no penal enforcement mechanism, one has nothing to fear from underfulfillment. Consequently one does not need to build safety factors into one's promises. The fulfillment activator, moreover, is the participator's individual perception that since everyone else is going to do *his* bit, it is *most profitable* to do one's own bit. There is no centralized fulfillment bonus.

Blueprint formulation and blueprint implementation are in this model a continuous process, conducted by the same people without much lapse of time. No one is bound for a year ahead to do very specific things, and if the blueprint looks wrong, it is quite light-heartedly revised. In a command economy, on the other hand, one is so bound over quite a long period. If something does go wrong at the enterprise, so that the plan must be revised, the center will be very sticky about it. Revision is in any case quite likely not to result from enterprise representation but from some a priori change in the planners' intentions. Planners and managers are functionally distinct.[24] It is possible, though not necessary, that there will be much more detail.

The French problem is, on the contrary, to prevent the blueprint from becoming purely epiphenomenal. It is claimed that if the economy strays from the concerted blueprint or seems to be drawing up the "wrong" blueprint in the first place, the weapons of RM, taxes, subsidies, and open-market intervention by the government prevent this. One is justified, however, in questioning this, especially since the Treaty of Rome. It is plain that blueprints sit ill with RM. One might also object that if the blueprint is *merely* the sum of all enterprise suggestions, it is by definition epiphenomenal; only insofar as the government's reconciliation service causes changes in these proposals can we speak of a true blueprint. But this is not to speak ill of French planning, for it is incredible that entrepreneurs would have put precisely these proposals into practice if they had not first heard the comments on them of other entrepreneurs. Most likely in their get-togethers they will talk each other into proposing greater expansion than they would have dared to separately. If the resulting blueprint merely corresponds to what everybody wants, (1) that is not a fault, and (2) they would have wanted less, and done less, without it.[25]

Our whole semiconscious image of what planning is must be altered to admit the French *économie concertée*, and it is worthwhile, at some slight cost in relevance, to linger on this point. If the activators are not different from those in other models; persuasion does play a somewhat greater role; but the main casualty is not Benthamism itself but its first cousin, formality. The process of French planning is difficult to describe, and its style varies greatly. Thus France itself is a large country with a strongly rational tradition. So the planning is located in a definite office, which has a formal timetable of work. But in any small advanced country there will be and always has been, of necessity, "French" planning. Thus when Mr. Wallenberg meets the Swedish cabinet at the Prime Minister's country seat (what is known as *Harpsunddemokrati*), about 50 percent of the Swedish economy is automatically represented, and any agreement is a national plan *ipso facto*. In Yugoslavia too there is a much looser and more informal consensus, through consultation, especially via the League of Communists. And in Mexico the country's mysterious Establishment, of which so little is known, undoubtedly concerts most large private business and even some government departments into a loose and unscientific "national plan," different from the more detailed and less important one that is published.

## THE CHOICE OF PLANNING MODELS

How are economic and social policy affected by this array of planning models and activation models? First, the models themselves are quite as often ends as they are means. The passions and ideologies of men directly determine the models we use, far more than their varied suitability for the achievement of other ends. Humanity is (to my mind, ludicrously) divided into those who think markets, supply, demand, and profit are immoral and those who think government is immoral.

Ends other than these are innumerable: economic growth, social justice, full employment, stable money, borrowing abroad, lending abroad, private ownership, decentralization, centralization, rational resource allocation, low administrative cost, social stability, rapid modernization, armed might, the rule of law, political freedom—the list is infinite. Nevertheless, we have to judge our activators, however briefly and dogmatically, in the light of some of these ends. Most of the ends, for reasons of space, we must omit altogether as substantially unaffected by the choice of activator. Two deserve each a separate section. In this section we discuss such ends as are affected, but only mildly, by the choice of activator.

*Ownership* is almost irrelevant. It matters only insofar as it affects (1) management and (2) the sentiment of the people toward the property they are administering. As to management, Yugoslavia and the Soviet New Economic Policy (NEP) demonstrate sufficiently that Socialist managers can compete, seek profits, invest, etc. Per contra the war economies of capitalist states show the compatibility of CI with private ownership, though not in my opinion in the long run or in peacetime; market socialism is surely much more stable than command capitalism. The activators, then, whatever they may be, seem to work reasonably well under all types of ownership. But when we come to graft and theft, it may be different. Statistical proof is, of course, unavailable, but it is obvious that the sentiment of care and responsibility, so important in innumerable minor day-to-day ways, is stronger among small private proprietors and very weak indeed among the employees of large public enterprises. The sixty-four-ruble question is how the property of large private enterprises fares by comparison. It is my impression that employees in all countries respect private property slightly but significantly more than public; i.e., they respect someone else's property more than everyone's property.

*Growth* is largely a matter of the policies pursued, not the institutional model used, and *pro tanto* does not concern us. It is not, for instance, true that CI makes possible a greater investment volume or a more growth-promoting investment pattern than a sufficiently determined RM.[26] The prompt sharing of inventions and an adequate level of technical education are similarly independent of CI. The only advantages quite specific to CI are planner's tension and control over the balance of payments, discussion of which is prevented by limitations of space.

### Rational Microallocation of Resources

*The rational microallocation of resources* is an end—if *end* is the right word for anything so clearly instrumental—of economic policy far more intimately dependent on the choice of activators. I define *economic rationality* here as the use of scarce resources in such a way as to yield the largest income possible, "income" being either consumer satisfaction,[27] foreign affairs, and defense satisfaction, or investment and research likely in future to yield either of these. The *micro* indicates that we are not asking about the allocation between these broad categories, but that we do insist on wise choice *between* investment projects and *between* weapons as much as between consumer goods.

In FM and RM profit is not only the activator but also the criterion. One chooses profitable rather than unprofitable actions, so that profit determines the shape of the economy, and one's motivation for so doing is that one keeps the profit oneself. In CI, on the other hand, activator and criterion are divorced, as we have seen.

The choice between FM and RM depends upon whether one feels that the consumer or investor knows his own interest and that this in turn coincides with the public interest or whether the "man in Whitehall knows best." Into this hackneyed subject we must refuse to enter. Suffice it that both FM and RM aim at a situation where resources are pushed just so far along each line that in *someone's* reasonable judgment they could not be better allocated, and that they get fairly close to this aim. Typical examples of the difference between FM and RM are the swingeing taxes on alcohol that the latter imposes and the subsidized government investment programs of backward countries.

The blueprint of a thoroughgoing CI has more difficulty in being microrational. The blueprint, to be rational, would have to reproduce the ideal allocation brought about by FM or RM, whichever we prefer. It seems to be agreed by all parties that this involves "perfect computation"; the central compilation of information on demand and supply at least as good as that currently available to entrepreneurs in a market and the simulation therefrom of the market by linear programming. And this is as yet (note the qualifying phrase) beyond the resources of man. Therefore, all blueprints have been and remain microirrational. To repeat, they may be consistent, in the method-of-balances sense, but infinitely many such consistent blueprints are possible. Only one of them is rational, i.e., optimal for the given preference system.

A centralized-market system, on the other hand, could well be rational, if communications were rapid enough. Only there would be, as we have seen, no blueprint. We must ask *why* decisions should in that case be centralized, for all demand information is gathered at the periphery, and each enterprise is provided with the correct supply information automatically by the internal accounting system of the socialist sector which we have already posited. Sending it up to the center is not going to improve this information, so the decisions might just as well be taken at the periphery in the first place. So long as they are taken on the correct principles, it is pointless to wait for orders. But if decision making is peripheral, we have market socialism, and there is no CI. One reason for persistence in face of this objection is purely ideological: decentralization is held to be immoral. The other is that the point of CI is to take decisions *different* from those that the market would have taken. Although all the information is locally available, the subordinate organ will probably not act upon it in the desired way, i.e., use the right "criterion." For example, it will raise prices and restrict output where it has a monopoly, as in Yugoslavia, or neglect social costs and send up factory smoke. So the activators normal to the command economy have to be used constantly, because profit and other spontaneous activators lead to the wrong results. Wherever competition works reasonably well or the manager is so imbued with "Socialist consciousness" that he does the right thing automatically, centralized market is indeed unnecessary. The "right thing" would presumably be to push output until marginal cost equals price; this is Lerner's Rule, the output criterion of Western marginalist socialism. But this is not the same as profit; indeed, it often entails loss. Therefore, in many but not all cases the planner must forbid profit as a criterion and add some such activator as a criterion-fulfillment bonus. Hence centralized market is the preferred model of such Socialists.

Thus from the point of view of rationality there are three types of command economy: First comes the dream, which it still is, of perfect computation, in which computers and teletype machines improve upon the most perfect of existing markets. How would people be activated in such a system? They would simply do what they were told. The perfection of the center would reduce us all to automatons, and we should doubtless be rewarded by order-fulfillment bonuses. For the state that has enough power to handle all these data and orders probably also has the administrative resources to reward and to punish. The widespread notion is false that activation above all else should be decentralized to be efficient. Rather the contrary: decentralization, as for instance under Liberman, requires that particular pains be taken over activation. At any rate, perfect computation might be tolerable because efficient, but it would reduce society to an ant heap.[28]

Secondly, there is centralized market, which is more or less practically possible here and now. The trouble with activation under centralized market is that people may well not see why they should wait upon the center. That independent action may lead to irrational results is a consideration unlikely to restrain ordinary unregenerate humanity. For example, we may well act monopolistically, equating marginal cost with marginal revenue rather than with price, as under Lerner's Rule. There are two reasons for this: (1) Rationality is a very complicated and controversial concept; few understand it, and only economists, certainly not enterprise managers, bother about it. (2) Even given a high level of economic training it is not obvious to a subordinate manager that his decisions are irrational: he needs an overall view. Hence our third possible type of command economy, ordinary arbitrary planning, has in fact functioned under Stalin, with all its manifold defects; centralized market, were it ever tried, might well not.

The rationality of intermediately centralized systems is discussed in the next section. What, however, if CI, though thoroughgoing in its sphere, embraces only a part of the economy? The answer is that it almost invariably does only that. The remainder of the economy,[29] like the possibility of foreign trade, is a cushion for the government's errors, and provides, through its prices, indicators of the true scarcity of everything, indicators which the government would be well advised to use, though it seldom does. For these uncontrolled markets tell us the cost of marginal supplies, and though their prices are not those that would reign throughout the economy in the absence of CI, they undoubtedly tell the government in which direction to move.

### Centralization and Decentralization

Of all the possible desiderata mentioned, the most intimately linked with the activation system are *centralization* and *decentralization*. Let us not examine but take for granted the varied tastes that make men prefer the one or the other. Completely to decentralize is to leave the choice of activators to spontaneous decision at the periphery; this leads mostly to profit, as we have seen. This activator works equally for FM, RM, and JI, since in all of them there is a market. The only kind of centralization that affects us here is that in a command economy.

First, completely to centralize is, by definition, to give detailed orders that leave no local option, and the activators that ensure that these orders are carried out must also be imposed at the center. As we have seen, these may or may not include profit. But complete centralization, not so much of the activators as of the decisions, is still far beyond human capacity.

More interest inheres in *partial* centralization. For reasons of space limitations and its own intolerable complexity, one type of this, where a subordinate planning body intervenes between center and enterprise,[30] will not be discussed. What, however, if some decisions are devolved all the way down to the enterprise? That would leave us with FM or RM at a low level, each enterprise being restrained by such commands as the center still chooses to give. The other decisions are then left to profit, the great spontaneous activator-*cum*-criterion. But the center can also impose any set of criteria upon the enterprise that its fancy devises and use any activator to enforce them, and this is an invariable feature of the command economy in practice, since the means of communication fall very far short indeed of making complete central control possible.

How, then, when some freedom is left to it in a system of command, can the enterprise be activated to follow the right criteria? It is not easy. The question introduces us to the immense and sprawling field of *blueprint avoidance,* a subject extremely like tax avoidance and equally difficult to generalize about. There is one basic principle: we fulfill our blueprint *formally,* with as little effort as possible, in order to earn the plan-fulfillment bonus. Space does not permit further detail; I only quote my own conclusions: [31]

> All this suggests a generalization that is at least attractive. A command economy will begin by decentralizing a fair amount of decision to enterprises, and imposing a comparatively simple set of indicators. The biases that these set up will compel it either to increase the complexity of the indicators or to decentralize the system towards more market-like forms. . . . The two single-indicator systems, then—the wholly decentralized one of profit and the market and the wholly centralized one of detailed physical commands—are the best in that they set up fewest objectionable biases; and a command economy will tend towards the one or the other, being restrained only by its ideological repulsion from one extreme, and by its administrative incapacity for the other.
>
> Where intermediate systems obtain, the presence of more than one indicator at a time is possible, indeed almost certain, and it is almost certain that they will "indicate" different things. The choice then arises for the

unfortunate manager, which of these indicators he shall most obey. In a permissive, essentially democratic society which nevertheless had a command economy for some reason, the solution of this problem would be institutionalized for the manager. He would be allowed to treat it openly as a maximization problem with two variables, just as a consumer subject to the British wartime system of "points" rationing had to economize both his "points" and his money, compromising between the different optima they indicated. But in the totalitarian economy of Communism the manager cannot frankly plead the material contradiction of his indicators and get the central planners to admit it. Instead, he quietly sets up a political system of priorities among his indicators, according to his understanding of the basic ideology of his masters, of any short-term changes in the party line, and of the likely consequence to himself of falling short in this rather than in that respect.

In the past, this system of priorities has been rather stable and could be described as follows: Where there is contradiction physical targets come first, technical ratios second and money targets third, especially if they are profit targets, as opposed to gross output targets. In conformity with the ideology underlying this, the manager's bonus is principally dependent on the physical output of his firm and he needs only to ensure so much profit as will make it possible for that bonus to be paid.

Moreover, in a very growth-conscious economy like the Soviet, the planned outputs will be impossibly high by whatever indicator they are measured; so that even a single-indicator system is self-contradictory by virtue of what we call "planner's tension," the making of impossibly high demands on establishments. Then there arises a choice, not between indicators but between customers to satisfy. Here, too, a political system of priorities has grown up which has long been rather stable: defence customers have priority over heavy industry customers, and light industry and agriculture come at the bottom. Plan under-fulfilment has less serious consequences if only uninfluential customers remain unsatisfied. In recent years, both profit in the first scale of priorities and agriculture in the second (and, under Malenkov, light industry) have gained in informal political importance.

None of this is very impressive. Nor would it necessarily be good to substitute a share of profit for the plan-fulfillment bonus as the main activator. This would, of course, entail making it the main indicator as well: there would be little point in promising the director a fixed share of the profit and then telling him to pursue some other indicator. Profit would still be calculated on the bogus input and output prices that Communist systems [32] develop, just as is the case when it is an indicator alone; i.e., unless the price system were reformed, it might not even be an improvement.

Clearly a great difficulty here is that prices are still set centrally and neither the final consumer nor any other customer can influence them. In other words the planner has decentralized power to the producer only; in everything not centrally ordered, in all matters of detail and interpretation, the customer's wishes are quite secondary. Communists accuse capitalism of producing for profit, not use, thus failing to see that competitive profit *is* use. A truer accusation is that Communists produce for plan, not use, or, in decentralized matters, for production, not use. Could an indicator directly represent the customer's wishes?

The answer is that it would have to be very different from the kind of thing so far discussed and would in particular suffer from being neither measurable nor overfulfillable. We are looking, in fact, not for a new indicator but a new allocation model. Such a thing is the "system of orders." In this case, in place of the contract, the customer has the right to give any orders he pleases in respect to the detailed specification. This is a much more flexible procedure, as it cuts out the central planner except insofar as the general category of the goods to be produced by the enterprise is concerned. We are still, of course, very far from rationality, because under the centrally fixed prices we have no guarantee that the customer's demands are rational; moreover, his demands may be due to centrally fixed output targets as well. But at least he now gets what he needs; [33] the system's efficiency rises.

The trouble with this system is that it is inordinately hard on the producer, and interferes with his plan-fulfillment, since it cannot itself be made a statistical measure of such fulfillment. In recent years little has been heard of it, and the basic reason is clear: the center cannot clothe the desire to help the consumer with a suitable activator. For of course the only suitable one is profit, which, though ideologically disagreeable, is now coming in. Previously, without any activator more powerful than persuasion, the whole notion of direct consumer satisfaction received only lip service. One could hardly even call such a failure plan avoidance, for the neglected goal had hardly been incorporated into the plan in the first place.

Plan avoidance, then, is the almost inevitable result of partial centralization, whether the "small" decisions are devolved right down to enterprises or—the case we have omitted—halfway down, to intermediate authorities. Moreover, irrationality, meaning here the failure to satisfy the consumer, is another result. For the grand central view, which is a *sine qua non* of rationality, is sacrificed, and innumerable "small" decisions are taken in isolation from each other. Thus two steel enterprises at opposite ends of the country must both decide, let us say, the diameters of the pipes they make. It might well be best for each to specialize, but it is quite certain that under intermediate decentralization neither will. Each has his row of customers to supply, named in the plan; each will produce the whole range. And it is not simply large decisions, such as who shall make steel, that must be rational. The requirement is almost equally urgent for small decisions, such as who shall make ⅜-inch steel pipes. Perfect competition and computation would each have solved our problem, although the only practical way out, obviously, is still the former. For a perfect market provides such a grand central view, for decisions of whatever "size," since all supplies and demands meet in one place and there is only one price. Perfect competition decentralizes the activators and the criteria, but it actually centralizes the information.

### Investment Scatter and Regionalism

Partial decentralization has nowhere more devastating effects than in the construction industry. We have often referred above to investment scatter.[34] This is a rather new subject in Western economics, although Communist economics has lived with it since 1917. Nevertheless, it is as evident in Madrid as in Moscow:

why are both cities so full of unfinished buildings?   The answer is not merely the great construction activity of these two growing economies but also quite simply wastefulness and lack of discipline: *it is much easier to start a project than to finish it.*   Scatter can be so great as to bring growth to a complete stop, as in Czechoslovakia in 1962–1963, where projects in progress had grown so much more rapidly than projects completed that current output plans, based of course on projects being completed, were hopelessly underfulfilled.

To what is scatter due?

1. To the inefficiency of builders, who never begin on time and always take longer than they promise once they have begun. Anyone who has "had the builders in" will readily understand.
2. In market economies, to the ambition of builders, who capture more contracts than they can fulfill, thus overextending their resources.
3. To cheap money, and still more to the Communist practice of allocating capital free of charge. In these ways no one is hurt when an enterprise pays a builder an installment long before it can use the building. We arrive thus at the paradox that higher interest rates raise "investment," meaning that they reduce new project starts and thus, while there are uncompleted projects, release factors of production to hasten their completion.
4. To the ambition of local bosses, especially party bosses, who want to build up their area. The sure way to do this is to get funds to get the project started. You can then appeal to the conscience of the planners to finish it. Not otherwise were medieval cathedrals built, including those still unfinished. Indeed, to start a project with insufficient funds is almost a *sine qua non* in public and charitable enterprises.
5. To the patriotism of national minorities, demanding a share of everything.
6. To the fiscal practice of yearly fund allocation. Clearly cause 4 would be much less likely if funds were allotted, once for all, to cover a whole project.

All these causes, it will be noted, operate under RM and FM as well.   We have no figures, but it seems obvious that in advanced market economies scatter is unimportant.[35] Possibly, however, in backward market economies with long lists of government projects it is as bad as in the U.S.S.R. Also in two more advanced market economies that use detailed blueprints we note the notorious overinvestment indulged in by local Yugoslav bosses [36] and the somewhat less virulent French *saupoudrage*. A whole structure of regional authorities is growing up in France largely as an attempt to counter *saupoudrage*, which was, however, itself unknown until the concerted economy began.[37] For, clearly, if investment and location are a market process, not a political process, there will be less political protest from regions that consider themselves neglected. Moreover, scatter is a vice quite additional to all those discussed in the previous section, which also apply to construction under CI.

I have mentioned investment scatter particularly because it is perhaps the most important kind of blueprint evasion. When it increases, there is a crisis; when it falls, there is a boom. It can be defeated, presumably, in two ways: by charging the buyer of the capital asset a rate of interest or by strictly planning the period of construction, with fines for overstepping it, such as are often written into Western contracts. The existing Communist systems of activation and, I suspect, those used in the public sector elsewhere are powerless against it, even strongly encourage it.

We have here, then, two problems: certain peculiarities of the construction industry and its financing, and the inordinate interest of all politicians in *location*. We can say in general that production decisions (e.g., the choice between woolen and cotton textiles) are not especially political and are therefore quite economically rational, under both RM and CI, but that location decisions are very political indeed and so devoid of economic rationality wherever there is not FM. Whether they are in that case subject to a higher rationality or to none, we forbear to ask.

## PLANNING AND THE SOCIAL ORDER

### The Administrative Cost of Planning

It is striking proof of the backwardness of economic science that no empirical study compares for us the *administrative cost* of the various economic systems. It seems obvious to the Western mind, especially to the Western-trained minds of refugees from communism, that the command economy has an immensely greater administrative cost than any FM or RM. The principal reason seems simple: since decision is centralized, information and activation must be centralized; the very assurance of mere consistency has to be made into a conscious process—and centralized; the partial decentralization just discussed undoubtedly saves something but leads to enforcement problems; and everything has to be centrally audited, moreover, in ways unnecessary in a market economy (i.e., for plan fulfillment).

Yet astoundingly enough, the only even partially serious attempt to count bureaucrats finds proportionately more in the United Kingdom than in the U.S.S.R.[38] Nove's work certainly flies in the face of common sense, refugee evidence, and tourist impression. Yet it is, after all, based on an attempt to study the statistics. My own belief is that, just as some Soviet economists say,[39] the number of Soviet administrators is very large and rising. It would follow that the official figures, which show a steady decline, are wholly the product of manipulation and worth nothing at all, that administrators are concealed wholesale in the ranks of "productive" workers.

After all, even if there were good will, it would be an immense task to render such employment statistics comparable. Consider the complications. FM and RM require stockbrokers, advertising agents, comparison shoppers, traveling salesmen, and a monopolies tribunal, while CI with planning requires plan preparers at enterprises, planners at the center, plan-fulfillment auditors, *tolkachi* (enterprise representatives at the planning center), price controllers, black marketers, and economic policemen.

All three systems require, though in different quantities, market researchers, dispatchers, tax collectors, commercial lawyers, insurance agents, ordinary accountants and auditors, sales managers, editors of trade journals, retailers, wholesalers (albeit of different functions), and bank clerks (ditto). Furthermore all these people require varying amounts of communications facilities, office space, and clerical assistance, plus the degree of technical development reached in these sectors by each country;

thus the United Kingdom uses cash registers and the U.S.S.R. abaci.

It is evident that activation, e.g., *tolkachi,* policemen, is precisely what is costly about CI, whether centralized or not. When we come to information, the list of administrative types solely brought into existence by a market is impressive and sobering. If advertisers and traveling salesmen could be got rid of in a more perfect and rationally organized market, no doubt it is not more unrealistic to say that *tolkachi* and policemen would be dispensable in a more perfect and rationally organized command economy. Much, too, of our perception of increasing bureaucracy in the U.S.S.R. simply follows from the increasing technical complexity of industry and the larger number of draftsmen, chemists, engineers, etc. Such types are not included in our list above. Their rise and the parallel decline of the blue-collar worker are common to all economies. Nevertheless, and in the absence of all solid data, I maintain my faith that markets require *much* less bureaucracy.

## Economic Freedom and the Rule of Law

We turn to *economic freedom and the rule of law* (democracy, of course, is related but distinct). At present, let us confine ourselves to the rule of law in the economy, reserving larger questions for later. Economic freedom means "I may do what I like with my own." If this *own* is maldistributed, we have economic injustice, not economic slavery. Thus economic freedom is by no means necessarily a good thing. On the contrary, it may by almost anyone's value judgments be very bad. No absolute property right is implied by the word *own:* as it is defined here, freedom of management and control are enough.

The rule of law I take to mean that government relies far more on statutes, passed at long intervals, than on administrative regulations; that these statutes are subject to judicial interpretation, if not revision; that the government may easily be sued for breach of statute and *ultra vires;* that it may make no ex post facto law; that it must behave similarly in similar cases; that it must publish its laws and its judicial proceedings; etc.

It is a truism, though a vastly important one, that *the command economy is incompatible with the rule of law in the economic field.* For where the government is invariably giving and countermanding orders, without regard to the profits of enterprises or perhaps even to their continuous existence, and where even without the direction of labor it can and does alter the conditions of a man's livelihood at the stroke of a pen, and all by virtue of delegated powers against which there is no appeal, there by definition law has ceased to rule. An important exception is that one enterprise may sue another in the U.S.S.R. for breach of contract, but only if they belong to different ministries. This legalism does not, however, trammel the central planner, who can certainly not be sued. For the rest *inter arma silent leges:* a command economy is in many respects always a war economy. Indeed under communism there is no distinction between civil servants and enterprise managers. They are all officers of one vast enterprise, of which the Council of Ministers is the Board of Directors.

Within RM we observe a historical drift away from the rule of law. The characteristic nineteenth-century government control was an indirect tax or tariff, unlikely to change even from budget to budget and certainly published in a statute book. There followed the less popular and more personal, but essentially similar, income tax and the factory and health acts. Meanwhile, however, central banking grew, a wholly administrative affair, though at first an unimportant one, governed largely by automatism and scarcely "affected with a public interest." But, gradually, central banks have grown to horrendous proportions and have come to fulfill innumerable functions. Nearly indistinguishable from treasuries, they yet retain the secrecy and executive rapidity of a private business. They almost entirely escape from the rule of law. Exchange control and building licenses complete the picture: the government departments that exercise them are almost as untrammeled as central banks. The Keynesian freedom from the necessity of balancing the budget is a further retreat from automatism.

Over and above the rule of law there is the question of consent. Governmental economic policies are like other laws; if democratically decided upon and not grossly offensive to minorities, they do enjoy consent.   The impersonal forces of the market certainly arouse less heat most of the time, since they indicate no one for the aggrieved to shoot at, but people can live with a government that takes economic decisions they do not like.

But what of the activators and of the execution of these decisions?   It is one thing to vote for, or vote against but tolerate, a forced investment program or the prohibition of alcoholic beverages or the development of the virgin lands.   It is another to be taxed, or arrested in a speakeasy, or shipped to Kazakhstan.   Often, then, the manner of enforcement, i.e., the choice of activator, is more politically important than the policy decided upon.   For instance, a subsidy to wages in Kazakhstan is unremarkable; the direction of labor thither [40] is possible only in a totalitarian state.   A heavy tax on alcohol gives rise to a lot of moonshining and smuggling; a flat prohibition shook society to its base.   If the money for investment is raised entirely by taxes, we squeal; if some of it is raised by borrowing, we only grumble.   Indeed, the holders of the new debt do not even grumble.

In fact, within RM there are important distinctions: the open-market operation, such as the purchase of an easement or the balancing of the budget by borrowing, is far milder than such measures as zoning and taxation.   The rule of law is not enhanced—indeed, there is usually more executive freedom in open-market operations—but consent is.   In each case, of course, the milder activator leads to a smaller direct result.   But the payoff in political contentment is very high, and redounds to the government's advantage in the myriad small ways known as tax discipline, social solidarity, law-abidingness, etc.   It follows that the unpopular program itself may have a better chance in the long run if more mildly activated.

We must distinguish here from the activation model the uses to which it is put.   A heavy burden of forced saving characterizes not CI but communism.   Any government, using any system, that demanded so much work and abstinence of its citizens would have to be totalitarian.   For instance, under RM the heavy tax burden would probably be enough; there is clearly a variable and high but still real limit to taxation in a democracy.

Government intervention of all kinds has also direct constitutional consequences.   The first is that it is an *executive, not a legislative, function.*   Only a few old-fashioned controls in RM are so stable and inflexible that they can be tolerably left to the legislature: taxes, subsidies, and flat prohibitions.   Even these often require so much executive interpretation that it is impossible to speak of "a government of laws, not men."   For the rest, virtually everything a government does under RM and CI it must do executively, in exercise of broad powers granted it.   Secondly, judicial check is mostly out of the question.   Suppose, for instance, a Polish enterprise has for years produced the generously priced article *A* and legally diverted considerable profit into the enterprise fund.   It is then ordered to produce the low-priced and difficult article *B* instead: has it a legal claim for compensation?   At present, of course not, but the suggestion has been made.   To my mind it is absurd; it would plunge the whole of Poland into litigation.

*No activator can enforce a government decision exactly.* Things always come out differently.   There are many reasons for this:

The orders are inconsistent with each other or with the basic resources available, because the method of balances has been violated.

Government servants, especially the public auditors, are too few in number to catch up with violations.

The detailed orders are unpopular.

The government's general policy is unpopular.

The orders come late, are unclear, or obviously refer to a situation other than that actually obtaining.

The activators are simply inefficient, as discussed on pages 142–146.

To a Western mind, especially one trained in law and constitutional history, these are crushing objections to the multiplication of activators by the government.   Positive activators are particularly objectionable, since they have to be so flexible and are so apt to be mutually contradictory   And certainly if the rule of law and the respect for law are overriding aims, CI is out of the question, and RM has grave limitations.

But it is a fallacy that unfulfillable orders, and especially those only in part unfulfillable, serve no social function. Such orders can be persuasive, hortatory; they can make an enterprise do more nearly what is wanted than under *laissez faire;* they can inspire or exact obedience to the spirit, even if the letter is violated or impossible. In particular, they can cause greater economic effort and are a prime stimulus to growth. Anyone who thinks unfulfillable orders self-defeating should remember his army days, from the absurdities barked by the sergeant on parade to the heroically impossible demands of the lieutenant leading his platoon in battle, or should reflect that a 30-mile-per-hour speed limit probably keeps him down to 35 miles per hour.

## Economic Crime

The subject of *activation and economic crime* has already been approached in the discussion of blueprint avoidance earlier in the chapter; economic crime, however, is blueprint evasion. It was also fringed in the discussion of the administrative cost of planning and the virtual impossibility of combining CI with the rule of law. But now, facing graft directly, I am shocked and daunted by the absolute nonexistence of an economic literature on it, and I ask the indulgence commonly extended to scouts sent ahead into unexplored territory. First, some general propositions:

I define *graft* as an illegal or dishonest exchange in the productive or political process, for whatever reason, by means of a bargain. Graft, then, involves by definition three parties: *A*, who is cheated or disobeyed, *B*, who cheats or disobeys him, and *C*, who pays *B* to do so. Theft is also an illegal or dishonest transaction, also for whatever motive, but without any bargain. Only *A* and *B* are involved, and *B* simply takes by force or fraud, giving nothing in return.[41] There is also simple law violation, involving neither theft nor graft. All three may be directed against either the enterprise or the state.

Our interest is in men's motives for these three types of action. The most obvious motive is personal gain, but a second one is to help one's enterprise along, a third is political or moral disagreement with the law, and a fourth, paradoxically, genuine concern for the state plan. For we may agree in a general way with the blueprint, but observing its minor inconsistencies, we may choose to violate it, steal something, or bribe someone in a small way in order to achieve its greater goals. No doubt there are also other motives.

Now (1) theft and illegality for personal gain do not concern us. They depend on many things, especially individual morality, the number of policemen, and the absolute standard of living and its direction of change, but hardly on the economic model.

But (2) the possibilities of graft for personal gain are enormously enhanced by all large-scale economic organization. For such organization sets up *ipso facto* a conflict of interest in the individual. Communism and CI, or big Federal government and RM, have no monopoly here. Thus the buyer for any large enterprise can be bribed to spend his employer's money in some way not optimal for the enterprise; or virtually anyone—the auditor of an enterprise or a member of a municipal planning body—can acquire information of economic value. Government intervention adds little here: the conflict of interest inheres in large organization as such. Only individual businesses, each with one boss-*cum*-worker, avoid conflict of interest. In such a case to buy the dishonest employee is identical with legitimately persuading the employer.

What government intervention does enhance is (3) economic crime for the sake of one's enterprise. This is merely as much as to say that the enterprise stands vis-à-vis the government in RM or CI much as the individual stands vis-à-vis his employer.

Most interesting for us here is (4) economic crime directed against some minor provision of the blueprint in order to fulfill the major goals. This must be distinguished from the blueprint avoidance discussed on page 164. For such avoidance was for personal gain, yet within the letter of the law. We now speak of more serious "offenses" with more honorable motives. It is difficult to exaggerate the frequency of such things under CI, and even under RM. I recall hearing a British exporter, encouraged by the government to export as much as possible, complain that packing cases were rationed and unobtainable; was it not his duty to buy them on the black market? They have in fact an equivalent under FM itself: if everybody else commits graft, anyone with a particular project must do so, too. This kind of economic crime, then, is good, at least in economic terms.

Lastly (5) we may have conscientious objections to government policy. In this case we shall hardly indulge in graft or theft, but we shall practice illegality on a large scale. For example, we may have political objections to strategic export controls or social objections to prohibition. A Soviet manager, again, may hold that the planned wage levels are too low for the workers' welfare.

Theft and straight legal violation are easy concepts; graft is not. If a politician rearranges taxes for money, that is graft. If he lies because he is about to devalue the pound and must protect it, that is not. If a Soviet manager fails to fulfill the plan (which is, of course, to break a law) through incompetence or because it is inconsistent with itself, that also is not graft. If he sells surplus material to help another enterprise and pockets the money, that is. So it is when a British alderman buys up land he knows will shortly be rezoned for housing by his own planning committee; but if he buys it up in ignorance, say in the area of another local authority, that is merely speculation.

There are no statistics of economic crime, but when "everyone knows" that Wisconsin is superior to Massachusetts, we need not doubt it. As a guess, the order of magnitude for income derived from this source in the United States is 5 percent of the national income. Larger figures, often quoted, refer to turnover, not income. Thus turnover in illegal gambling alone might be 20 percent of the national income, but it is a statistical blunder to compare turnover and income in this way.

If everybody else commits graft and steals, great entrepreneurs must, as we have seen, also commit graft and steal. The more economic crime there is, the more there must be. This is all the truth there is in the common American admiration for the shady characters who built the United States economy. Had such crime not been rooted in government and people, railroads could and would have been built by honest men. Similarly if the command economy sets up an unfulfillable blueprint, managers have to break the law. That is, economic crime is good only if society is bad.[42] Since command blueprints must in practice be self-contradictory, CI makes economic crime inevitable. RM makes it merely probable; much depends on the height of particular taxes. FM confines such crime to that conducted by employees against their private bosses.

Economic criminality varies for reasons unconnected with economic models. In England, Scotland, Northern Ireland, Germany, the Netherlands, and Scandinavia the level has for a very long time been rather low, which is presumably due in some way to Protestantism. In other advanced capitalist nations it is middling. In the rest of the world it is high. From time to time governments arise that diminish graft: China in 1950–1959,[43] Egypt in the early days of Nasser, Singapore immediately after British rule, etc. The permanent success or failure of these "turn the rascals out" campaigns is not our concern. The definition of graft varies with cultural change. Chinese and Soviet Communists tend to call tipping graft; Polish, Hungarian, and Yugoslav Communists accept it. Few United States citizens regard the use of inside knowledge for private profit, without harming one's organization, as graft, but such use has led to formidable public inquiries in the City of London. A full treatise would iron out these differences and, in particular, strip the rationalizations from the face of concealed graft.

When all is said and done, then, do we actually want there to be economic crime? I am inclined to say, "Where it appears not to be functional, prosecute; where it does, change the system and then prosecute whatever crime continues." For these things are quite simply immoral, and in a way that affects more than the notorious minimum of "two consenting adults," and so they are appropriately not only sins but also crimes. Moreover, their economic advantages are heavily offset by the fact that they block the flow of information and command; they make proper management impossible.

Now while this argument seems reasonable in such cases as Prohibition, it seems very harsh in two separate cases: The first is where graft is psychologically endemic, regardless of all economic models. Among advanced countries the United States is in this respect notorious. No change of model could help us here. In such a case we must at least admit that police work is also an economic input, which cannot be indefinitely big, and that men are evil and not to be rendered perfect by any education, religion, or propaganda. So long as we do not try to rationalize or white-wash our frailty, we must then permit graft (though surely not theft) and only try to suppress its major manifestations.

The second exception is the command economy. Since the blueprint must be somewhat self-contradictory and planner's tension is endemic, there must be some form of illegality; it is a technical necessity. One's hope is to confine these violations to those that are individually moral, i.e., pursue enterprise rather than personal gain. But undoubtedly a strict, overriding regard for law and private morals must condemn the command economy out of hand.

Illegalities within the command economy are a movement toward the market. Where they are mere blueprint evasion for personal gain, they have no limit and may end up in making the planning epiphenomenal. But where their object is to achieve the major lines of the blueprint or to earn legally the bonus it promises, the extent of the movement is limited.

Even if economic crime is functional, as in (4), or conscientious, as in (5), we shall surely withhold our approval from the redistribution of income that also results; for, of course, while graft is exceedingly profitable, it is also very risky, and only shady characters benefit by it. We may, however, take a lenient view of some income redistribution in a command economy, e.g., when graft diverts scarce materials from the profits of state enterprises to the consumption of the people.

### General Political Freedom

This leaves us with the largest question of all: if under central control there can be no rule of law in the economy, can *law rule or people be free anywhere* in the society? There is doubtless no bigger or hotter potato in all social science than this. Let us first clear away certain misconceptions. First, there is such a thing as the rule of tyrannical law: all freedom might be legally suppressed. I include this here along with the arbitrary and extra-legal suppression of freedom. Secondly, almost no government has *first* instituted a command economy and *then* abolished political, intellectual, and religious freedom.   If CI, or something near it, comes in during a war and the social freedoms, as we may call them for short, are suspended, both FM or RM and the social freedoms usually return with peace.   They were suspended only "for the duration," with the very specific aim of victory.

On the other hand, Fascist and even Communist governments are more hostile a priori to social freedoms than to the market.   Titoism and the Soviet NEP excellently illustrate this.   So did Mussolini, who actually abolished many government controls during his first years of office.   Even if CI did determine totalitarianism as a Marxist "base" determines its "superstructure," it is certain that FM and RM are compatible with any kind of superstructure.

Nevertheless, it is very impressive how invariably men lose their noneconomic freedoms where the command economy rules and how any partial restoration of the market in a Communist country seems to be accompanied with relaxation elsewhere. Surely CI must be to some extent cause and the social unfreedoms effect.   I can think of several reasons why this must be so:

First, it is humanly difficult for politicians and civil servants not to let their social hand know what their economic hand doeth. It is not psychologically easy to take strong measures here and be very tolerant there, to take innumerable executive actions here but be bound by laws there.

Then there are inescapable technical connections between the two fields.   Those who would exercise political, intellectual, and religious freedom need incomes, books, telephones, newsprint, churches, access to broadcasting facilities.   The government has these matters automatically in its hand, since they are part of the command economy (they can also be interfered with under RM).   The temptation to cheat in allocating resources is overwhelming.   Indeed, the more tolerant Communist governments actually cheat more than the less tolerant.   Thus in the U.S.S.R. inconvenient intellectuals are simply forbidden to publish and removed from editorial boards; in Poland they are told there is a shortage of newsprint, at the very moment when other journals are founded.

Per contra the social freedoms may be used to attack economic policy or the economic model. Now if the model is FM, the government is being criticized only for inaction: its day-to-day economic machinery does not suffer, because it has none. But under RM and especially under CI, there is immensely much to criticize, and criticism impedes current operations. An enlightened government should welcome most criticism, since not otherwise can its mistakes of policy and decision making be corrected. But there is another prerequisite of the command economy that makes free and universal criticism genuinely counterproductive: the blueprint, once drawn up, must be obeyed. This means that the citizens must display a great deal of discipline in action, which any Army officer will confirm is impossible to combine with total "indiscipline" in discussion.

This point is immensely strengthened if actual secrecy is essential to the operation of CI. Communist governments have hitherto held that this is so. In the U.S.S.R. the very tax rates are concealed, not to mention many merely ex post facto statistics of performance (the 1963 harvest, the equality or inequality of incomes, many figures on the prewar period, etc). To me this secrecy seems almost entirely counterproductive. It was used neither during war communism nor during the first Soviet Five-Year Plan, and it has been almost abandoned in Poland and Hungary. Its sole rationale is to conceal economic failure from the world. For the rest, it springs only from paranoia, but, whatever its causes, it creates an atmosphere in which the social freedoms are bound to die.

The original Hayek thesis [44] was that one control leads to another: RM slips inevitably into CI, as the free citizenry try to wriggle out of the grasp of their interventionist government and so must be more and more strictly brought to heel. The process is irreversible and engulfs all other freedoms too. Although not impossible, this is a piece of inverted Marxism which history does not exemplify by a single instance. The slipping of RM into CI is indeed exemplified by innumerable capitalist war economies, but when wars cease, the process is regularly reversed. Nor does Hayek show exactly why the command economy abolishes the social freedoms, as we have tried to show above. As to peacetime

CI, history records no case of a government that was dedicated both to that and to social freedom.

As an attack on RM, Hayek's *The Road to Serfdom* seems to me to fail altogether, even though indirect controls are becoming more and more complicated and less and less subject to the legislature. But as applied to the command economy, and perhaps to CI in general, it is essentially successful, though not in a rigorous or historical way. I suggest that the facts are as follows: Everybody really knows that political opposition, free speech, the rule of law generally, etc., are incompatible with a command economy. No government dedicated to the former attempts the latter, except in wartime. At the end of the war, it is the "superstructure" of social freedom that wins out, reversing the economic "base." Per contra, no government dedicated to the command economy [45] attempts to grant or preserve social freedom, but it is highly significant that nearly always when such governments slightly relax their grip in one field, they do so also in the other. However slight the technical connection between economic freedom (about which I do not feel passionately) and the social freedoms (about which I do), regimes hostile to both do treat them as indivisible.

## NOTES

[1] Cf., however, chaps. 19 and 20 of Peter J. D. Wiles, *Political Economy of Communism*, Harvard University Press, Cambridge, Mass., 1962. The formulation discussed here owes much to Oskar Lange's *Political Economy*, The Macmillan Company, New York, 1963, chap. 5.

[2] An excellent example of this dichotomy is Chester Barnard, *The Functions of the Executive*, Harvard University Press, Cambridge, Mass., 1938, chap. 11.

[3] See Chap. 7, "Activating National Plans."

[4] On request. If the arbitrator is imposed, this is a "legal command."

[5] This is in essence the model I call *Capitalist War Economy* (CWE) in Wiles, *op. cit.*, pp. 70–71. The model shades into CI if the government uses its own nationalized construction enterprise or otherwise relies upon administrative force to get the projects completed.

[6] That is, I can see nothing in the word *unbalanced* but a straightforward old-fashioned *disequilibirum*. See Wiles, *op. cit.*, pp. 206–209.

[7] In *Economic Development and Cultural Change*, July, 1961.

[8] This is not to say that profit is perfect under these circumstances. What,

for instance, is the cost of a prototype? How much fixed cost, how much research and development must it bear? What is the demand for it, how do we know "what the market will bear"? In cases of great complexity, where too little is known, obviously all criteria are likely to mislead. Profit, then, also becomes more misleading than usual, but perhaps its advantage over criteria increases, too.

[9] In Communist CI there is also a perennial lack of spare parts. This, however, is quite inexcusable and by no means a direct product of the system. A simple change in the orders given would make factories produce more spare parts, fewer complete articles.

[10] This point has merely empirical validity. Technical progress might reduce the number of settled types, but it happens to increase them. On all this cf. Leon Smolinski and Peter J. D. Wiles, *Problems of Communism*, United States Information Agency, Washington, D.C., 1963.

[11] It has similarly been observed that in any society it takes good labor relations to make sophisticated products. For that matter slavery, the classic case of only one activator, could make only the simplest products.

[12] Wiles, *op. cit.*, pp. 73–75, slightly amended.

[13] Cf. Chap. 2, "The Institutional Context." But, per contra, it may draw attention to deadlocks, involve the government unnecessarily in private quarrels, and generally offend against the excellent principle of *quieta non movere*.

[14] Wiles, *op. cit.*, p. 75.

[15] If a government could be realistically conceived of in FM, it would engage in "neutral" taxation; i.e., it would tax to raise revenue alone, and in such a way as to leave the proportions of everything unchanged.

[16] The Communists retrospectively dubbed the period 1918–1921 "war communism" not because at the time there had always been war (there had not) or because the system was then thought of as temporary (it most certainly was not), but after it had failed, as an excuse. If this is dishonest, they are nevertheless in order when they date the inception of "planning" not from 1918 but from the foundation of GOELRO, the body for long-term electrification (1920).

[17] Wiles, *op. cit.*, p. 36.

[18] *Ibid.*, pp. 79–80.

[19] Wiles, *op. cit.*, chaps. 17, 18. I miss there, however, the essential point that socialism and communism are distinguished precisely by the change to moral activation.

[20] To every generalization its exception: during the first Soviet FYP enterprises used to send up "counterplans" (*vstrechniye plany*) to the center. Owing to the general excitement and pressure, and in particular owing to the anxiety of local Party officials to distinguish themselves, these proposals exceeded those made by the center. The same happened during the Chinese Great Leap Forward of 1958. In the first enthusiasm of their noncommand planning, Tanganyikan authorities have done the same thing.

[21] *Wealth of Nations*, vol. I, p. x.

[22] Cf. John M. Montias, *The Czechoslovak Economy*, Princeton, 1962, privately circulated.

[23] Marshall I. Goldman, "Economic Controversy in the Soviet Union," *Foreign Affairs*, April, 1963; Harry G. Shaffer and Rush V. Greenslade, "Problems of Economic Reform," *Problems of Communism*, June, 1963.

[24] Even though, under communism, they belong to the same career hierarchy. In France, on the other hand, the functional distinction is blurred, while the career hierarchies diverge into those of civil servant and capitalist executive.

[25] On the obvious possibilities of monopolistic restriction in this system, I am unable to speak from evidence.

[26] See Wiles, *op. cit.*, chaps. 13–16. I do not, however, share the Chicago school's opinion that FM would do as well or better, if people were simply to save more. This seems to be untrue, on the simplest Keynesian grounds.

[27] Assuming, alas, the addibility of satisfactions among consumers—as every economist interested in results must.

[28] Unless people ceased to worry about economic life. If everybody except planners, politicians, and economists agreed that the whole subject was beneath their attention and if all interest were concentrated on the use of leisure, an economy that deprived us all of all economic initiative might be psychologically tolerable. Prerequisites would be extreme affluence, high educational levels, and short working hours. Even so it is difficult to imagine a whole nation devoid of, for instance, the instinct of craftsmanship.

[29] For example, in the U.S.S.R. the *kolkhoz* sector and the secondhand and black markets.

[30] Cf., however, Wiles, *op. cit.*, chaps. 7 and 8, for the first tentative steps in analyzing this.

[31] *Ibid.*, pp. 82–85, 89–90.

[32] Other command economies, not based on Marxism, might not have this vice.

[33] Subject, of course, as in all economic models, to his having the requisite income. We abstract, as always, from the justice of income distribution, which is irrevelant to this argument.

[34] Russian, *raspylenie;* Czech, *rozestavenost;* French, *saupoudrage.*

[35] A notorious exception is the numerous "political" roads and Army bases of the United States.

[36] Wiles, *op. cit.*, p. 152.

[37] See Chap. 11.

[38] Alec Nove, *Manchester Statistical Society*, January, 1962.

[39] Quoted in Smolinski and Wiles, *Problems of Communism, op. cit.*

[40] This is in fact done not by legal command but by various forms of persuasion.

[41] It is also possible to combine theft and graft: when *B* promises some illegal action to *C*, takes the bribe, and then fails to perform, i.e., does not "stay bought."

[42] Unless it is, in individual psychology, an outlet like juvenile violence.

Thus a psychologist might argue that Robespierre was a mass murderer because he was incorruptible.

[43] The hunger is said to have reestablished "squeeze."

[44] Friedrich A. Von Hayek, *The Road to Serfdom*, The University of Chicago Press, Chicago, 1944.

[45] As the U.S.S.R. moves away from the profit and law activators of the command economy to the merely persuasive ones of full communism, it is the obvious intention that social freedom should increase. But it may well turn out technically necessary that it should decrease, since only a brainwashed population will respond to persuasion alone.

# 7

## Activating National Plans

*Bertram M. Gross*

The problem of implementing plans in any country at any particular period is always a unique problem, one that can be rationally dealt with only by diagnosing the specific obstacles and fashioning an implementation strategy in terms of estimated feasibilities. Furthermore, even the most laudable steps to carry well-designed plans into effect may result in a considerable degree of frustration. Any economy, and particularly the social system in which it is embedded, is only partially controllable. Unforeseeable complications may always produce unpreventable shortfalls.

To analyze the process of plan implementation, we must first introduce the concept of activating as an alternative to the more traditional concept of command. We shall then analyze the obstacles to effective activation, and the processes of building an *activation base*, developing an *activation mix*, coping with conflicts, and developing campaign strategies. This analysis will lead us into many delicate areas usually glossed over by those who approach economic planning in the restricted terms of economic analysis or "nuts and bolts" administration. It will bring us face to face with such "unmentionable" realities as interest conflicts, the distribution of power, and the strategy and tactics of influence.

## ACTIVATING: THE BASIC CONCEPT

Any study of plan implementation, unfortunately, is seriously impeded by certain immaturities in the popular approach to government administration. Many people think of administration as a small-*a* affair involving nothing but staff tools and formal structures, rather that as a large-*A* affair involving the guidance of complex systems in difficult environments. Many too readily accept, and even act in accordance with, overrigid dichotomies between planning and administration, between policy making and execution, and between ends and means. They fail to see the intimate and indeed inextricable interrelations among the administrative processes of planning, activating, and evaluating.

Indeed the traditional language of both public and business administration places an inordinate emphasis upon command (or orders, directions, or instructions) as the way of getting action.[1] "After an organization has been formed, it must be made to work," wrote Fayol, "and this is the function of command."[2] "Directing" was the central element among the seven processes in Gulick's famous POSDCORB.[3] Many more recent analyses of administration, or management, approach the problem of getting actions with the concepts of (1) command, (2) control (usually conceived of either as command in the first instance or else subsequent commands to correct action not in accordance with plans), and (3) coordination (usually conceived of as commands to keep different actions in conformance with plans). The same spirit is inherent in such terms as *the chain of command* and the *span of control*. This tendency to get away from the many difficulties involved in initiating action has often been reinforced by modern theories concerning problem solving and decision making. The analysts of decision making and rationality often prefer to limit themselves to cognitive processes and get away from the nastier problems involved in deciding how to get people to act in accordance with the decisions that are made. The same tendency is promoted by exaggerated ideas of the great power that a Prime Minister, President, or Cabinet Minister could exert if he really made the effort, if he really chose to use the directive power allegedly at his fingertips.

In actual practice, however, as every experienced administrator knows, people cannot be moved to action by commands alone. First of all, command is one-directional: one can give orders to a subordinate but not to an associate, superior, or competitor. A government agency may give orders to people who are not in its employ, but usually only in accordance with certain customs, laws, or regulations that subordinate certain people and activities to its command. As a form of feasible action, therefore, command tends to be relevant mainly for people in the higher hierarchical positions and, in a general sense, only for the chief of state himself. Reliance on command as a means of getting action, therefore, may readily produce the very inaction that seems to inhere in overcentralization.

Secondly, the power of a command rests upon the receivers' assumption that evasion or disobedience will be punished. Few people can draw upon all the punishments needed to back up reliance on command as the sole means of activation. This is particularly true when available punishments may be evaded. Hence the finding of Dahl and Lindblom that "command is possible only under conditions of social organization that prevent subordinates from fleeing the reach of the superior." [4]

Thirdly, if command is relied on too much, it can readily lose effectiveness. Punishments may lose their sting. Indeed, they may be converted by the punished into badges of glory.[5] Both commands and punishments may be evaded, sometimes with impunity. When not evaded, the aftereffect may be to undermine initiative or even to bring people and organizations to a point where they may lose their ability to act without instructions from others. In the case of some people and organizations, the very whispering hint of command may lead the proud and headstrong to refuse to take action that they might otherwise have wanted to take of their own accord.

In contrast, a full-blooded approach to the implementation of national plans requires attention to *all* the methods whereby the major actors on the national stage take steps to get action. Commands must be included but must be put into focus by being set alongside other methods of influencing human behavior. The concept of activating provides an effective instrument for doing this. As shown later in the chapter, under "Using Influence: the Activation Mix," *activating* may be defined generally as the use of influence and more specifically as something done through any combination of various methods of persuading, pressuring (which includes commanding), and promoting self-activation.

Before discussing these methods of activation, however, it is necessary to identify the major obstacles to activating and the process of mobilizing sources of influence by building an activation base.

## ANALYZING OBSTACLES TO ACTIVATION

Like any other problem, the difficulty of implementing a national plan is often responded to in an irrational manner. The existence of an implementation problem may at first be denied. When admitted, it may be handled in terms of a habitual reaction without an effort at diagnosis. The attempted treatment may be irrelevant to the disease or may even accentuate it. Indeed, irrational responses of this type seem inherent in the growth of national planning. The rationality of technical calculation, so essential to effective national planning, seems to develop more rapidly than the rationality of dealing with institutional deficiencies, human resistance, and defective processes of planning, evaluation, or activation.

A rational analysis of the obstacles to plan implementation will often point to improved ways of activating plans by overcoming resource deficiencies, human resistance, and defects in evaluation and activation themselves. In many instances, however, such analysis will indicate that the plans, as presently constituted, are simply impossible to carry out. This will necessitate an adjustment of time schedules or, indeed, major changes in the substance of the plans and the process of their formulation.

### Resource Deficiencies

In a poor country the greatest obstacle to the activation of any plans for making it richer is its poverty itself. This is particularly obvious in any country that lacks such basic natural resources as good soil, water, forests, and minerals. Heroic efforts are needed to overcome these deficiencies, but the poverty created by such deficiences is itself a major obstacle to such efforts A vicious circle is thereby created.

In part, these obstacles are technical. They can be overcome by science, technology, and know-how. In this respect, they are not absolutes. Their difficulty is relative to the current state of knowledge and skill. Indeed, with modern processes and machinery it is technically possible in any country to achieve results, whether in agriculture, mining, construction, manufacture, or transportation, that would have been regarded as impossible a few decades ago. In the not-too-distant future it will certainly be feasible to implement plans for the elimination of cancer, the desalination of salt water, and the widespread control of the weather. In the developed nations of the world it is already possible to abolish involuntary poverty.

But there are no purely technical obstacles. Knowledge and skill are human attributes. Agricultural and industrial objectives cannot be achieved in a given country just because the required knowledge and know-how exist somewhere in the world. People with these capacities must also exist in, or be brought to, that country. Natural resources are meaningless without human resources. Underdeveloped human resources are the most serious of all resource deficiencies.

Although overlooked in the formal accounts used by economists, institutional resources are also of critical importance. Natural resources cannot be used effectively by people acting as individuals alone. Significant plans for progress become feasible only when people are brought together into organizations capable of exploiting and extending available knowledge and knowhow. The absence of adequately staffed and adequately administered organizations is as much an objective difficulty as any deficiencies in soil, minerals, machinery, science, or technology.

The more ambitious the plans, the greater the resource deficiencies seem. To make the desert bloom, to control a mighty river, to build a progressive steel industry, to develop a national transportation system, to provide good housing for the majority of the people, to explore the moon—these are the stuff that national plans are made of. While they may be easy to dream about, they can never be accomplished without facing one or another form of resource deficiency.

Unfortunately, human and institutional resources are often neglected by so-called "planning experts." Plans are often conceived of in scientific and technological terms alone, particularly by scientists, technologists, and laymen whose adoration of science and technology blinds them to the social instruments through which science and technology become useful.

### Resistance

Still more remote from solution through science and technology alone are the obstacles created by human resistance to the carrying out of plans. In one form or another such resistance is inevitable.

In its mildest form the energy of planners and activators is pitted against the inertia of others. People and organizations are not easily moved. They are weighed down by habit and custom, just as physical objects are weighed down by their mass. As with physical objects, any effort to move them even a little is apt to create friction. An effort to move them far or quickly is apt to create active resistance and bring counterplans into being.

The most active form of resistance is based upon a felt conflict of interests. In the case of cross-sectoral plans a certain kind of resistance can reasonably be anticipated from the very nature of the plans themselves. Thus, the plans below will probably be opposed by the groups opposite them:

| *Plans for* | *Groups Opposing* |
|---|---|
| Higher taxes | Taxpayers |
| Wage controls | Wage earners, particularly their labor union representatives |
| Price maxima | Sellers |
| Price minima | Buyers |
| Higher interest rates | Borrowers |
| Lower interest rates | Lenders |

| *Plans for* (continued) | *Groups Opposing* (continued) |
|---|---|
| Nationalization | Private enterprisers (except those eager to be "bailed out" at a good price) |

The nature and intensity of the opposition will depend, of course, upon the specific circumstances and upon the degree to which the "injured" interests are organized. Sectoral and areal plans emerge out of competition for scarce resources by organizations in different sectors and areas. While the distribution of these scarce resources among the various sectors and areas provides the wherewithal for satisfying certain interests, it inevitably implies, at least in part, the denial of resources to others. The process of resource allocation has its negative side also—the distribution of dissatisfactions. These inevitably give rise to efforts to change official plans or impede their implementation.

Moreover, plans for technological progress always produce serious interest conflicts.

> Technological change of any significance whatsoever is a threat, real or imagined, to the power or security of someone. . . . In its more obvious aspects, any technological change which enables the production of similar output with less labor threatens to reduce employment. But even where such an effect can be counterbalanced by expanded production or by transfers to other work, the change itself threatens established positions and expertise. It renders obsolete the accrued capital of knowledge in the hands and minds of those who operated in accordance with previous processes. It may even suggest that the people responsible for the previous processes are inferior individuals, as compared with the wiser souls who promote the new processes. Furthermore, it may turn upside down the whole world of established relationships and lead to a complete reorganization of work groups, tasks, responsibilities and individual status.[6]

Finally, plans for changes in social structure, whether they are explicit objectives or merely the corollaries of performance objectives, lead the planners into the heart of deep-felt social conflicts. The elimination of caste or class distinctions, the control of monopolies, the regulation of any powerful interests, the reorganization of industry or agriculture, the promotion of new cooperatives, trade unions, or trade associations, the "leveling down" of privileged groups, the "leveling up" of the underprivileged—all such objectives pit planners against plan opponents. Under such circumstances it is a rare thing if the social conflicts inherent in (or provoked by) certain plans for changes in social structure are not reflected to some degree by conflicts among the central planners themselves.

To analyze the human opposition to national plans, it is essential to identify the interests and groups directly and indirectly involved in these conflicts and estimate the influence, or power, they may exercise under various conditions. Yet a serious obstacle to such analysis is provided by technocratic conceptions of planning as something divorced from anything so sordid as social conflict. "There has always been a tendency in economics," as Myrdal has pointed out, "to gloss over interest conflicts." [7]   As planning advisers, economists usually use dehumanized models abstracted from interest conflicts. Indeed, many planning technicians see national planning as a blackboard problem exercise far removed from the real world of clashing interests and competing influence strategies.

### Defects in Planning, Evaluating, or Activating

Another set of obstacles is always provided by the behavior of those engaged in the very processes of national planning, evaluating, and activating. These are extremely complex processes that have thus far been subjected to little more than superficial study by social scientists. Most practitioners are guided mainly by hunch, intuition, and trial and error. At best, adequate is associated with inadequate planning, good with bad evaluating, and brilliant with wretched activating. It is unlikely that any foreseeable increase in human knowledge and skill will prevent such defects. Although a full survey of major defects of this kind would be beyond the limits of this chapter, brief mention may be made of some of those that seem widespread.

*Overcommitment.* "Once settled," Von Moltke told the Kaiser with respect to the Schlieffen Plan for Germany's World War I offensive against France, "it cannot be altered." [8] Similarly, once an overambitious goal had been set for steel output during India's third-plan period, fear of criticism prevented the planners from reducing the output targets and thereby accentuating the great progress that had, in fact, been made. The other side of the coin is the tendency of planners to accept the credit for over-fulfillment when a sudden change in international markets leads to more foreign-trade income than had been hoped for; to revise goals upward in the light of new opportunities would deny them the illusion of false achievement.

Action-oriented planning, in contrast, is a far cry from the rigid idea of a stable, automatic, and highly predictable system. It is rather a highly dynamic process leading from one point of disequilibrium to another. "The best laid schemes o' mice and men gang aft a-gley." The gap between desired and actual performance is usually rather high. Even the best of planners always fail to anticipate certain new situations. The most successful plans always have unanticipated consequences. The most rational methods always create unanticipated conditions. All these factors lead to unanticipated changes in planners, plans, and planning methods.

Above all, in action-oriented planning there is no "master plan." The planning documents, important though they are as instruments of communication and as ways of recording sequences that could not otherwise be arranged in an orderly fashion, are rarely up to date. They can never express the major elements of purposefulness. By the time these points are written down and double-checked, they are usually out of date. A written master plan can only be up to date when it represents a planner's vision upon which no action is being taken or an abstract scheme remote from all operational detail. If the master plan is beautifully printed, with elaborate charts, tables, and pictures, one may be sure that it does not represent what is going on or that, as is often the case, nothing is going on.

**Projectismo.** In discussing Mexican culture, Fayerweather [9] defines *projectismo* as:

. . . constructing plans without much critical analysis and then assuming the plans to be an accomplished fact . . . the individual is caught up in belief and identification with his schemes as a form of reality. . . . *Projectismo* is part of reality for many Mexicans. Listening to one of them describing a plan, you realize that, however unlikely or uncertain of success the plan may be, the man is experiencing in its conception the same type of satisfactions which a man of action would realize only as he carried it out. And for him the satisfactions are the greater because a plan which exists only in his mind does not need to suffer the buffeting of conflicts and obstacles.

Fayerweather explains *projectismo* in Mexico as a compensating element to offset the frustrations of life throughout Mexican history.

Yet it would be an absurd mistake to regard as a purely Mexican phenomenon the propensity to derive satisfaction from goals in a way that diverts attention from goal attainment. This is, rather, a universal tendency. It is a widespread phenomenon in the public life of all industrially underdeveloped countries, where dreams are easy to concoct but the conflicts and obstacles to achievement are tremendous. It is probably just as widespread in the private fantasies of millions of frustrated or neurotic people in the industrially developed countries. In fact, many of the growth-rate projections developed by frustrated technicians and ritualistically publicized by political leaders can best be described as *projectismo*. They often consist of macrogoals for employment or GNP, without being related to any specific or identifiable means of attainment. They may be abstract projections unrelated to any specific projects. It is also *projectismo* when planners propose major development "projects" without the engineering specifications needed to make a decision concerning them, let alone to get them under way.

Another form of *projectismo* is based upon utopian commitments to desired situations that are simply impossible to obtain. In this latter case, the elaboration of presumed methods of attaining the unattainable may serve to make the plan more plausible, even though not a bit more feasible. Yet the fact that a plan may be utopian need not prevent its reaching the stage of central decision and commitment. National political leaders often make "pie in the sky" promises as the only way to distract attention from current suffering. While such promises may lead to bitter disillusionment, they may also start the wheels going around on more realistic planning processes.

*Document orientation.* Overconcentration on documents is one of the occupational pathologies of planning technicians. The preparation of major plan documents is the central task of many technicians. This task is particularly important when the planning documents formulate specific purposes and serve as an essential link in the process of communication among leaders throughout a country or even among the people at large. The written word is essential to record the actions that are to be taken and the reasons for them. Without it, there is no possibility of supplementing the defective memory of people and of providing effective communication among them, particularly on details. The written word, especially if laden with an impressive array of statistics, also has tremendous symbolic value. It may be of great value in mobilizing support.

Yet plan documents by themselves can never express all the elements of human purposefulness. Some of the more important purposes can never be properly or fully expressed in writing. They must be sensed and felt. Moreover, many points that are clearly written are sometimes out of date by the time of printing. Others are out of date just a little later, and the plan documents can never be brought up to date. In planning, as in the drama, "the play's the thing" and not the script. When the script is taken for the whole show, a major gap develops between plan formulation and action under plans. Plan documents may even be used not so much as an instrument of planning but as a preliminary to planning at some later date or as a substitute for planning at present.

*Underevaluation or overevaluation.* How well (or badly) is the plan progressing? How effective (or ineffective) are the actions of this organization, in that sector, or in that multisectoral program?

To ask these questions and find answers to them is an integral essential to good planning. Administrators may rarely assume such perfection in planning and activating that the satisfactory nature of ensuing action may be taken for granted. To compensate for past errors and adjust to new conditions, control efforts are invariably needed in the form of additional activation, changes in plans, or both. These, in turn, may require certain changes in personnel or organizational structure. By evaluating past and current action, administrators may complete the "feedback loop" and undertake these control activities.

Sustained evaluation, however, is often neglected. Performance information is often hard to obtain. When obtained, it may prove unreliable. If reliable, it may prove tedious or unpleasant, particularly in comparison with the more heady exercise of concocting new plans. If fully analyzed, the evaluation data may stay in the offices of technical personnel and never get to the more responsible planners. A glaring example of what may happen when attention is not given to actual performance is provided by the following story: "An Egyptian platoon commander who had been in charge of a number of Archers (British tank) was asked why, when abandoning his guns, he had not spiked them. He insisted that he had done so; he really believed it. And when he was taken back to his own guns and shown them intact and in perfect fighting order, he could not understand it. Of course they had been spiked; he had told somebody to do it." [10] In national planning where matters are usually more complicated than in war, events like this are always happening.

The other side of the coin is that overemphasis on evaluation may serve to impede the kind of action it is supposed to promote and promote the kind it is presumably designed to control. As pointed out earlier in the chapter, many planners and plan theorists have no concept of activation whatsoever. They may thus tend to think in the limited terms of "planning and evaluation" or "planning and control." Accordingly, when it becomes obvious that for the sake of implementation something else is needed to supplement planning processes, they will often move forward vigorously but unwisely into ill-conceived evaluation and control measures. There are, indeed, many cases in developing countries where faulty plan implementation has been made more faulty through the advice of "foreign experts" who, with little attempt at diagnosis, have prescribed Western control systems as the remedy for defective activation. In some cases the "foreign experts" may themselves be totally lacking in practical experience in the handling of evaluation and control activities in their own country.

In diagnosing such obstacles to plan implementation, it is important to keep in mind the major difficulties that may be created by evaluation activities and control systems.

The first is the danger that an overdose of evaluation or control may unwittingly serve to undermine plan implementation. Evaluation and control may divert an undue amount of time and energy from concrete implementation steps to the filling out of forms, the conducting of endless studies, and exhausting appearances before evaluation boards or investigating commissions. They may provoke a debilitating sense of resentment and antagonism against the evaluators, undermine the initiative of the evaluatees, and—what is still worse—even destroy their sense of responsibility for their own actions. In reporting on the lack of initiative shown by public enterprises in Burma, Walinsky tells how the government established a high-level, discreetly quiet "Board of Boards" to investigate their operations.[11] In reading his report, one cannot help but wonder if the investigation itself nay not have reduced the initiative and self-reliance of the public enterprises under study. In this connection it should be kept in mind that close supervision and intensive investigation (particularly by legislative committees) have often been favorite devices whereby interests hostile to a government program may, in the name of helping it, take action to undermine it.

The second is the ever-present possibility that where tight control is exercised with respect to defined criteria, the result may be "action distortion," that is, compliance at the cost of neglecting other aspects of performance that cannot be so readily measured. Thus in Soviet planning, control figures expressed in terms of quantitative targets for output have often had the effect of promoting the neglect of quality, production costs, or both.[12] This tendency has also been amply documented with respect to control systems in United States government and business.[13]

Third, evaluation and control systems have an innate tendency to produce "data distortion" as well as action distortion. In providing information under control systems or in response to investigations, administrators often select or "color" information to enhance their own performance, "pass the buck" to others, or tell their superiors what they would like to hear. "Events that may be interpreted as failures, if reported at all, are skillfully underrated and sandwiched between successes," reports Redfield. "Through experience the subordinate learns how much to report, what interests the boss the most, how far one can safely go in confession of his own failures and in pointing out the boss's mistakes, and how co-workers at the same level report." Even statistical and financial reports, despite their appearance of cold objectivity, may be based upon a certain amount of fabricated or distorted information at the point where the primary data is first recorded. As these data move through the various channels of processing and interpretation, the distortion may grow. "Distortion is a cumulative process, starting at the bottom and growing as it ascends the hierarchy, because those at the top foster it through a multitude of expressions and actions." [14]

Finally, the sheer bulk of information collected through evaluation activities may clog the communication channels of the central planning machinery. This has tended to happen in India, where the creation of evaluation boards and committees has become an almost automatic response to problems of faulty implementation. The writing of an evaluation report, in addition to becoming a substitute for action, merely adds to the growing number of reports which pile up on the desks of people too busy to read them.

*Administrative Myopia.* Planners often get lost in the clouds by losing sight of the organizational basis for both planning and implementation. On the other hand, they often tend to exaggerate the importance of one particular agency (usually their own), thereby losing sight of the major planning roles to be played by many others among the central cluster of national institutions with major roles in national planning. This myopic self-concentration becomes most dangerous when the effort is made to solve problems of coordination by doses of major reliance on stronger doses of formal hierarchic authority. On the other hand, preoccupation with building a central planning organization often diverts attention from the need of building many new organizations throughout the society. Many economists still make the mistake of seeing capital investment as a disembodied process, without giving enough attention to the human organizations needed to invest capital and use it productively. Many educational plans have been drawn up with little attention to the required investment in the educational institutions needed to train teachers, to provide education, and to employ highly trained scientific and technical personnel.

Another form of administrative myopia is nourished by over-sharp dichotomies, both personal and temporal, between planning and activating. The personal dichotomy arrays planners and proposers on one side and doers and disposers on the other. The temporal dichotomy regards planning as something that comes first and implementation (or activation) as something to be thought about afterward. Such conceptions create or magnify the fact that doers and deciders always have a role in formulating plans. They ignore the fact that the process of formulation has tremendous implications for implementation. They therefore create or magnify obstacles to plan activation.

Finally, administrative myopia takes the form of totally unrealistic conceptions of what is involved in the management of complex organizations and the still more complex interrelations among such organizations. Many planners seem to have a mental picture of administration based on the twin glories of central omnipotence and central omniscience. They envision all-powerful, all-knowing figures seated on a high pinnacle in a hierarchical heaven, with the rules of reason (as they expound them) carried out by lesser folk. If, in their ignorance, politicians, workers, farmers, and bureaucrats do not cooperate, they must be "educated." If they will not be educated, this goes to show the depths of man's ignorance and the perversity of the world.

In real life the administration of national planning is quite different. Both power and knowledge are dispersed. There is always competition between divergent interests and purposes, and different methods of activation. Above all, there is competition between competing planners. The idea that planning is noncompetitive, something entirely different from market competition, is rather remote from the realities of planning, just as the classical economist's picture of free competition is remote from the realities of actual market practices. Naturally, the competition that exists under planning is not free and unbridled. It is rather competition which is resolved through various combinations of integration, compromise, domination, deadlock, and avoidance. It is structured by the common interests, institutions, and procedures that bind groups together and by the interlocking roles that define group conflict. In this sense national planning is always some form of "structured competition." The administration of national planning always involves the management of conflict.

## MOBILIZING INFLUENCE: THE ACTIVATION BASE

In warfare, strategic plans are not limited to military operations that may be conducted against various enemies. They also provide for a buildup of the forces to be used and the maintenance of vital supply lines.

Similarly, plans for implementing national plans are not limited to what the activators do. They also provide for mobilizing the support and acceptance that make it possible for the activators to do anything. *More specifically, they involve the development and maintenance of a network of supporting groups and widespread popular acceptance.* These two elements together comprise the activation base.[15] The nature and strength of these elements are largely determined not after national plans are decided upon but in the basic processes of formulating national plans and building the national planning system.

### The Support Network

"If you want to implement national plans, you have to organize specific support for them." This is one of the working axioms underlying the efforts of those concerned with plan implementation. It applies to all societies—democratic, authoritarian, and totalitarian.

In any society, however, this practical axiom is subject to misinterpretation. Support may be mistakenly thought of in terms of passive supporters alone, of the "governed" whose consent or acquiescence is somehow or other obtained. The identity of the "you" that wants implementation or seeks support may be narrowly regarded as limited to a small circle.

A support network, however, may be more realistically thought of as consisting of three concentric circles:

1. *Key activators.* These are the people and groups comprising the "you" in the axiom, those who take the lead in both building the activation base and in using the influence thus acquired.
2. *Active allies.* These are the key people and groups with the power to carry out, or obstruct, various areal, sectoral, or cross-sectoral plans. Their support is vital for various components of a national plan, although they may indeed be passive or antagonistic to other components.
3. *Passive collaborators.* These are the large numbers of people and groups who "go along." Their acquiescence or neutrality is of tremendous importance, in contrast with the situation which might arise if they should become plan opponents.

The building of a support network is necessarily a selective process. In a totalitarian society, where the key activators will try to mobilize the entire society, there will always be certain individuals and groups who will remain outside (or be pushed outside) the network. In a democratic society the sources of organized opposition will usually be much stronger. In both, there are significant limits on which groups can or should be brought within the inner circle of key activators or the second circle of active allies. In all societies the design of a support network takes into account the differential power of people and groups. Special mention must be made of the following:

1. *National leaders.* The chief of state, his personal advisers, and any informal "kitchen cabinet" are of tremendous importance for the inner circle of key activators. Even apart from anything he does, the support of the chief of state is essential to give legitimacy to the plan and to the activation efforts of others.

2. *Financial management agencies.* The various government agencies playing financial management roles are of strategic importance because of their power over budgets and the money supply. Plan implementation is usually endangered if all these agencies enter the picture only as passive collaborators. On the other hand, the vitality of plan may be endangered if they all enter the circle of key activators.
3. *Major national ministries or departments.* These are usually the most important intermediaries in a national planning system. With tremendous amounts of money and people at their disposal, they can determine the success or failure of major plan components.
4. *Other national organizations.* The most important of these are usually the national organizations representing enterprises in one or more sectors of production and distribution (chambers of commerce, industry groups, farmers groups, cooperative federations, etc.). Labor organizations may also be of great importance, particularly when they are the only mass organizations concerned with cross-sectoral problems of employment, income, and living standards.
5. *Political parties.* Whenever a support network includes strategic people and groups from among the four preceding categories, some degree of party support is assured. More may be needed. Under one-party dominance it is dangerous not to enjoy the support of key leaders in the party organization. Under competitive party conditions multiparty support is desirable. One of the greatest tests of party leadership is its ability to win bipartisan or nonpartisan support for major parts of a national plan. In governmental systems in which significant power is exercised by legislatures, legislative party leaders may occupy a crucial role in the support network.

To a certain extent, the design of a support network fits into the hierarchical structure of government and—if there be such—of society as a whole. The support of subordinates, such as ministries and departments, cannot be taken for granted. It must be won and maintained through specific actions taken by their superordinate national leaders.

But major parts of any support network are made up of coalitions, blocs, or alliances that cut across, and often tend to confuse, the major lines of hierarchical relations.   Some of these coalitions may be formalized through coordinating committees and councils and serviced through joint staffs.   Many consist of informal, collaborative relations.   In more authoritarian regimes the dominant coalition tends to be a discrete alliance—say, among party activists, key bureaucrats and managers, military leaders, and the secret police.   In more democratic regimes the pattern is usually one of overlapping coalitions.   In idealized form these two pat-

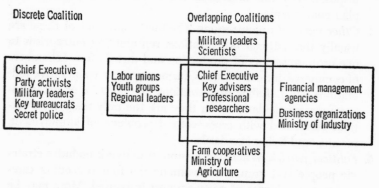

Figure 5. Patterns of coalition.

terns are illustrated in Figure 5.   When examined more closely, however, even the discrete coalition may turn out to be composed of a set of smaller, overlapping coalitions.   The central cores of two or more overlapping coalitions are rarely identical; some advisers and professionals will belong only to one or another.   With both types, the coalition structure tends to change over time.   In both cases, there is a tendency to exclude groups that may threaten the power position of the key activators and a countervailing tendency to coopt into positions of power those groups whose energy and resourcefulness represent a greater threat if they remain outside.   In both, the necessities of the activation base may bring together people and groups that may seem to be and indeed behave like strange bedfellows.

Finally, the organization of a support network cannot always be limited to those groups already in existence. New organizations must often be established: new planning research agencies, new ministries, new public or private enterprises, new forms of agricultural organization, new associations of producers or workers. Organizations must be expanded or replaced. Accordingly, whether or not this is deliberately done on ideological grounds, the very process of building the activation base involves some degree of change, if not reconstruction, in a society's social structure.

## Unorganized Opinions and Attitudes

Any strong activation base also includes, in addition to a network of supporting groups, a broader and less structured form of support, or acceptance, from large numbers of people in their individual capacity. This is what is often referred to as a "favorable climate of public opinion."

> Yet the term "public opinion" is misleading and dangerous if used to refer to some mythical organic entity that comprises the entire society, or to some artificial average that purports to represent all opinions in the society. . . . Different opinions are inevitably held by different people. Under most circumstances, except for a few broadly stated issues during a period of national crisis, there will always be less than complete consensus in opinion. There will usually be at least two different opinions on a single question—and often many more. There may be any one of a varying number of patterns of dispersion among these various opinions. Hence, any meaningful discussion of public opinion must start with a recognition of diversity. It is in this sense that people often talk about the opinions not of the public but of specific "publics." [16]

The opinions of key elite groups in strategic positions of power have already been dealt with in the discussion of the support network. We are now left with the opinions and attitudes of unorganized publics. These publics are the various crisscrossing groups (in the sense of logical categories rather than specific organizations) into which the population may be divided on the basis of age, sex, race, religion, caste, class, kinship, area, sector, occupation, education, wealth, and income.

One reason for the importance of these publics is that their opinions and attitudes have decisive effect on the position of support or opposition taken by specific organizations. Unorganized opinion may always be reflected in the activities of organized groups. It may lead to the organization of new groups or coalitions. It may indeed include the views of the rank-and-file of large organizations and thereby affect the power of the leaders of such organizations to help or impede plan implementation.

Moreover, even in a highly organized society individuals have important roles. Compliance with laws and regulations, enthusiasm or indifference on the job, voting behavior in free elections —all these are strongly affected by the attitudes of individuals.

As with the support of organized groups, favorable opinions are usually sought on a selective basis. Although a great charismatic leader may win the support of an overwhelming majority for himself as a person, this support is never automatically transferable to the major components of a national plan. Although most groups may support some aspects of a plan, on other aspects the support of some groups can be won only at the cost of sacrificing support elsewhere. Thus, in a looser and cruder form the strategy of building general support through the favorable opinions of unorganized groups mirrors the coalition strategy of organizing the network of supporting organizations.

## USING INFLUENCE: THE ACTIVATION MIX

If command is not the only way to get plans carried out, what else can get things done?

This question may best be answered by regarding command as merely one form of pressure. In addition, an activator may use various forms of persuasion. Also, instead of directly applying persuasion or pressure, an activator may try to get people and groups to activate themselves. The activation mix is the particular combination of these various forms of influence that activators may use in any particular situation. Its composition depends not only on the skill of the activators but also on the activation base, on the resources and energies on which they must rely.    In turn, influence must be used to mobilize and maintain sources of influence; the activation base can be built only through the use of an effective activation mix.

## Persuading

When *A* tries to persuade *B* to do *X* (a course of action), he wants *B* to regard *X* as a way of satisfying or gratifying *B*'s interests (or of avoiding some form of dissatisfaction).    If the satisfaction is contingent on something that *A* or someone else may subsequently do (which we may call *Y*), then this is pressure.    If it is inherent in the relation between *B* and *A*, this is true persuasion.

The following forms of persuasion—informing, expecting, providing an example, proposing, and propagandizing—may be roughly ranked in an ascending order of vigor on the part of *A*.    The effectiveness of each depends not only on its combination with other elements in the activation mix but also upon *A*'s and *B*'s perceptions of *B*'s interests.

*Informing.*    One of the most effective methods of persuasion is the presentation of data relevant to a desired course of action.    Sometimes advisers and others, instead of making specific proposals, will merely present data indicating the desirability of a definite course of action.    Often the process of informing may be quite detailed.    In legal briefs, position papers, budget justifications, and plan proposals, data are presented (1) to explain the details of a proposed course of action, (2) to indicate how and why it will satisfy the interests of the "activatees," and (3) to show how and why alternatives are unfeasible or undesirable.    Where no counterdocuments are presented, these documents may be extremely persuasive.    When many such presentations are made, no point of view will be taken seriously unless backed up by some sort of brief.    Even if a brief is too long to be read or too complicated to be understood, its very size and the presumed competence of its compilers may serve to inspire confidence in the proposal.

In a still more pure form the provision of information may be dissociated from any specific proposals. In this sense the annual Economic Reports of the President, by providing basic information on economic trends and possibilities, undoubtedly have a long-run persuasive effect on the key centers of power in America. Similar forms of persuasion have been adopted in the Netherlands and other countries. The "indicative planning" of the French, by involving more business leaders in the process of information interpretation, goes still further. Even in the Soviet Union there is no doubt that the information in basic plan documents *qua information* establishes outer boundaries within which more vigorous forms of activation are used.

*Expecting.* People may also be activated simply by expecting that they will behave in a certain manner. This is particularly effective when the expectation is shared and expressed not only by the activator but also by many others. The tremendous power of mere expectation is illustrated by the extent to which people cling to behavior patterns expressed in traditions and in informal roles and codes. This power stems from the dissatisfaction created by disapproval and the gratification resulting from approval. It is greatest when the expectation is shared by the activatees themselves. It is weakest when there are conflicting expectations and other strong incentives bearing upon them.

Even when unspoken, expectations tend to communicate themselves in mysterious ways. Thus, national planners may promulgate a new program to reduce tax evasion. But if they themselves expect the program to fail, their expectations may turn out to be a "self-confirming prophecy."

*Providing an example.* Another powerful, although often overlooked, form of activation is providing an example to be followed or imitated. An administrator who "loafs" has a hard time getting others to work hard. The example that he sets may be more influential than anything else he does.

The power of example rests in the satisfactions that people obtain from identifying themselves with a person or group whom they admire or envy. This has often been referred to by political scientists as the *bandwagon effect*, by economists as the *demon-*

*stration effect.* Moreover, providing an example has the additional advantage of communicating far more clearly than may be possible in words the exact nature of the action to be taken.

In national planning the power of example is particularly relevant to such matters as austerity, diligence, and hard work. High government officials who lead a life of conspicuous luxury may thereby undermine plans that call for widespread sacrifices by all the people. Example is also important in improving administrative performance throughout the planning and implementation system. If central planners want more administrators to promote initiative and creativity in the lower ranks of their organizations, they, in their own behavior, set some concrete examples of how this may or may not be done. Conversely, a technical-assistance agency which tries to improve public administration in a developing nation may undo all its good work by providing, in its own operations, a conspicuous example of red-tape rigidity or corruption.[17]

*Proposing.* One of the major functions of advisers is to propose courses of action. This may be done by a direct recommendation or by indirectly discussing alternatives. The incentive lies in the implicit assumption, which may or may not be clearly stated, that acceptance of the advice is in the interests of the advisee. Advice is most readily accepted when it shows people how to do what they want to do or to organize their conflicting wants. The process of acceptance is usually quicker if the advisee is led to believe that the suggested course of action is really his own idea.

Sometimes, as with command, proposals will be listened to only when coming from someone authorized to offer them. The authoritative nature of a proposal also has a major bearing on the likelihood of its acceptance. When a person is confident that professional advisers are directly concerned with his interests and that there is no conflict among them, the presumption is that the rejection of an authoritative recommendation will lead to some form of dissatisfaction. Under these circumstances, which are fulfilled in many practitioner-client relations, an advisory proposal may have tremendous power.

The making of proposals is a vital part of planning and plan implementation. Some proposals are backed up by commands or other forms of pressure. Some are backed up by other forms of persuasion. Many stand on their own feet, with little supplementation. Often, the great merit of a concrete proposal by national planners is that it may inspire others, including key implementers, to come up with counterproposals that are more feasible, if not even inherently more desirable.

*Propagandizing.* In a colloquial sense the word *propaganda* is often used to refer to someone else's efforts at persuasion, while one's own are described as informational or educational activities. Even in a more technical sense the line between propagandizing and informing is hard to draw. Data must always to some extent be structured. They clearly become propaganda only when the facts are strongly "slanted" or a serious effort is made to appeal to emotions and feelings. Any symbols, slogans, or acts identifying the desired course of action with the interests and aspirations of the activatees may be used to do this.

Some administrators become effective leaders within their organizations by themselves becoming the personal symbols of their followers' interests. Those who have learned this secret of modern-day charisms do not merely persuade people; they convince people by establishing an emotional link with their deeper interests. Similarly, many organizations try to become symbols of interests widely shared by large publics. This is the object of institutional advertising.

It is not always easy to tell whether propaganda is designed more for a broad or for a narrow audience. Much public relations and publicity ostensibly for external consumption has its greatest utility in keeping the members of an organization persuaded. Election propaganda, it has long been observed, is often listened to mainly by a party's supporters. The public relations activity of the United States Forest Service "is intended to affect the internal forces acting on the Rangers while it strengthens 'inside' them, by heightening their identification with the organization, their tendencies toward conforming with agency decisions." [18] Some planning propaganda probably has its greatest effect upon the self-image and self-confidence of the central planners and their key allies. The most effective propaganda is that which is directly geared to efforts at building the network of organized support and popular acceptance by unorganized publics.

### Pressuring

As already suggested, the difference between persuasion and pressure is that, with the latter, $A$ makes $X$ more desirable (or less undesirable) by promising or threatening $Y$ (subsequent action by the activator in the form of a reward or punishment). The difference between the two forms of $Y$ is not always sharp. The unused stick may be seen as a reward, the withdrawn carrot as punishment.

The following forms of pressure—bargaining, manipulating, command, and physical force—may be roughly ranked in an ascending order of "toughness" by an activator. As with the forms of persuasion, the effectiveness of each depends on its position in the total activation mix and upon $A$'s and $B$'s perceptions of $B$'s interests.

The degree of certainty is also important. Severe sanctions (or great rewards) mean little when there is no likelihood of applying (or receiving) them. On the other hand, if the reward-punishment system is automatic and no follow-up is needed, all the activator needs to do is demonstrate the inevitable results of a given course of action. Pressure has thus been reduced to persuasion.

*Bargaining.* In bargaining the process of using pressure works in both directions. Both the activators and the activatees wield incentives. Each modifies his promises or threats in the light of the actions of the other. Moreover, the desired actions themselves, as well as the rewards and punishments, are also subject to negotiation.

The power of bargaining as a form of activation lies in this flexibility. Both the quid and the quo may be adapted to the actual needs and strategies of the people and groups involved, as these needs are discovered and modified in the light of shifting relationships. The activators escape many of the resentments and frictions that may easily result from one-way activation. Bargaining on specific points becomes the basis of such cooperative relations as reciprocity, logrolling, or the exchange of favors. It also enters into the formation of longer-term alliances and coalitions. Bargaining between buyers and sellers constitutes some form of economic market.

Bargaining is an inherent part of the process of making and implementing national plans. Under more dictatorial planning there are fewer bargainers. Under more democratic planning more people and groups are involved in the endless process of negotiation, maneuver, and reciprocal adjustment, much of this taking place in various markets. At times, however, ultrarational planning technicians may deny any place for bargaining in their own services with respect to plan formulation. By this act of self-denial they may thereby decrease the rationality of the bargaining process iself.

*Manipulating.* In manipulation the activators use pressure to get action without directly stating what they want done. They create situations and influences that impel the activated to move in the desired direction. The successful coquette may use negative signals in order to induce positive action by the ardent male. A central bank may manipulate the money supply and the interest rate in order to obtain, without direct commands, certain desired changes in economic activity or price levels. "Because command is a more ostensible, direct, person-to-person relationship, perhaps it can offend status, self-respect, and dignity of individuals more than does manipulating of operating penalities," Dahl and Lindblom observe. "Manipulation of field seems to be more suitable for creating 'permissive situations,' i.e., situations in which a particular response is attained although the individual can choose among a variety of rewards and penalties." [19]

The manipulation of markets has always been a treasured device of money making by powerful market operators. It is now coming to be regarded as an invaluable device for plan implementation, even when its use may mean the extension of old market situations or the promotion of new ones.[20]

*Commanding.* A command (order, regulation, instruction, or direction) is a direct presentation of the desired course of action backed up by at least an implied threat of punishment if the action is not taken. Because other forms of activation are so widely used, command is often a residual method, used only when nothing else will do. When used, moreover, it is often closely associated with persuasion and with other forms of pressure.

Under some circumstances, command is the best method of activation. No other method can be as useful in times of emergency or in any situation when rapid action and coordination are needed. Some people will respond only to command. On some programs, above all, nothing else is conceivable. Strip command from a tax plan and it becomes a plan for seeking voluntary contributions.

There are many preconditions for the effectiveness of commands. As military officers learn in their training schools, a command must clearly specify the action to be taken. It must be feasible; the impossible can be expected of no one. If there is time, a command may also be explained and justified; one's action in carrying out a command is not hampered by being persuaded of its desirability. It must come from a legitimate source; an Army officer will not usually obey an intelligible, feasible, and well-justified command given him by a newspaper reporter. It must be acceptable. In the language of Barnard and Simon, it must be within the receiver's "zone of indifference" or "area of acceptance." The command giver must be prepared to check on the action taken and to take corrective action wherever needed. In national planning, let it be added, these requirements may become extremely onerous, particularly because of the great complexity often involved in the course of desired action, its explanation and justification, evaluation systems, and the handling of specific sanctions.

Above all, there is a difficult relation between the frequency of commands and their effectiveness. If national planners and activators go too far in issuing vast numbers of regulations and orders, their quantity may quickly outrun the available supply of meaningful rewards and punishments. Resentment and opposition may be promoted. Widespread evasion and deception may result. On the other hand, the art of issuing firm regulations and orders cannot be developed without sustained use. The value of command as a "last resort" can never be exploited if the "gun behind the door" is allowed to grow rusty.

*Using physical force.* The use of physical force, or coercion, is one of the oldest means of influencing the actions of others. It is based on two unpleasant but unavoidable facts. The first is that the application of force usually creates intense dissatisfactions which, when felt or feared, may serve as incentive or deterrent. The second is that when applied in certain forms, such as confinement, crippling, murder, or destruction, it may reduce or eliminate the recipient's capacity to act at all.

With the advent of the industrial and administrative revolutions and the accompanying decline in slavery and forced labor, physical force has declined as a conspicuous form of activation. Even the most authoritarian administrators of the modern world no longer dream of relying on the whips of the taskmaster. More effective modes of pressure are always available and are generally used. Even when used as a last resort, physical force is accurately seen as something that at best has negative value only and at worst may unleash counterforces that may damage if not destroy its users.

Although the area in which physical force is used has narrowed considerably, government's traditional monopoly on the legitimate use of organized violence has been maintained. Police forces and courts are indispensable instruments of government, and also of national plan implementation. In fact, together with military forces, they are often essential to provide an environment of law, order, and national security, an environment which, whether in peace, war, or in-between stages, is essential for the implementation of national plans.

### Promoting Self-activation

One of the unique characteristics of people and human organizations, as distinguished from machines, is that they are more self-activating. Although dependent upon their environment for necessary inputs, they can take steps by themselves to obtain these inputs. They do not have to rely, as do machines, upon messages from makers and operators. Both the individual cells which form the organism and the organism as a whole are independent systems of energy, systems which will recharge themselves and even grow in power until the inevitable day of disintegration. There is thus a realm of self-activation beyond direct persuasion or pressure, seduction, or coercion.

To penetrate this realm, national planners may use persuasion and pressure to get people and groups to activate themselves by self-administered rewards and punishments.

*Encouraging participation in decision making.* The most immediate way to promote self-activation is to involve people in the process of themselves determining the desired course of action. To the extent that a decision or plan is regarded as one's own, activation boils down to getting oneself to do what one wants to do. Although this may not be easy, particularly when wants are conflicting and capacities limited, the problem of interpersonal influence is largely bypassed. Also, the problem of accurately communicating the nature of the action to be taken is tremendously eased.

Many studies have demonstrated that in the operation of single, large-scale organizations various forms of broad participation in decision making and planning have reduced turnover, eased adjustment to changes in production methods, raised output, and provided better environment for professional employees.[21] Selznick has demonstrated the value of external participation in building support for a controversial program.[22] Salter has shown its value in coordinating international operations.[23]

The framework for participation in national planning decisions is provided by the social structure itself, particularly by the distribution of power among various groups. The more decentralized the structure and the larger the role of economic markets, the greater the participation of each part in planning its own affairs. Within such a structure the use of persuasion, bargaining, and manipulation, as distinct from enforced command, may enlarge the possibility of such participation. This may be referred to as *dispersed responsibility*. In contrast, there is also *shared responsibility*, which usually involves some form of adjustment in the formal or informal structure. Within single organizations, such adjustment may be made by setting up management committees, management teams, or labor-management councils. In government it may take the form of formal or informal representation of nongovernment interests within government, both in the official personnel of government and in representative committees of various types.

Two interesting examples of the promotion of large-scale participation in national planning are provided by the short-lived National Recovery Administration (NRA) experiment during the early New Deal of Franklin Roosevelt and the more recent use of sectoral and cross-sectoral commissions in French national planning. Under the NRA each major industry in the United States was asked to organize a "code authority" which would develop its own code to maintain prices and prevent "unfair competition." Within very general policies, each authority, composed almost entirely of private business interests, was left on its own. By the time the whole structure was ready to collapse of its own weight, the Supreme Court destroyed its foundations by a decision that it was based upon an unconstitutional devolution of government power to private interests.

In French national planning, in contrast, the sectoral and cross-sectoral commissions have been given no formal power whatsoever, nor are they strictly advisory groups to advise the government. Indeed, each group contains a substantial number of government as well as private representatives. Their function is, rather, to work together in formulating joint goals and policies. The national plan is to an important extent the product of such joint effort. It is therefore not the *government's* plan so much as it is *du plan*. It belongs to all the participants. It is expected, therefore, that those who helped make the plan will do their best to carry it out. In fact, the clearest principle in modern French national planning is the principle of *"the participation in policy-making of those who will have to bear the brunt of the implementation of measures decided upon."* [24]

The use of such methods to promote self-activation is fraught with technical difficulties. Wide decentralization requires greater central efforts to keep decentralized operations in line with general policy. The more informal representative and consultative relations require large amounts of time and energy and still larger expenditures of patience and skill. The more formal ones seem to require long and frequent meetings, carefully prepared agendas, and strong supporting services. Both involve continuous experimentation.

The greatest difficulty, however, is the danger of either bluff or breakdown. On the one hand, "participative" techniques are often used to provide ritualistic rather than genuine participation. Planners may merely want to give private groups the *sense* of participation in order to manipulate them into accepting predetermined decisions and plans as their own. Similarly, many representatives on consultative committees, both intraorganizational and interorganizational, are mainly interested in the prestige accruing to themselves or their constituents through symbolic rather than actual participation. On the other hand, too much participation may lead to organizational breakdown. As Selznick points out in his TVA study, leadership needs participation in order to get cooperation, but "if participation is allowed to go too far, the continuity of leadership and policy may be threatened." [25] This danger is particularly great in the case of participation by external groups eager to penetrate government in order to exploit it for their own narrow purposes. This, in part, is what happened under the NRA. This will also happen whenever market mechanisms are relied upon for resource allocation in periods of acute shortages.

The possibility of avoiding these two extremes depends upon the capacities of both the national planners and those whose participation they may want to promote. The planner who favors wide participation must be able to cope with the fact that the plans and actions that emerge can never be precisely known in advance. He must be able to take the risk that the self-activators may decide to go in directions he had not previously contemplated. He must be willing to share power in order to help build a larger system of power. On the other hand, the other participants must be mature and self-confident enough to escape the tendency to rely overmuch upon central government (as in many developing nations) or to regard central government with ingrained suspicion and distrust (as is also the case in the United States and many developed nations). Above all, there must be enough organizations outside central government to make such participation conceivable. In some countries steps to build such organizations must be taken *pari passu* with efforts to promote their participation in national planning.

*Educating.* Education may promote self-activation by helping people acquire more knowledge, abilities, and interests. To the extent that this may be done, individuals and organizations will be more capable of rational participation in planning and implementation. They will acquire more confidence in the handling of their own tasks and in cooperating with others on shared tasks.

In a certain sense every national planning effort is a large-scale exercise in nationwide education. Planning documents and planning discussions raise the level of knowledge about important phenomena. Planning and implementation activities develop new and better abilities. The vision of future goals may awaken new and deeper interests. Moreover, both in the developed and the developing nations, increasing attention is being given under national plans to the expansion of formal education and training at all levels.

Nevertheless, two different approaches, sometimes combined, may be discerned. The first sees education as an instrument of conformity. This is much like the educational efforts in some large-scale organizations that aim to "control what goes on inside each individual organization member, to get them to do of their own volition what the managers want them to do, and to equip them with the resources of skill and knowledge for these duties." [26] Here education becomes a combination of general propaganda and indoctrination in the proper response to prescribed incentives. Self-activation is all right just so long as it takes place within carefully prescribed limits.

The second approach aims at the promotion of greater autonomy. Both individuals and organizations may be encouraged to learn how to deal with new and more challenging situations.

They may be helped to broaden their perspectives and seek creative solutions of their own, even if this means challenging approved plans.

The second approach can rarely become significant if the national planners see themselves as the repositories of high wisdom and regard education as something needed only by others. One of the most important things that good national planners learn from experience is the shocking extent of their own ignorance. One of the greatest contributions they can make to the nation-wide process of learning through planning is to set a clear example of people who are diligently trying to educate themselves through research, theory, and the fearless examination of their own failures and successes. A dramatic example of such an attitude was provided by President Nyerere of Tanganyika in a public speech to the effect that "we all must learn." All Tanganyikans, he maintained, must "accept that they knew nothing" and continue their search for knowledge. Many conferences, he held, were needed to show the people, including parliamentary secretaries, that "they knew nothing." The newspaper reports indicate that Nyerere drew cheers when he told the gathering "that he himself was learning to be President. He had been a teacher earlier, and he was now learning his new job." [27]

## COPING WITH CONFLICTS

National planners and plan activators, it has already been emphasized, are inevitably involved in handling conflicts among people, groups, organizations, and underlying interests. In building the activation base, they prepare for conflict. In using any series of activation mixes, they aim at certain conflict outcomes.[28] The implementation of national plans, therefore, may also be seen from the viewpoint of the types of outcomes that are sought and attained.

### Victory-Defeat

Victory by one party to a conflict (or defeat to others) is the neatest of all outcomes. The victor receives a clear-cut gain. The defeated suffers an unambiguous loss.

It is also a highly circumscribed form of outcome. Even in games and debates, where there are agreed-upon rules of keeping the score, a victory in one round may be quickly followed by defeat in the next, and vice versa. In more complex forms of conflict, the possibility of such change is still greater. Clear defeat may be transformed into a psychological victory by propagandistic success in calling it something else, as when President Nasser of Egypt embellished his political victory over the forces that had seized the Suez Canal by convincing Egyptian supporters that it was military superiority which forced the withdrawal of the invaders from the canal region. The very act of surrender, as Coser pointed out, may involve an "assertion of power." [29] It may be used to establish conditions for subsequent gains. The anguish of defeat may, in fact, be a contribution to future victories by providing the unseasoned with an invaluable baptism by fire and by teaching lessons that could otherwise never be learned. Above all, victory or defeat on one issue may be inextricably associated with defeat or victory on other issues. Under such circumstances, either one is merely one aspect of a compromise outcome. Accordingly, national planners can rarely afford the luxury of seriously seeking a complete victory in all their battles. To do so would be to risk far too many defeats.

### Compromise

A compromise occurs when each party to a conflict wins something and loses something. It may take place with respect to a single issue, or it may emerge as the aggregate of a set of specific victories and defeats on various issues. It is thus the most widespread outcome of conflict resolution. The shaping of compromises is thus an inherent part of both formulating and carrying out national plans.

The necessity of compromise is something that can never be learned painlessly. It is particularly difficult for those who have discovered the ease with which a purely logical problem can be solved through the processes of deduction but have not learned the difference between such a problem and a genuine social conflict. For these, who may play extremely important roles in national planning, compromise is often seen as an unmitigated evil. If it is to be tolerated, the condition is often laid down that at least there be no compromise on matters of principle. But principles are usually the first things to be yielded, for the simple reason that they are so rarely a clear-cut expression of fundamental high-priority interests. Because they are sometimes willing to sacrifice principles which are not directly related to basic interests but are rather propagandistic devices for the extension of support, the most effective national leaders often appear to be totally unprincipled men. In a world of sharp divisions and dispersed power, they may even have to yield on basic interests. It may be added that since interests and principles are always multiple and diverse, the safeguarding or serving of some invariably requires a yielding or even sacrifice of others.

At the same time, to laud compromise as a value in itself may lead to an eating away of moral value and the growth of a cynical "anything goes" attitude that may undermine the integrity of national planning. It may also lead to an oversized role for those planners and activators who are skillful in serving as brokers and go-betweens. These are people who usually care more about making a deal or keeping peace for its own sake than about making progress toward achieving substantive goals.

### Integration

As Mary Follett pointed out long ago, integration is a conflict outcome in which the interests of all sides have found a place without any side's sacrificing anything. The process of working toward an integration involves getting behind the symbols that may hide the state of true affairs and bringing conflicts out into the open so that the underlying interests can be analyzed and reexamined.[30] This is very close to the "working through" process developed by psychoanalysts. Its application to organizational conflict is well illustrated in the way in which consultants of the Tavistock Institute of Human Relations helped bring about an integration, thus resolving certain managerial conflicts in the Glazier plant.[31] Its application to national planning is envisaged by Follett's discussion of achieving integration through a continuous process of interpenetration and "reciprocal relating" at many levels.[32] Such a procedure is approximated in many ways by the national planning system in France. Thus, the French plan, to an important extent, represents an integration of major interests in the French society.

Enthusiasm for integration should not lead one to believe that it is possible to resolve all or most conflicts in this manner. Although such an outcome is generally more desirable and although integration probably plays a much greater role than many cynics would think, there are undoubtedly many occasions when nothing is possible except some sequence or combination of avoidance, deadlock, victory-defeat, or compromise. An integration of any complex conflict, moreover, is a multisided operation that usually must include within it some elements of mere compromise.

One of the reasons for the difficulty of attaining integration as an outcome of conflict is that it always involves a broadening of the framework. It requires the conflicting parties to become involved in issues beyond the current agenda of attention. It takes into account the many and diverse interests of the combatants, apart from those which are the basis of contention. It is based upon an examination of new and hitherto unexamined courses of action. This requires on the part of at least some of the planners and activators a broad perspective toward life and a varied acquaintance with the total environment. To get beyond the narrow confines of mere compromise, one must be able to analyze the wide range of people's interests and have a sense of what is and is not feasible in a complex environment. These are not common capacities.

### Deadlock

Deadlock is such a negative state that it may be difficult to regard it as an outcome. As with the stalemate conclusion of a chess game, no side can win. But unlike chess, the broader game of social conflict can often continue in a state of deadlock for long periods of time. "The possibility of deadlock—or to use a closely related term, stasis—is inherent in the democratic process of peaceful group conflict. When few victories are ever complete, when power is widely dispersed among many 'veto groups,' when every solution is a compromise that is objectionable to many, and when every settlement itself creates new problems, you have the makings of a stalemate." [33]

The negative aspect of deadlock is probably one of the reasons why peace is not always as attractive as the hatred of war might suggest it should be. A "no win" peace is never as appealing as a victory. It becomes more desirable only when the dangers of defeat make "no loss" seem more comfortable. "Peace through stalemate, based on a coincident recognition by each side of the opponent's strength, is at least preferable to peace through common exhaustion." [34]

From the long-term perspective of protracted conflict, however, deadlock may have more positive aspects. It may keep an opponent's energies concentrated upon a certain front, while one tries to advance on other fronts. It may provide a breathing space, with or without withdrawal, during which one mobilizes forces for renewed efforts or, as with many plans for land reform in developing nations, for substantial modification or even withdrawal of ambitious plans.

### Avoidance

Interest divergence among human beings and groups is so great that it is highly doubtful whether social intercourse would be even tolerable without many forms of avoidance. In fact, withdrawal from conflict seems to be one of man's most natural and traditional ways of coping with conflicting interests. Internal conflicts may be unconsciously repressed. Family conflicts may be avoided by having children sleep in separate rooms, taboos on the discussion of delicate subjects, or, as in some societies, rules against husbands talking with mothers-in-law. Within organizations interpersonal conflicts are avoided by people's "keeping out of each other's hair," by developing codes of non-interference in another's "territory," by suppressing deeply felt differences of opinion. and by postponing or evading decisions. In conflicts among nations avoidance is achieved through disengagement, a *cordon sanitaire,* isolationism, or the division of disputed territory into spheres of exclusive influence. At the national level, avoidance takes the form of regarding certain desirable courses of action as taboo, or at least as not to be incorporated in planning objectives for the present.

If avoidance is carried to an ultimate extreme, it may indeed mean the end of conflict, as when a central government avoids dealing with a runaway inflationary crisis. Under such circumstances the price of peace may mean the end of both planning and plan implementation. Yet always, within bounds, many issues must be dodged, at least temporarily. The only alternatives may be defeat, deadlock, or an unsatisfactory compromise.

## DEVELOPING CAMPAIGN STRATEGIES

For the purposes of analysis it has been necessary in the preceding sections to discuss in an artificially separated manner the interrelated processes of mobilizing sources of influence, using influence, and resolving conflicts. In actual practice these processes are combined in a series of interlocking events that move toward or away from various objectives in national plans. The more effective activators see these events not as single, sporadic acts but as a series of campaigns (or designed operations). To conduct these campaigns in the face of obstacles, inertia, and uncertainty, they develop various campaign strategies. In the eyes of a few national leaders these separate strategies may be seen as part of some overall grand strategy for the implementation of national planning as a whole. For the major activators, however, the important things are specific campaigns to carry out certain parts of a national plan. Grand strategy has meaning in the sense of interrelating major campaigns on such matters as agricultural production, industrial expansion, export promotion, price restraint, tax revision, and improved education.

### Exploiting Crisis

One of the most delicate aspects of campaign strategy is the use of crisis situations. A period of widespread complacency does not lend itself easily to the accomplishment of great social changes. At the time of sharply perceived crisis, however, many things are feasible that might otherwise be impossible. Leighton explains the difference as follows: [35]

> Communities under stress, with their labile and intense emotions and shifting systems of belief, are ripe for change. While this is a situation fraught with danger because of trends which may make the stress become worse before it gets better, there is also an opportunity for administrative action that is not likely to be found in more secure times. Skillful administration may be able to seize the moment not only to guide spontaneous shifts in constructive directions but even to achieve extensive changes that would otherwise be impossible or extremely difficult. . . .
>
> At periods of great emotional stir the individual human being can undergo far-reaching and permanent changes in his personality. It is as if the bony structure of his systems of belief and of his habitual patterns of behavior becomes soft, is pushed into new shapes and hardens there when the period of tension is over.

The opportunity for initiating extraordinary action is created by this softening. In exploiting this opportunity administrators can, by seizing the initiative, both unify their followers inside and outside the organization and divide and surprise their opponents. As Hirschman has pointed out in his discussion of social reform in Latin America, "crisis may make it possible to take action against powerful groups which are normally well entrenched and invulnerable, [and] . . . may stimulate action and hence learning on a problem on which insight has been low and which for that very reason has not been tackled as long as it was in a quiescent state." [36] Above all, in time of crisis administrators themselves must act. The crisis calls a halt to the many prior acts of postponement and avoidance. In discussing United States participation in international relations, Cleveland points out that "the President, the Secretaries of State and Defense, the Director of Central Intelligence and several dozen other men do spend a very large part of their time working on the crises of the moment." He adds that "it is often at moments of crisis that the most basic long-range decisions about foreign policy are made." [37]

The same observation is relevant to the top officials of government in their handling of domestic plans.

To exploit crisis, national planners are usually continuously alert for sources of stress. To be forewarned is to be forearmed; the penalties are great for not recognizing a crisis until too late. Long-range planning, particularly contingency planning, provides one way of getting prepared to deal with crises. Yet planners often fail to anticipate the profile of the actual crises that emerge. Contingency plans "must normally deal with many contingencies which do not, as things work out, come to pass." [38] The utility of the plans, rather, is that their preparation may help develop a more "ready" organization or at least a set of organizations better geared to facing uncertainties.

The only sure way to anticipate a crisis is to bring it into being. Thus *crisis creation* has become a widespread instrument in the implementation of plans. In a narrow sense the planners create a sense of crisis within the planning system whenever they initiate a difficult and extremely risky operation; the sense of crisis emerges from the fear of failure. In the Soviet Union the system of setting high-output norms for sectors and enterprises is an institutionalized method of creating and maintaining a sense of crisis in all major subsystems of the society. This is what has been referred to by Wiles as "planner's excess demand" or "planner's tension." [39] In a broader sense, a sense of crisis has been maintained throughout the nation by sustained international tensions and by the attitudes toward the external world developed by national leaders. The theory of capitalist encirclement, the post-World War II drive for the extension of communism in Eastern Europe and other parts of the world, the ideology of the cold war, and, more recently, the theory of competitive coexistence—all these in different ways have contributed to the sense of crisis. Similarly, in many countries of the industrialized West, plan activators have often been obliged to describe their plans as weapons in the cold war or competitive coexistence. In a still broader sense the national leaders in industrially underdeveloped countries have often found no way to combat the apathy and inertia of tradition-ridden masses other than the active awakening of discontent with low living standards. The elite who spread the "revolution of rising expectations," by stirring up aspirations for the immediately unattainable, deliberately create personal crisis in the lives of the high aspirers.

## Timing

Time is the medium in which operations are led. "What time is it?" is the ever-present question in the minds of the plan activators.

A major question is when to start—or expand—a campaign. If one waits until plans are perfected and all the needed support is obtained, valuable time may be lost. The best way to improve a plan may be to test it in action. The best way to get support may be to demonstrate that something is really under way. On the other hand, it is sometimes better to wait until a situation "boils over" and people are complaining about the lack of leadership. This may provide the most favorable situation for leaders to initiate action.

By bringing together a host of area, sectoral, and cross-sectoral plans, national planning may provide a highly rational picture of the most desirable course of development. The picture is still more rational if feasibility takes its place alongside desirability. When this is done, it usually becomes evident that it is not feasible to initiate all desirable programs at the same time. It is even less feasible to time operations in such a way as to have each one support and supplement the other. When opportunities arise to move ahead rapidly in one campaign, it is often wise strategy to act even though this may result in mining more coal than the railroads can move or bringing more students into school than the present teaching staff can handle. To wait until similar opportunities develop on all other fronts may slow up everything and may, indeed, postpone the day when there will be enough freight cars or schoolteachers. Thus to a certain extent unbalanced development is made inevitable by what we might call the *principle of differential feasibility*.[40] This principle is particularly applicable to planning in industrially underdeveloped countries. Here it is extremely difficult to do anything important, because of the great shortage of appropriate organizations, manpower, and physical resources, and the great resistance offered by custom and tradition.   Anything important may seem unfeasible, and the choice becomes one between *differential unfeasibilities*.   Under such circumstances the higher rationality of plan implementation often suggests the desirability of a vigorous campaign for action at any points of *least unfeasibility*.

## Maintaining Positive Stance

One of the greatest dangers to the implementation of plans is that a cumulative series of failures or shortfalls will put the planners in a negative and defensive position.   This is what seems to have happened in India during the middle of the third-plan period (1961–1966).

To maintain a positive stance it is important to keep the initiative.   In simpler operations this means maintaining a style and tempo of action that provides continuous results, even if only small ones.   It means setting deadlines and dealing directly with problems that might lead to a breakdown.   But in the panorama of national planning as a whole there are always breakdowns.   If these are allowed to get out of hand, the results may be disastrous.   One way of keeping them in hand is to conduct enough campaigns at points of least unfeasibility, as discussed above.   Another is to direct greater public attention to advances and successes rather than allow them to be neglected.   There is a general tendency under national planning for the escalation of public criticism, as the national planners become the conspicuous targets for dissatisfactions which would otherwise be vented in smaller circles.   As a countermeasure, national planners must "pat themselves on the back" by advertising their successes. This is most effective when it is not done by themselves but when, indeed, the credit is taken by, and given to, people and groups that play a major role in the activation base.   Direct and conspicuous self-congratulation can undermine the support for national planners and their plans.

In situations of conflicting pressures and bitter controversy, a major problem is how to respond to criticism and attack.   To keep the initiative it is often essential to ignore some attacks, refusing to be put on the defense.   Sometimes the best defense is a counterattack on another front, the formation of a new alliance, or capitulation on one front in order to advance on another. When a detailed defense is needed, it is often more appropriate if it comes not from the national planners themselves but from their active supporters or, indeed, from those who have previously been neutral bystanders.

### The Art of the Improbable

Politics has often been called the "art of the possible." This phrase calls attention to the necessity of trimming the sails of desirability to the winds of feasibility. In national planning, where the political arts are required to the highest degree, the phrase is particularly applicable.

Yet in the politics of national planning, as in any other art, there are many degrees of artistry. At one extreme there are the novitiates: learners or bumblers. In the middle there are the steady, reliable craftsmen. At the other extreme there are the great artists. One's place on this scale is not determined by occupation or hierarchic rank. We may find novitiates and bumblers among political leaders as well as among technicians. Although the best opportunities for the exercise of great artistry may arise in or near the offices of chiefs of state, some of the greatest artists are often found among the career-service bureaucrats and the leaders of intermediate or peripheral organizations.

In this form of art the criterion of greatness is results achieved in the face of serious obstacles, both technical and human. The lesser artists are those who manage to break through the feasibility barrier at various points. The bumblers are those who break their heads on the barrier or else (in a burst of epiphenomenal planning) merely usher in what was already inevitable anyway. The great artists are those who transcend the limits of small feasibilities and achieve results that, in the eyes of careful observers, might have been regarded as highly improbable, if not impossible. By developing flexible campaign strategies for analyzing obstacles, building an activation base, using an appropriate activation mix, and resolving human conflicts, they become the masters of the art of the improbable.

## NOTES

[1] The concept of activating has been more formally presented within the framework of general management theory in Bertram M. Gross, *The Managing of Organizations*, The Free Press of Glencoe, New York, 1964, in chaps. 10, "The Management of Organizations," and 29, "Rationality: Administrative Processes"; the materials in the present chapter also draw upon the discussion of conflict resolution in chap. 11, "The Conflict-Cooperation Nexus."

[2] Henri Fayol, *General and Industrial Management*, trans. by Constance Storrs, Sir Isaac Pitman & Sons, Ltd., London, 1955, p. 97.

[3] Luther Gulick, "Note on the Theory of Organization," in Luther Gulick and Lyndall Urwick (eds.), *Papers on the Science of Administration*, Institute of Public Administration, New York, 1937, p. 13.

[4] Robert A. Dahl and Charles E. Lindblom, *Politics, Economics and Welfare*, Harper & Row, Publishers, Incorporated, New York, 1953, p. 103.

[5] Gresham M. Sykes, *The Society of Captives*, Princeton University Press, Princeton, N.J., 1958.

[6] Gross, *op. cit.*, chap. 15, "People in Organizations: Formal Aspects."

[7] Gunnar Myrdal, *The Political Element in the Development of Economic Theory*, Harvard University Press, Cambridge, Mass., 1954.

[8] Barbara Tuchman, *The Guns of August*, The Macmillan Company, New York, 1962, p. 97.

[9] John Fayerweather, *The Executive Overseas*, Syracuse University Press, Syracuse, N.Y., 1959, pp. 77–78.

[10] Robert Henriques, *A Hundred Hours to Suez*, The Viking Press, Inc., New York, 1957, p. 58.

[11] Louis J. Walinsky, *Economic Development in Burma, 1951–1960*, The Twentieth Century Fund, New York, 1952, pp. 465–474.

[12] Joseph S. Berliner, *Factory and Manager in the USSR*, Harvard University Press, Cambridge, Mass., 1957.

[13] Peter Blau, *The Dynamics of Bureaucracy*, The University of Chicago Press, Chicago, 1955; Edmund D. Learned, *Executive Action*, Harvard Graduate School of Business Administration, Boston, 1951, p. 132.

[14] Charles E. Redfield, *Communication in Management*, The University of Chicago Press, Chicago, 1953, pp. 131–132.

[15] The direct observation of influence, or power, is so difficult that one must often appraise it indirectly by studying the activation base. Thus, in Herbert A. Simon, *Models of Man*, John Wiley & Sons., Inc., New York, 1957, p. 69, Simon suggests that "if we can measure the magnitude of the influence base, we can infer from this the magnitude of the influence. E.g., if wealth is the principal influence base in a particular situation—the principal means of exercising influence—then in that situation we may measure influence indirectly by wealth)."

[16] Gross, *op. cit.*, chap. 17, "The Immediate Environment."

[17] The author of this chapter has seen this happen in a number of countries.

[18] Herbert Kaufman, *The Forest Ranger,* The Johns Hopkins Press, Baltimore, 1960, pp. 196–197.

[19] Dahl and Lindblom, *op. cit.*, p. 121.

[20] Market manipulation often involves firm commands (or regulations) at certain points. The manipulation inheres in their indirect effects.

[21] Among the more relevant of such studies are Temple Burling et al., *The Give and Take in Hospitals,* G. P. Putnam's Sons, New York, 1956; Lester Coch and R. P. French, Jr., "Overcoming Resistance to Change," *Human Relations,* vol. 1, pp. 512–532, 1947–1948; F. Mann and C. Williams, "Observations on the Dynamics of Change to Electronic Data-Processing Equipment," *Administrative Science Quarterly,* vol. 5, pp. 217–256, 1960; and Seymour Melman, *Decision-making and Productivity,* Blackwell, Oxford, 1958.

[22] Philip Selznick, *TVA and the Grass Roots,* University of California Press, Berkeley, Calif., 1949.

[23] Sir Arthur Salter, *Allied Shipping Control,* Oxford University Press, London, 1921.

[24] John Hackett and Anne-Marie Hackett, *Economic Planning in France,* Harvard University Press, Cambridge, Mass., 1963, p. 365.

[25] *Op. cit.*, p. 261.

[26] *Op. cit.*

[27] "We All Must Learn," *Tanganyika Standard,* Mar. 17, 1964.

[28] The term *conflict resolution* could also be used. Yet *resolution* (like *solution* and *problem solving*) suggests a finality inconsistent with the on-going process whereby every desired conflict outcome creates new problems. It also suggests a purely intellectual operation that could be handled with a computer.

[29] Louis Coser, "The Termination of Conflict," *Journal of Conflict Resolution,* vol. 5, p. 36, 1961.

[30] Mary Parker Follett, *Dynamic Administration,* Harper & Row, Publishers, Incorporated, New York, 1940, pp. 30–49.

[31] Elliott Jaques, *The Changing Culture of a Factory,* Tavistock Institute of Human Relations, London, 1951.

[32] *Op. cit.;* see particularly "Individualism in a Planned Society," pp. 295–314.

[33] Bertram M. Gross, *The Legislative Struggle: A Study in Social Combat,* McGraw-Hill Book Company, New York, 1953, p. 26.

[34] Liddell Hart, *Strategy,* Frederick A. Praeger, Inc., New York, 1954, p. 370.

[35] Alexander H. Leighton, *The Governance of Men,* Princeton University Press, Princeton, N.J., 1945, pp. 369–370.

[36] Albert O. Hirschman, *Journeys toward Progress: Studies of Economic Policy Making in Latin America,* The Twentieth Century Fund, New York, 1963, p. 261.

[37] Harlan Cleveland, "Crisis Diplomacy," *Foreign Affairs*, p. 3, August, 1962.

[38] *Ibid.*, p. 4.

[39] Peter J. D. Wiles, *The Political Economy of Communism*, Harvard University Press, Cambridge, Mass., 1962, pp. 259–261.

[40] The case for unbalanced development is presented with considerable illustrative detail in Albert O. Hirschman's *The Strategy of Economic Development*, Yale University Press, New Haven, Conn., 1958, and his *Journeys toward Progress*, Twentieth Century Fund, New York, 1963.

# 8

## Developing National Planning Personnel

### INTERPLAN Executive Committee[1]

### THE PLANNERS TOO MUST LEARN

In every country of the modern world, no matter what the level of industrial development or the type of political system, national government has accepted an important degree of responsibility for the guidance of significant economic change. Persistent efforts at national economic planning and implementation are the result.

The differences in the types and degrees of such central government responsibility are tremendous. It is quite clear that there can be no one style or form of national economic planning implementation and no "one best way" automatically applicable to all countries.

Yet in all countries this new responsibility has presented an unprecedented challenge to the capacities of key personnel involved in planning, activating, and evaluating programs of national economic change. *This challenge has created a need everywhere for the development of great capacities on the part of both present personnel and the younger people who will replace them.*

233

In part, this need may be reduced or made more manageable by the development of improved institutions and/or by greater reliance on various market mechanisms. To a considerable extent it may be met also by the learning that should take place as people go about their regular work in formulating and implementing national programs.

In large part, however, special educational programs are required to help people face responsibilities. Such programs may, indeed, help people learn more from practical experience and contribute to their activities in improving institutions and utilizing market mechanisms.

*This chapter deals with the preparation of educational programs, geared to the unique needs and conditions of individual countries and regions, to help develop more effective national planning personnel.*

### The Planners' Blind Spot

It is now widely recognized that successful efforts by central governments to promote rapid economic change, whether through detailed controls or general policies, require a vast array of educational and training activities. This recognition is evidenced by the inclusion in national economic plans of specific programs for general education at all levels, the training of technicians and trainers in various "strategic" areas, and the training and development of administrators of public, private, and mixed organizations.

There is somewhat less recognition, however, of the fact that the *central planners too must learn.* Indeed, there is often a tendency for national policy makers and administrators to regard education and training as being *needed by others, not by themselves.*

In contrast, one of the most important educational currents in the modern world is the growth of educational programs for executives. These new management-development programs are based upon the proposition that the learning processes of top policy makers and administrators are too important to be left to chance. Every year, in more and more countries, management and administrators respond creatively to uncertain and rapidly changing environments. Today, a hallmark of any well managed organization is that its higher officials realize that they too must learn. Indeed, the recognition that the higher officials must also learn is indispensable in creating an atmosphere conducive to learning and adaptation throughout an organization. A myth of infallibility and omniscience on the part of the people at the top may produce stultification and routinization throughout the lower levels.

This exciting trend has, for the most part, barely touched the central agencies involved in the guidance of national economic change. Their use of training for planners has been limited mainly to the indirect encouragement of programs undertaken by universities and independent institutes for the development of economic technicians and public administrators needed by various government ministries. In a few cases, of which Venezuela's CORDIPLAN is a conspicuous example, they have directly promoted training in the economic techniques of central programming. Most such programs, however, have been oriented toward remedying acute shortages in the supply of junior economic technicians. A few, as with France's INSEE, are oriented toward the preparation of senior technicians.

Yet even an abundant supply of economic technicians, senior as well as junior, will not provide the range of skills and knowledge needed to formulate sound plans, implement them, and adjust them to meet new conditions. This point is increasingly recognized at the level of the individual enterprise, where general management training is rapidly expanding. This point should also be recognized by the central agencies of government—the chief executives and their aides, the specialized planning and economic advisory boards and commissions, and the central agencies of financial management. To develop a general atmosphere of creativity and innovation the central-guidance-cluster leaders should set a personal example. They should disclaim any pretensions of infallibility and omniscience. They should demonstrate that they are interested in developing their own abilities, knowledge, and interests.

## Economic Planning Transcends Economics

The need for learning on the part of national planners has often been obscured by/the fallacious idea that economic planning involves economics alone: "Since it's all economics, just get good economists and let them get on with it."

This idea stems from the obvious fact that national economic plans are oriented toward many objectives that must be expressed in terms relating to national income and product, levels of employment and prices, investment and consumption, demand and supply, fiscal and monetary policies, and the balance of payments. It has at times been encouraged by extravagant claims made on behalf of new methods of computerized econometrics (often by people who understand them the least).

But national economic planning is always subordinated to certain objects that transcend economics. Among these may be (1) the building of a new kind of society, (2) human dignity and personal development, (3) social justice, (4) national or personal security, (5) cultural, artistic or religious values, and (6) political stability.

Moreover, the attainment of even purely economic goals always involves instrumental objectives of a noneconomic nature. Among these may be (1) nation building, (2) the development of new institutions, (3) the adaptation or elimination of old institutions, (4) the formation or strengthening of a domestic power base, and (5) participation in various international alliances and coalitions.

All these matters are the very lifeblood of national economic planning. This was recognized in one of the major propositions in the document "What Is National Planning?" [2] as developed during the July, 1964, conference of the International Group for Studies in National Planning: "Many of the conscious objectives and unintended consequences, as well as many of the means required for goal formulation, implementation and evaluation, are usually political, cultural, social or biophysical rather than merely economic."

The implications are clear. Techniques of economic calculations, no matter how valuable, are not enough to provide a sound basis for either formulating or implementing national economic plans. Action is needed to develop the capacities of national planning personnel (economists included) in the complex tasks of decision making and communication with respect to planning, implementing, and evaluating programs of national economic change.

In our judgment such action should include not only "learning through doing" as part of daily tasks but also special educational or development programs that take people away from, and give them a better perspective toward, their daily tasks.

## THE LEARNERS

If we adopt the principle that planners too must learn, how can we identify the planners?

This question *cannot* be answered by simply referring to the personnel of some "central planning organ."

There is a great variety of different functions performed by the organizations designated as central planning organs in various countries. These functions may include one or more of the following: (1) the technical preparation of economic studies and proposals, (2) the coordination of interministerial (or interdepartmental) policies and programs, and (3) the representation of the views of major groups in the country.

In addition, tremendously important functions in the guidance of national economic change are usually played by (1) such powerful financial institutions as finance ministries and central banks, (2) some other ministry or department that may, because of some peculiar circumstance, exercise supraministerial influence of national programs as a whole, (3) the chiefs of state and their immediate assistants and advisers, and (4) the national leaders of political parties or powerful nongovernmental interest groups. It is this network as a whole which is referred to by the phrase *central guidance cluster.*

In addition, we must also include the surrounding ring of the many organizations that maintain the closest contact with a central guidance cluster, provide it with basic information and indispensable support, and, indeed, constitute its major reservoir of skilled personnel. These are the central government's many ministries, departments, and commissions, the country's major nationwide enterprises (both private and public), and the regional or local units of both.

In this context, therefore, the term *planners* is not confined to the personnel of a specialized planning agency or even of the government itself.

Let us now identify more specifically the five interdependent types of planning personnel who may be regarded as the clientele of special development programs. It is fashionable to point to one or another of these groups as the real "powers that be." Yet we know of no objective way of singling out one group as opposed to the others. In their own way the members of each group play roles of tremendous significance in the guidance of national change.

### Specialists

This group includes the large and usually increasing number of experts who handle the increasingly complex tasks of central government and technologically based nationwide organizations. It includes an increasing number of people who have been professionally trained in engineering, agronomy, education, public health, medicine, law, statistics, and the natural sciences. It includes an increasing number of economists and people with other social science backgrounds.

In each of these fields specialization is intensifying with subdisciplines multiplying rapidly. In each, major roles are played by specialist-administrators who coordinate the work of subspecialists. While the bulk of these specialists are to be found in the many agencies of central government, some of the most influential—and most in need of broadened perspectives—are always in the central guidance cluster.

### Leaders of Interdisciplinary Teams

The development of major policies and programs always requires intensive work by various interdisciplinary teams. Sometimes these are within specific organizations; often, they are interorganizational bodies set up on a permanent or *ad hoc* basis.

The working leaders of these teams are often specialists themselves—economists, engineers, experts on various agency programs, etc. Yet the tasks of leadership require knowledge and skills reaching far beyond their field of specialized competence or training. The lack of such knowledge and skills is a factor in contributing toward the frequent "group think" sterility of such team operations, their proclivities toward interminable red tape, and the adoption by team members of frozen positions in defense of narrow bureaucratic interests.

## Top Executives

These are the highest-level career administrators in the central guidance cluster and its surrounding ring of nationwide organizations. They are the generalists who must work, on the one hand, with the political leaders of the country and, on the other hand, with the specialists and the interdisciplinary team leaders. Some of them may, indeed, come from, or end up in, the sphere of national politics or specialist expertise. They face the most difficult problems of large-scale management and administration, particularly in the interrelating of complex programs and the detailed balancing of divergent interests.

The first hurdle with this group is the old-fashioned idea that they have nothing to learn from advanced management conferences. Once this hurdle is overcome—and this is beginning to happen in many countries—the second hurdle is the attitude "We're too busy—we have no time." This hurdle often can be overcome by a series of short conferences or workshops in which they may appear as major contributors, discussants, or debaters.

The participation of this group in educational activities of this type can be crucial in developing a "learning atmosphere" on the part of specialists and interdisciplinary team leaders.

## Political Leaders

This group includes (1) major political appointees in executive-branch organizations, (2) elected members of the national legislature, (3) national party officials and staff members, and above all (4) the Chief Executive (whether Prime Minister or President) and his immediate staff.

This is the hardest group to involve directly in educational activities, in part because of the tremendous time pressures generated by political life, in part because of the old-fashioned assumption that they need know nothing but the skills of political maneuver, in part because of the anti-intellectual orientation of the old-fashioned politician. The first of these factors is a tremendous difficulty. The others are weakening, as the complexities of modern society tend to create a new breed of politician.

We believe that in many countries it is possible to include political leaders (with the sole exception of the Chief Executive) in special educational programs. In some cases they may take part in conferences arranged for top executives also. In other cases special programs may be arranged for and with legislative committees—indeed, even in the form of special legislative studies and investigations.

### Interest-group Leaders

These are the leaders of the major federations of enterprises, trade unions, professional groups, educational institutions, etc., apart from or outside the government apparatus. In many countries these leaders are called upon to play major roles in formulating, reviewing, or legitimatizing national policies and programs. Yet they are often completely unprepared to play such roles. Participation in national planning processes may itself be a major educational influence, particularly by helping interest-group leaders obtain a better appreciation of other interests in society. But this participation could be greatly facilitated and indeed be made more meaningful and less ritualistic if accompanied by participation in special seminars and conferences of the type to be discussed in the next section.

## SOME LEARNING OBJECTIVES AND METHODS

Just what can these various kinds of people hope to learn from special educational programs?

One way to answer this question is to summarize the substantive content of the special educational programs now being conducted in developing nations or for people from developing nations—often in, or with assistance from, more developed nations. Valuable information on substantive content may be obtained from various publications of the Organization for Economic Development and Cooperation and the Economic Commission for Latin America. Similar information on the various development institutes in Eastern Europe has not yet been developed.

Yet with but few exceptions these programs are currently oriented mainly toward the training of economic specialists, and often junior specialists at that. Rarely do they attempt to help specialists learn how to make a multidimensional analysis of planning problems, recognize the uses and limitations of noneconomic techniques and disciplines, or handle conflicts among competing interests (even competing forms of economic analysis). Still more rarely are they oriented toward the learning needs of interdisciplinary group leaders, top executives, political leaders, or interest-group leaders. Often, these programs are too much based upon general approaches developed in other countries and not sufficiently adapted to the special conditions, political and social system, and goals of the country concerned.

Moreover, we have as yet found no instance of educational programs to meet the needs of the more highly industrialized problems in the guidance of social change, the former in overcoming institutionalized resistances to modernization and social mobility, the latter in overcoming poverty and building a "Great Society." The tendency of top government personnel in both countries is to approach their problems with the narrow tools and concepts of a previous generation. Education of central policy makers and programmers is regarded as appropriate for others (that is, people from developing nations), not for themselves.

Nevertheless, we have found many encouraging currents. Some of the best economists are the very first to point out the limitations of economics and the need for education in transeconomic matters. Some of the institutes for development planning are experimenting with new and broader subject matter. Many interesting new approaches are to be found at the Institute of Social Studies at the Hague and the University of Pittsburgh's Economic and Social Development Program.

As we have tried to understand these new currents, we find that they flow in three directions. They may be briefly summarized as the development of educational programs designed to help people learn something significant about (1) the multidimensional analysis of planning problems, (2) the uses and limitations of specialized techniques, and (3) the arts of conflict management.

Further progress in these directions undoubtedly requires much more experimentation and innovation by many different kinds of educational institutions in many parts of the world. It undoubtedly requires a much stronger foundation in empirical research (both basic and applied) and in the development of more relevant concepts and theories concerning the formulation and implementation of plans. Above all, it is essential that educational programs of this type be geared to the unique conditions in individual countries. There is no general formula that can be automatically applied without very considerable adjustment to both industrializing and industrialized countries, to both Socialist and non-Socialist countries.

The following suggestions are designed to encourage a variety of educational programs in many different countries.

## The Multidimensional Analysis of Planning Problems

In the managing of national change there is no such thing as a purely *economic* problem, a purely *political* problem, a purely *legal* problem, a purely *cultural* problem, or a purely *technological* problem. Real-life problems are exceedingly complex. They invariably fall into all these categories at once.

A major goal of special educational programs, therefore, should be to help the various types of planners learn how to define and analyze these problems in many dimensions.

Toward this end we suggest consideration of the following possibilities:

*Problem-oriented workshops.* There are many fundamental national problems that are widely mishandled because of a tendency to analyze them, at least formally and explicitly, in unidimensional terms. Among these are the following:

*The development or appraisal of specific programs.* Much work has been done by economists on criteria for the evaluation of major investment programs. Some of this falls under the heading of "cost-benefit analysis." Yet the benefit side of such analysis is typically very narrow, with too much attention to direct, as distinguished from indirect, benefits and to benefits that can be expressed in monetary terms as distinguished from those that can properly be expressed only in nonmonetary terms. Much of this work suffers from a major unstated premise that somehow or other all the considerations may be reduced to some single-valued index number or "utility function."

The cost-benefit analysts can make a major contribution toward the evaluation of major investment programs. In our judgment one of the best ways for this contribution to be made is to arrange seminars or workshops in which their work is used as a "starting point" to develop multidimensional analysis of, let us say, agricultural programs, or new educational programs, or new programs of scientific research. The participants in these conferences, who might include many different types of planners, would then be challenged to include in the analysis such factors as:

1. The actual and potential support for the proposed program or major variations thereof
2. The political, social, and cultural benefits and disadvantages accruing to various groups as a result of the program (in other words "whose nest would be feathered" and "whose ox would be gored")
3. The various areas in which there might be presently unanticipated consequences, for good or for bad
4. The managerial and administrative factors that might affect the feasibility or the content of the program

*Preparing an annual budget geared to long-range plans.* The current government budget or the next year's budget is in most countries the core of long-range planning. Yet there are invariably certain understandable tensions and jurisdictional conflicts between the budget units of government and those who specialize in developing or coordinating long-range plans. Although some of these tensions are both unavoidable and healthy, progress often depends upon much better work in making the budget an instrument of long-range planning. To do so, however, involves relationships that go far beyond the central guidance cluster and vitally affect the work of individual departments. It also involves the development of new concepts of mission definition or program formulation, concepts that deal more adequately with the quantity and quality of government services and with presumed effect upon various aspects of social structure and social performance. All this, in turn, requires the participation of many kinds of people from many departments or ministries, from legislatures, and from universities. In a country like the United Kingdom, workshops on this subject could not only help educate the old-time bureaucracy in the Treasury; they could also help democratize the entire structure of governmental planning. In the United States such workshops could help the major departments make the difficult transition from financial budgeting to genuine program planning. In developing nations they could help develop budget machinery that would play a much more vital role in planning for the governmental sector.

*Institution building.* National change requires many new institutions and considerable adaptation in existing ones. How is this to be done?

This subject also can be taken up in specific terms, as with conferences on how to build effective public enterprise corporations, how to strengthen the tax-collection organization, how to establish the institutions required for a securities market, or how to promote innovating of service-oriented corporations in the private sector. Some of these subjects may best be dealt with through international workshops covering major regions of the world.

*Mobilizing resources.* This essential subject is usually handled as a technical problem in the field of tax policy and borrowing.

But taxation is also a political process par excellence. So is borrowing. It would be exceedingly helpful to develop ways of dealing with this subject in language stripped of "double-talk" and oriented squarely toward analyzing its political, administrative, and cultural aspects.

It would be still more helpful if conferences and workshops in this area also dealt with the fundamental problems raised by developing nations in mobilizing external resources from the developed nations and from international agencies. This would mean dealing with "trade versus aid" in a framework of the direct identification of the pressure group and institutional obstacles in developed nations to trade policies that promote economic growth in "poor countries." It would mean dealing frankly with the various alternatives involved in "playing one side against the other."

*Handling essential controls.* Development programs often involve various approaches to the direct or indirect control of nongovernment activity. Among the most universal of these are "wage policy," "income policy," or "price policy." In some cases these verge on direct wage control or price control. In most developing nations (and some others) there are various controls over foreign currency or foreign investment.

Here again we find phenomena that are political, administrative, and psychological but are usually discussed as though they were only economic or legal. Here again we need conferences or workshops that produce multidimensional analyses.

*Obtaining improved statistics.* This is a problem in every country and in some countries a desperate problem, but it is only in small part a problem that can be handled by statisticians. The training of statisticians qualifies them mainly to process data that has already been obtained. Obtaining data that is worth processing is an entirely different matter. Statistics are tremendous sources of power. The building of machinery for collecting statistics sets up new channels of communication between different sectors of society. These are processes that should be faced "in the round."

**Seminars on the social system of a country or region.** Planners, more than any other people, should understand the country in which they live and for which they plan. To help develop this understanding special seminars or courses should be established, particularly for technicians and group leaders. Such courses should deal with the kind of subject matter found in *The American Society*,[3] by the Cornell sociologist Robin Williams, Jr. They should analyze the resource base of the country, family stratification and mobility, economic institutions, political institutions, communication network, education, business, agriculture, labor, religion, values, science, technology, and major currents of social, cultural, economic, and political change. Immersion in basic facts about their own country would help overcome tendencies among planners to analyze problems in overgeneralized terms.

In countries where frank analysis of the power structure and institutional change might touch upon ultrasensitive areas, it might be more feasible if such seminars were set up internationally to deal with a group of countries.

*Conferences on social, as distinguished from economic, accounting.* National economic accounts, although invaluable, can provide but a pallid reflection of the substantive changes sought or attained by major programs of economic and social change. Indeed, overemphasis upon quantitative economic information may serve to detract attention from more qualitative and equally significant information. The remedy to this problem is not to cut down on economic data (which, on the contrary, usually needs expansion and improvement) but rather to compile and disseminate noneconomic data as well. One possible way to do this is to prepare *annual social reports* as parts of, or supplements to, the annual economic analyses that are regularly prepared in most countries.

Such reports cannot be prepared in ivory towers. The basic concepts require new thinking along lines that are still far from clear. We believe that conferences on this subject, cosponsored by universities and United Nation agencies, would help people think and learn together. Those participating in such conferences should include a wide variety of specialists, executives, and social scientists from the academic world.

## The Uses and Limitations of Specialized Techniques

Economic analysis is at the very heart of national economic planning. Accordingly, it is essential that the professional economists in national planning agencies continuously refresh and improve their professional skills.

It is also important that the noneconomists be given nonprofessional training concerning:

Elementary economic concepts and principles, particularly in relation to development, resource allocation, money and taxation, motivations of investors, consumers and workers, international trade and spatial economics

The use and manipulation of economic data, particularly of national income accounts, at the national level

The major disputes and major new directions in the economics of development, growth, and planning

The kinds of questions that should be put to economists

The kinds of errors and bias to which different kinds of economists are prone

Successful economic planning increasingly requires the talents of specialized technicians in many other fields. This has been more widely recognized in such fields as engineering, agronomy, industrial technology, scientific research, medicine and health services, education, public administration, and business management. Much greater recognition is needed of the potential contributions of specialists in political analysis, anthropology, sociology, psychology, social psychology, and psychiatry. Political leaders and administrators need to learn how best to develop these valuable specialties, how to get the specialists to work together, and how to integrate their divergent views. The specialists themselves, particularly the economists, need to learn how their skills may be supplemented and invigorated by people from other disciplines.

We recommend special attention to the following already recognized academic disciplines:

Statistics (methods and data; no theory apart from elementary probability; special reference to errors and reliability)

The necessary mathematics (functions; the principles of input/output; linear programming; econometrics)

Sociology (human behavior theory; social structure theory; urban and rural sociology; sociology of work)

Political Science (organization theory and management; public administration; political theory and the main ideologies; parties; pressure groups, especially trade-union and military; international organizations)

Regionalism (spatial economics; land use; regional geography)

Also, for our purposes, the following vocational subjects are of equal status with academic disciplines:

Social welfare (education; health; unemployment; social gerontology; penology; urban renewal; youth problems)

Finance (budgeting; project presentation and evaluation; fiscal management)

Public Law (constitutional and administrative)

Planning techniques and procedures

There should further be in each country at least one body responsible for all this education. Whether it gave all the courses itself or contracted with others to give them would depend on local circumstances.

Finally, there should be a few international colleges, such as the one in Santiago, Chile. These should have a specialized resident faculty, as well as a high turnover of visiting faculty.

## The Arts of Conflict Management

The formulation and implementation of national plans and policies involve the resolution of conflicting interests and divergent plans under conditions of imperfect information, ambiguity, changing pressures, and turbulent environments.

This requires continuous improvement and innovation in the arts and techniques of:

1. Negotiation, bargaining, compromise, and creative integration
2. The organization of groups and coalitions
3. Individual and mass persuasion
4. Command and regulation
5. Evaluation and control

Although experience is indispensable to the development of these arts, there is nevertheless an important role for special educational programs, particularly if geared to the specific needs of individual countries and regions.

*The specialists.* In many specialized fields, particularly those which seem more scientific in nature, there is a dangerous tendency for the specialists to become rigid and narrow.

To help specialists make their full contribution it would be helpful to provide a serious course (preferably at a university or independent institution) dealing with the cognitive, personality, and environmental aspects of *real-life decision making.*

The cognitive aspects of the course would present heuristic models of research. As against deterministic models that assume certainty and simplicity, they would stress the necessity of coping with uncertainty and complexity. They would recognize the role in decision making of power, influence, habit, and cultural norms. They would also stress the importance of problem analysis, problem definition, and "problem creating," as against mere problem solving. For this purpose, detailed problems, case studies, and stimulation-discussion exercises would be very useful in supplementing lectures.

The personality aspects of the course would try to develop among the participants:

1. A tolerance of ambiguity
2. The capacity to live with dissonant alternatives until possibilities for choices become clear
3. An awareness of the importance of permissive psychosocial climates
4. An interest in immediate feedback and in continuous evaluation
5. A willingness to learn, unlearn, take risks, and admit errors
6. A feeling for the occasions that warrant the stronger forms of persuasion

For this purpose many of the methods used in human relations training would be useful.

The environmental aspects would deal with:

1. The need for environmental scanning
2. The awareness that environmental information will always be imperfect and require interpretation
3. Acclimatization to the emergence of the unexpected or the uncontrollable

4. The possibilities of adaptation to new conditions without giving up the most important objectives

Case studies and simulation-discussion exercises may also be useful here.

*Team leaders.* Here the educational task is to help people make a difficult role transition from specialist to the leader of a group of specialists.

Such people need a program of planned management education that opens up the best available knowledge from the behavioral sciences and other disciplines on small-group dynamics and the management of complex formal organizations.

The group-dynamics aspect of the program should deal with role differentiation; communication; the conditions of group cohesion, conflict, and creativity; and leadership styles.

The managerial aspect should deal with the details and dynamics of formal and informal organization, financial and other dimensions of organizational performance, and the process of planning, activating, and evaluating. It should deal directly with the differences between various organizations, particularly between those organizations that do not sell their output and those that do. Attention should be given to relations with legislatures, pressure groups, and political leaders.

*Top executives and other leaders.* These people are continuously immersed in complex conflict situations. Many of them may be better qualified than anyone else to help specialists and team leaders learn more about the arts of conflict management. Yet this does not mean that they themselves cannot learn more or that special educational programs cannot contribute to their learning processes.

Four types of educational programs should be given particular attention:

First, internal conferences or workshops should be organized to help executives and other leaders explore the major problems within their own organizations, whether these are problems of "hardening of the arteries," the lack of managerial personnel, "bureaucratic feudalism," low morale, or low productivity. External advisers or consultants can often be helpful in this connection.

Secondly, broader conferences and workshops can deal with such ever-practical problems as the organization of a "support base" (or activation base) for major programs. Attention can be given to the strategies needed to develop effective coalitions or alliances, overcome apathy or organized resistance, and lead effective action campaigns.

Thirdly, under "social island" conditions, top executives, political and interest-group leaders, journalists, professors, and other opinion leaders can be brought together for mutual confrontation in exploring such problems as (1) opinion formulation, influence, and alienation, (2) policy making, and (3) the theory and practice of institution building.

Fourthly, political leaders and interest-group leaders especially should be provided with organized opportunities for (1) learning about their country's plans and planning institutions and (2) meeting and working with their country's top planning executives and specialists. At times this has been done through conferences organized by the central planning institutions themselves. In many circumstances, however, it may prove more fruitful to arrange for less official undertakings under the sponsorship of international bodies, universities, or independent institutions.

## SPECIFIC SUGGESTIONS

Action along the lines discussed in the previous section requires initiative and imagination on the part of individuals in a variety of organizations: national planning agencies, the United Nations and other transnational organizations, universities and other educational and research institutions, and national or international planning associations.

Accordingly, some of our major suggestions will now be briefly restated in terms of the agencies that might consider acting upon them. In formulating suggestions in this manner, of course, we are very conscious of the fact that many such agencies are already moving along the lines suggested. Indeed, some may already be taking action that is superior to, or at least different from, any of the proposals herein contained.

### To National Planning Agencies

We feel that much more ambitious action along these lines is required on the part of the specialized national agencies concentrating upon the coordination of national economic policies and programs. In some countries this is a national planning commission; in others, a Ministry of Finance, Treasury, Bureau of the Budget, or Council of Economic Advisers. We suggest that these agencies consider such specific steps as the following:

1. A senior official should be charged with preparing a long-range plan for the development of the planning personnel.
2. Widespread agency and staff support for such a development program should be mobilized, with incentives to encourage active participation by all ranks in the various courses, seminars, and other development activities.
3. The development program should include specific provisions for such activities, among others, as:
    a. Refresher courses in the various planning disciplines, especially for the technical-professional staff
    b. Workshops on decision making, conflict management, social change, and planning ecology for middle and senior ranks
    c. Residential seminars and longer study courses, to be held at universities or other research and training institutes
    d. Job rotation, assignment to private or other public agencies, study abroad and similar activities designed to broaden experience

### To the United Nations and Other Transnational Organizations

We also suggest major extensions of the work already started by the United Nations, some of its specialized agencies, regional organizations, and other transnational organizations. Such agencies should consider taking the following steps:

1. Initiate, hold, and aid international seminars and round tables to prepare detailed proposals for the development of national

planning personnel (as defined earlier in the chapter, under "The Learners"), including illustrative curricula for courses and lists of teaching materials.

2. Initiate and aid the preparation of comparative studies, cases, texts, and similar material to serve as educational aids in the development of national planning officials or as the basis for such educational aids.

3. Initiate, hold, and aid international seminars, exchange programs, and other activities to develop teachers and trainers for programs for planning personnel.

4. Initiate, hold, and aid international and cross-cultural seminars for senior executives of national planning units, as direct-training and staff-development activities.

## To Educational and Research Institutions

It is suggested that universities and other research institutions help out, where appropriate, by taking the following steps:

1. Reexamine the curricula of those subjects from which most planning personnel are recruited, such as economics, physical planning, and law. These curricula should be broadened so as to assure that the graduates have a basic knowledge in social sciences and are aware of the social functions and multiple dimensions of national planning.

2. Provide students generally with a broad view of national problems and the role of national planning in dealing with them.

3. Encourage the academic staff to engage in research relevant to national planning and to contribute to educational activities for national planning personnel.

4. In cooperation with national planning units, hold special courses, seminars, conferences, etc., for national planning staff.

## To Planning Associations

We believe that professional associations of planners should encourage their members to support staff-development activities and to participate in them. We also suggest that such associations hold symposia, round tables, and similar activities to broaden the competence of their own members.

Nonprofessional planning associations, particularly those composed of people from different walks of life, can play a major role in educating interest-group leaders and contributing to a more enlightened public opinion in this area.

## CONCLUDING COMMENTS

In conclusion, two major points deserve brief mention.

First, in any specific country or region the various agencies listed above should work out specific patterns of cooperative action. No one of these agencies can do the whole job by itself.

Secondly, the research foundation for the kind of educational programs discussed in this chapter is still lamentably weak. Major progress along the lines of these suggestions cannot be expected without a deepening and widening of current research activities—both applied and basic, both empirical and theoretical —in the entire field of national planning. This is a subject, however, which cannot be dealt with directly within the confines of this chapter.

## NOTES

[1] This report was prepared by the Executive Committee of the International Group for Studies in National Planning (INTERPLAN), based on preliminary drafts produced at an International Planning Conference, held in Warsaw, Poland, April 20–24, 1965, at the invitation of the Institute of Philosophy and Sociology of the Polish Academy of Science. It is a "preliminary" report in the sense that more specific—and improved—proposals will be developed on the basis of comments received from many countries since then and the reexamination of the subject at INTERPLAN's conference in Caracas, Venezuela, in November, 1966.

[2] See Chap. 9.

[3] Robin Williams, Jr., *The American Society,* rev. ed., Alfred A. Knopf, Inc., New York, 1960.

PART 2

# Vistas for
# Research and
# Theory

# 9

# What Is National Planning?

## Robert J. Shafer [1]

One of the greatest obstacles to significant research in this field has been the lack of a dynamic, action-oriented, realistic, and highly articulated concept of national economic planning. In some countries the term *planning* is socially acceptable only when referring to the plans of private business, state or local governments, or the activities of national government agencies within such traditional sectors as road and airport planning. When used to refer to the broad coordinating and promotional activities of a central government, the term is often a red flag. In the United States and Western Germany, particularly, it smacks of socialism or communism. It also brings back memories of centralized wartime controls in the former, of Hitler and the Nazis in the latter. Still more difficult is the fact that in most countries the term suggests many different things to different people. Where national economic planning is highly popular (and this includes the great majority of countries), *planning* has a mystical quality redolent of great visions and easy panaceas. For technicians and econometricians, *planning* has often come to refer to the limited process of making certain econometric calculations. Although vision and technique are both important aspects of the planning process, neither of these concepts provides an adequate guide to policy, analysis, or empirical research.

One of the great achievements of the Minnowbrook Conference was the formulation of a more useful "starting point" concept. This concept, based upon the preliminary studies already undertaken by the participants, dealt with (1) the planning process in general, (2) the national planning process, and (3) national planning institutions. At the beginning of the conference, however, conceptual agreement would have been impossible. It was only after three weeks of continuous examination of planning problems in individual countries that it was possible to prepare a set of propositions that could be accepted as a basis of discussion. This first set of propositions was then thoroughly reformulated by a special committee that shuttled back and forth between the preparation of committee drafts and plenary sessions at which the drafts were torn to pieces. Strangely enough, what emerged from this protracted process was not a watered-down compromise but twenty propositions setting forth a constructive integration of many previously divergent points of view.

## THE PLANNING PROCESS IN GENERAL

One of the most important points to emerge at the conference was the sharp difference between *planning* and *plans*. The former is a process of change and becoming, a process in which the planner is not himself "programmed." A plan, however, is itself a program and may be subject to little change or adaptation. The process of planning, moreover, is only *intended* rationality. Empirical examination yields many examples of irrational planning and of routinized, rather than creative, goal commitments.

This "process approach" to planning was set forth abstractly in the first six of the Minnowbrook propositions:

1. Planning is a process of formulating goals and developing commitments to attaining them, a process undertaken to some extent by all individuals and organizations.
2. Planning is a process of intended adaptive rationality in pursuit of goals. In practice it is usually intermingled with be-

havior which is spontaneous, inadvertent, or random, or behavior which is directed by habit, tradition, previous decision, or external pressure.

3. Planning, as foresight coupled to goals, policies, and action, inescapably grows out of, and is linked to, specific cultures (and especially to their characteristic patterns of action and authority relationships).

4. Planning has functions that are:
   *a.* Explicit, open, and manifest
   *b.* Implicit, hidden, and latent

5. The process of planning implies attention to implementation and to evaluation of both goals and performance.

6. In a formal organization, the concept of central planning implies not only planning for the entire system (enterprise, government agency, political party, trade association, union, etc.) but the promotion and coordination of planning by its component units or subsystems.

Although space limitations prevent a commentary on each of the propositions, it should be noted that by this concept planning involves "commitment" (Minnowbrook proposition 1). This is much more than merely formulating proposals or expressing vague desires. It also is closely connected with implementation and evaluation (Minnowbrook proposition 5).

## THE NATIONAL PLANNING PROCESS

The next nine Minnowbrook propositions spell out the multidimensionality of the national planning process. They identify the major variables which combine in different ways to produce the special—even unique—planning systems in different countries.

7. Central planning in a national system may include widespread initiative and participation by individuals and groups, both public and private, outside the central planning institutions of the national government.

8. National planning is an effort to promote or coordinate, through central planning institutions, the activities of:

  *a.* Intermediate bodies, such as national government departments, regional, state, or local government, business federations, and large nationwide enterprises
  *b.* Operating units, such as enterprises, associations, local
  governments, agencies, communities, families, and individuals

9. National economic planning consists of coordinated efforts by
   central institutions to develop some combination of:
   *a.* *Aggregate* planning for general levels of output and income, employment, price levels, consumption, investment,
   balance of payments, etc.
   *b.* *Cross-sectoral* planning for the supply or distribution of
   income and of such resources as manpower, goods, credit,
   or information
   *c.* *Sectoral* or *subsectoral* planning for such areas of activity
   as agricultural crops, mining, steel, road construction, rail-
   ways, electric power, education, health, and other specific
   sectors
   *d.* *Enterprise* planning by or for private, public, or mixed enterprise
   *e.* *Spatial* planning for the geographical distribution of activity

Therefore, separate national government activities in such
fields as taxation, expenditure, control of the money supply, regulation, mediation, information provision, or enterprise operation,
without coordinating efforts by central institutions, do not constitute national planning.

10. In some countries, the scope of national planning efforts is
    limited mainly to an integration of cross-sectional measures
    and aggregate planning with occasional or highly selective
    attention to sectoral or enterprise planning.   In other coun-
    tries, efforts are made at far-reaching integration of all the
    elements referred to in propositions 8 and 9.
11. National planning also varies from country to country and
    from time to time with respect to:
    *a.* The extent of compulsion or pressure, as distinguished

from suggestion and persuasion, that may be used by central government institutions
  b. The balance between centralization and decentralization
  c. The extent of reliance upon, or manipulation of, market mechanisms
  d. The degree of emphasis upon short-range or long-range considerations
  e. The degree of initiative and autonomy exercised by intermediate bodies and operating units
12. *Many of the conscious objectives and unintended consequences, as well as many of the means required for goal formulation, implementation, and elevation, are usually political, cultural, social, or biophysical rather than merely economic.*
13. National planning is economic planning to the extent that it deals with decisions on the allocation of scarce resources and the production and distribution of goods and services.
14. Many terms are used to refer to national planning, including:
  a. Coordinated economic programming
  b. Integration of national economic policies
  c. National resources budgeting
  d. Management of the economy
  e. National economic policy making
15. Although national planning documents are important elements in the planning process, any "national plan" can provide only partial representation of the significant commitments developed through the planning process.

## NATIONAL PLANNING INSTITUTIONS

One of the great popular fallacies of national planning is the idea that all the major functions involved in guiding an economy can be centralized in one agency of government. Although this idea is rarely stated so bluntly, it is nonetheless directly suggested by the tendency of econometricians to concentrate public attention upon a specialized staff agency involved in macroeconomic analysis and projections. This tendency is reinforced by the inclinations of political leaders to use such an agency (usually conspicuously labeled "the planning" board, commission, or council) for symbolic, ceremonial, or (when the going gets tough) sacrificial purposes.

This fallacy is clearly shunted aside by Minnowbrook propositions 16 through 20:

16. In any country, national planning functions are performed by a variety of institutions rather than by a single agency.

17. The names given to national planning councils, commissions, and boards often lead to the erroneous impression that such bodies are comparable or that they perform all national planning functions in their countries.

18. Some of the more important functions of central planning institutions are:
    a. Representation of major interest groups
    b. Adjustment of major interest groups in the society
    c. Technical appraisal of current trends and formulation of aggregate goals
    d. Preparation, coordination, or review of major projects
    e. Mediation among competing groups and national leaders
    f. National political leadership
    g. Central financial management (budgeting, controlling money supply, etc.)
    h. Handling of the critical issues of the moment
    i. Symbolic or ceremonial functions

19. Such functions are usually institutionalized in different ways in response to the conditions prevailing in different societies.

20. In some societies, informal arrangements and procedures may be the functional equivalents of more highly formalized central planning institutions in other societies.

Prime attention, therefore, must be focused upon the entire cluster of central institutions playing basic roles in the guidance of national economic activity. These roles, in turn must be analyzed realistically, with full awareness of the multiplicity of roles played by any one agency, of the changes in the role "mix" of any one agency over time, and of divergent perceptions of any particular role.

The twenty propositions set forth above are best regarded not as final achievements but as starting points for more sophisticated concept formulation (or "concept attainment," as the psychologists would put it) by scholars and planning administrators. A considerable period of competitive concept differentiation will undoubtedly be required before it will be possible to narrow down the possibilities to a widely acceptable set of sharp conceptual tools.

## NOTE

[1] The propositions in this chapter were prepared by a committee headed by Professor Shafer. The other members of the committee were Lynton K. Caldwell; Bertram M. Gross; and Thomas H. Rasmussen, graduate student, Syracuse University. The twenty propositions have also appeared in "The Great Vista: National Planning Research," *Social Science Information*, pp. 1–14, June, 1965.

# 10

## Some Fundamental Questions on National Planning

### Peter J. D. Wiles

The most difficult task faced by decision makers is not problem solving but problem formulating. This is particularly true for research, one of the more highly structured types of decision making.

In the field of national economic planning, however, the questions have been asked by government officials who needed answers yesterday. Social scientists have been expected to give quick, pragmatic answers. The bulk of research being done, therefore, has been largely restricted to economic analysis or to applied research with very little foundation in basic research. Most of the researchers have suppressed their own question-propounding inclinations and have concentrated upon answer giving which, while having the merit of being timely, has too often been highly superficial.

Despite the variety of viewpoints represented and presented at the Minnowbrook Conference, there was unanimity on the necessity of rigorous empirical research on national planning processes in different countries throughout the world. During the conference the participants presented and debated their own plans for empirical and theoretical studies, some limited to specific countries, some transnational in scope. These discussions led to a feeling that an inventory should be made of the major questions that might be asked about national economic planning in any country. A common set of questions might help the researchers overcome concentration on matters peculiar to individual countries, thereby facilitating comparative analysis.

Accordingly, a preliminary set of questions was prepared by the seminar director and divided among four committees comprising all the participants, together with a number of graduate students and research associates. All the committee reports were presented to, and discussed by, the entire group. Finally a new committee, under the chairmanship of Peter J. D. Wiles, produced the following set of questions on the basis of the previous lists and discussions:

## SOCIAL FRAMEWORK

### Emergence of Planning

In general, what conditions have led to the emergence, if any, of national planning? Specifically:

1. Who were the promoters, and who were the adherents?
2. Was the perception of imminent crisis a factor in the emergence of planning or the cause of inaction? What kind of crisis?
3. To what extent has the emergence of planning and the selection of its type been dependent upon political circumstances, cultural values, ideology, and technical and managerial abilities?
4. To what extent, and why, have planning concepts, methods, or doctrines been borrowed by one country from another or imposed upon it?
5. What attempts have been made to adapt transplanted concepts, etc., to local needs?
6. What was the role of foreign advisers in national planning?
7. What opposition has there been to the whole concept?
8. Has national planning simply failed to arise at all, because of:
   *a.* Hopeless goal conflict?

    *b.* Antiplanning ideology?
    *c.* General satisfaction with the existing state of affairs?
    *d.* Lack of personnel resources?
9. What, in terms of formal typology, is the planning system most like, e.g., *laissez faire,* regulated market, command economy, welfare capitalism, Titoism, Soviet-type economy?

## Social and Political Environment

1. What are the main divisions (class, regional, religious, etc.) in this society which most affect the process of planning?
2. What are the major interests, organized and unorganized, in the society? What values can be identified with them?
3. What features of planning can be traced to an ideology, e.g., communism, socialism, Gandhiism, Catholicism, *laissez faire,* fascism, nationalism?
4. To what extent is the economy dependent upon outside assistance, supplies, or markets, or subject to external pressures?
5. To what extent does the need for assistance or the desire for resisting external pressures lead to coalitions to improve the country's bargaining position, e.g., Afro-Asian, Latin-American groupings, the movements for federation to increase size?
6. How have the size and diversity of the country affected the planning?
    *a.* How do the geographic distribution of cultural diversity (ethnic, linguistic, etc.) and the existence of national minorities in distinct areas affect planning?
    *b.* How do (1) the geographical dimensions of the country, (2) the density of the population, or (3) the number of local or regional units of administration affect the planning process?
    *c.* Has the country's federal constitution, if any, affected planning?

## Economic Environment

1. How far have the existing economic structures affected planning?
    *a.* How big is the public sector, and in what branches does

it operate (including defense, education, medicine, insurance)?

b. How much of it is run by:
  (1) Government departments?
  (2) Public corporations?
  (3) Local authorities?

c. How much of the private sector is run by:
  (1) Corporations with limited liability?  How much by large corporations?  How much by small?
  (2) Partnerships?
  (3) One-man businesses?
  (4) Consumer cooperatives?
  (5) Producer cooperatives?

d. What is the extent of the subsistence sector?

e. How much labor is unionized?

f. Are the unions craft, industrial, employmental, general, other?

g. How are the free professions organized?

h. What is the banking system?

i. How extensive are the social services?

2. What is the dedication of society to the economic freedoms:

a. Of private entrepreneurial property?
  (1) Can property be confiscated?  If so, who sets compensation, if any?
  (2) How difficult do the plan and other laws make it:
    (a) To set up a new private enterprise, especially a peasant household or small shop?
    (b) To found a producers' or consumers' cooperative with rules of one's own making?
    (c) To found a syndicalist enterprise?
  (3) Have the planners right of access to private and/or public accounts?
  (4) Are tax assessments subject to review?
  (5) Is the refusal of a license subject to review?
  (6) What powers of search have the police for contraband materials?

b. Of labour?

(1) Can workers strike?

(2) Can trade unions organize independently without harassment?

(3) Is labor directed to new jobs?

(4) Is labor kept in jobs it happens to be in?

(5) How is military or prison labor used?

(6) Is there any noneconomic discrimination in hiring?

*c.* Of consumers?

(1) Are fraud, quacks, unqualified practitioners, monopolistic behavior, and advertising controlled?

(2) Is there rationing?

(3) Is the consumer sovereign in the economist's sense; i.e., is more produced of what he makes more profitable, and less of what he makes less profitable? In other words does the output mix follow the consumer's tastes, profit permitting?

(4) How easy is it to form consumer cooperatives?

(5) Is it possible to form consumer protective associations? If so, how much influence have they?

*d.* Generally?

(1) If the plan adversely affects the livelihood of persons and organizations in any way not listed above, is it subject to appeal?

(2) How much are planners restricted by the acceptance of any of these freedoms?

3. The performance of the economy:

*a.* Average net national income (or GNP) per capita in domestic currency

*b.* Movement of the dedication of society to the economic freedoms, over time (see 2 above)

*c.* Movement of population over time because of births, deaths, immigration, emigration

*d.* Residential breakdown of population

*e.* Occupational breakdown and skills (including, for purposes of comparability, the ancillary occupations of agriculture)

*f.* Educational attainment

*g.* Health

   *h.* Recent performance of consumer prices (not only retail prices but including rent)
   *i.* Distribution of income between rich and poor
   *j.* Distribution of private capital between the rich and poor
   *k.* Variation of average income between areas, between racial and religious groups
   *l.* Percentage of net national income spent or earned in foreign trade (including invisibles)
   *m.* Percentage of net national income (or GNP) spent on defense, education, net investment, other consumption

## The Geographical Environment

1. To what extent and in what ways do the following factors in the biophysical environment affect national planning?
   *a.* Density and distribution of population
   *b.* Endemic hazards to health
   *c.* Land-use potentiality (soil, topography, climate)
   *d.* Mineral deposits
   *e.* Situation in relation to international river systems
   *f.* Location with respect to import-export opportunities
   *g.* Ability to meet natural-resource requirements out of national territory
   *h.* Unique resources of scenic or natural-history value

## External Political Environment

1. Is there transnational or supranational planning? If so, how did it arise?
2. What effect has it had on planning within the country? Or vice versa?
3. To what extent do national planning goals depend on international planning or action?
4. Has national and/or international planning tended to disrupt international economic or political relations? Or vice versa?
5. How has the formation of common markets and economic blocs affected national planning in individual countries?
6. To what extent is the national plan drawn up with a view to appealing for foreign aid?

7. Is planning influenced by the country's desire to compete with others, e.g., in the rate of economic growth, social justice, the sophistication of its planning machinery?
8. What is the geographical situation with regard to defense?
9. To what military alliance does the country belong? Which countries are its enemies?

## General Attitudes

1. How much do people want the following national objectives?

| | |
|---|---|
| National defense | Rational regional distribution |
| National prestige | Rational use of physical |
| Economic autarchy | environment |
| Full employment | Population control |
| Price stability | Education |
| Economic growth | Health |
| Distributive justice | Racial and/or minority |
| A better balance between | integration |
| private and collective | |
| consumption | |

2. How much are people influenced by the following personal objectives?

| | |
|---|---|
| Religion | Economic freedom |
| High consumption | Leisure |
| Conspicuous consumption | Highbrow culture |
| Security | Lowbrow culture |
| Education | Vice as legally defined |
| Health | Sport |
| Family planning | |
| Politically guaranteed freedoms | |

3. What are people's general attitudes toward government plans and planning?

## GOAL FORMULATION

### The Hierarchy of Goals

1. What are the overriding goals, and how are lesser goals subordinated to them (accommodation, suppression, elimination, etc.)?

2. Is economic growth a means or an end in the plan? What various aims lie behind it?
3. To what extent do personal attitudes and objectives conflict with national objectives? Does the plan recognize and/or conciliate this conflict?
4. To what extent do the planners seek to further economic freedom (see question 1 under "Economic Environment," pages 266–267)?
5. Are they restricted in the pursuit of other goals by considerations of social discrimination, e.g.:
   *a.* Do the planners try to abolish or maintain sexual, racial, and religious discrimination in employment?
   *b.* Do they try to facilitate the social mobility of backward groups by investment in their areas, or do they maintain the *status quo?*
   *c.* Do they try to facilitate or prevent the geographical mobility of backward groups?
   *d.* Do they try to assimilate minority groups by investing in their areas, by encouraging immigration into them, etc.?
   *e.* Do they try to abolish or maintain educational discrimination?
6. Does ideology inspire or inhibit the formulation of *detailed* goals?
7. To what extent are there implicit, informal, hidden, or latent goals underlying the more explicit, formal, open, and manifest goals?
8. Precisely what groups, broad and narrow, pursue which goals?

### Interest Groups

1. Has national planning been consistent with a pluralism of needs and goals among different people and different subsystems?
2. What is the set of interest groups and the degree of their articulation?
3. Are these interest groups directly involved in the planning process? How do they get access to it?
4. Do governmental bodies outside the immediate planning structure form interest groups with a serious impact on national planning, e.g., other ministries, local authorities?

5. What notice do the planners take of the goals and interests of the broader publics?

## Types of Conflict

What are the major actual conflicts, e.g.:

Short-run incomes policy        Unemployment vs. sound
Budgetary freedom                  money
Regional                        Investment vs. consumption
Religious                       Racial
The basic class and ownership
    structure

## External Influences

1. Are specific projects determined by the availability of foreign capital, thus influencing the structure of the plan?
2. How does the desire to attract more foreign private capital affect the politics of the plan?
3. What are the problems posed for the planners by foreign capital already in the country?
4. How has the formation of common markets and economic blocs affected the details of national planning?
5. How has the formation of common markets and economic blocs affected national planning in individual countries?

# DECISION MAKING

## The Institutional Network

1. Is there an identifiable central planning complex wholly within, partly within, or wholly outside the government? If so, what is the relationship between it and the government as a whole? The central planning complex may consist, *inter alia*, of:
   a. Political leadership
   b. Financial interest representatives
   c. Special interest representatives
   d. Professional experts
   e. Mediating personnel
   f. Special roles created for dealing with issues of the moment

2. Are *d* and *e* on page 272 civil servants? How secure is their tenure?

3. What are the formal constitutional positions of the planning bodies, e.g., ministry, interministerial committee, unofficial advisory council to the President?

4. Is there any pattern to the frequent reorganizations that characterize agencies in the central planning complex?

5. What are the attitudes of the traditional departments of government to national planning and the planners?

6. Have the national planners tried to develop viable subsystems (e.g., local authorities, trade unions, trade associations)? If so, to what extent were they successful?

7. What is the position of foreign advisory groups in national planning?

8. What is the position of local or provincial government vis-à-vis the plan?

9. How, if at all, do the following pressure groups influence the process of decision making?
   *a.* Trade unions (which unions in particular?)
   *b.* Other professional organizations
   *c.* Youth and women's organizations
   *d.* Churches and other religious organizations
   *e.* Peasants' and farmers' associations
   *f.* Private business associations
   *g.* Intellectuals' associations

10. Are there any institutional provisions for consulting the above-mentioned or any other pressure groups during the decision-making process? At what stage of the process is the role of pressure groups most conspicuous?

11. What are the informal ways of exerting pressure on planning agencies?

12. What groups are most successful in making the pressure effective?

13. On what factors does effectiveness of pressure most depend?

## Political Parties

1. Have the political parties the right to participate in drawing up the plan?

    *a.* Do they actually participate?

    *b.* What interests do they represent, and to what extent do they act as direct agents of particular interest groups?

2. Is planning "nonpolitical," "bipartisan," or "above party"? If so, to what extent?

    *a.* If so, is it because the parties lack interest, or because they agree, or because they have achieved a permanent and satisfactory division of power inside the planning apparatus?

    *b.* If not, do the planners simply obey the party in power?

3. To what extent can planners resist political demands on "national," "technical," or other grounds?

4. To what extent do the planners influence party action? Can they be active party members?

5. What is the role of campaign speeches, party platforms, and party programs in planning?

## The Decision-making Process

1. What are the devices used to recognize and handle friction among various publics and institutions? How efficient are these devices?

2. How are the conflicts handled in the planning process, e.g., bargaining, compromise, insistence on victory or defeat, tolerance of prolonged deadlock, avoidance of crucial issues, coalition building, interest integration in the process of goal formulation?

3. Are there significant differences in goals and methods among member institutions of the central planning complex?

4. How and when do the planners use the following methods to effect coordination and overcome resistance among other bodies:

    *a.* Settling disputes by giving orders

    *b.* Asking them to settle disputes among themselves

    *c.* Deliberately promoting competition among them

    *d.* Creating new institutions

5. What are the particular forms of resistance and dispute?

6. How do the planners persuade each other?

7. Who are the key participants in the decision process?

    *a.* What are their personal motivations and goals?

    *b.* With what interests, roles, and values can they be identified?

    *c.* What are their bases of political support?

    *d.* How frequently do they shift from one issue and role to another?

8. What are the forms of participation by nonplanners? What aspects of the decision process are conducted in the open and what are conducted in secret?

9. To what extent is decision making routinized as contrasted with creative adaptation?

10. To what extent does the lack of trained people and relevant institutions limit the rationality of the system?

11. What is the role of economists and social scientists in improving the rationality of decision making?

    *a.* How accurate is the economic, sociological, and other information used by the planners? How accurate do they think it is?

    *b.* What mathematical models do the planners construct? What degree of accuracy would their underlying data require for the models to be useful? To what practical uses are the models in fact put?

    *c.* What deliberate biases are built into the information by the original sources?

    *d.* Does the plan come out punctually? If not, what do people do in the meantime?

    *e.* What role is given to social scientists, other than economists, in the central planning complex?

    *f.* Do social scientists take technological decisions or physical scientists social and economic decisions?

    *g.* To what extent are the planners' attention and goals determined by the availability of data?

## The Constitution and the Rule of Law

1. Is the plan a legal command?
2. How is nonfulfillment penalized?
3. What is the balance between statute and delegated powers?
4. In either case is the plan subject to:

  *a.* Judicial review?
  *b.* Administrative review?
  *c.* Review by the parliament or any other public body?
5. How much of the formulated plan is secret?
6. Is the factual material on which the plan is based accessible to the public?
7. To what extent are the planning negotiations public?
8. Has the constitution, or any legislation, or the rules of parliamentary or judicial procedure been altered for the sake of the plan?


## Politically Guaranteed Freedoms

NOTE: *Freedom* here is defined as "freedom from." "Freedom to" is implicit in other sections.

1. How easy is political opposition to:
   *a.* Details in the plan?
   *b.* The broad lines of the plan?
   *c.* The existence of the planning authorities?
2. How easy is simple evasion by those subject to control by the plan?
3. Has the number of controls tended to decrease or increase? If the latter, was it:
   *a.* In order to stop evasion of those already imposed?
   *b.* By "Parkinson's law"?
   *c.* For other reasons, e.g., increasing complexity of the economy, increasing efficiency of communications?
4. Has there been a drift from persuasion through market to pressure types of control, or vice versa (see question 1 under "Activators and Sanctions," on page 277)?
5. During the period of planning, how have the freedoms of speech, association, worship, communication, and political action for various social groups in fact fared?
6. Has increased planning gone hand in hand with a diminution of these freedoms?   Or vice versa?
7. Has planning undermined or facilitated the economic freedom of the organs relevant to question 5, e.g., made it difficult to build churches, publish newspapers?

8. Has a regime determined a priori to root out the freedoms in question 5 also imposed economic planning? In what chronological order?
9. Have the freedoms in question 5 obstructed or reduced the amount of economic planning? For example, has the public insisted on relaxing wartime controls at the end of a war?
10. What other connections are there between question 5 and economic planning in the country?

## IMPLEMENTATION

### Activators and Sanctions

1. What activators do the planners use on outside agents?
   a. Market: purchase and sale in the open market, plan fulfillment bonus, subsidies, direct taxes, credit licensing through the banks?
   b. Persuasion: informing, expecting, providing an example, proposing, propaganda, medals and honors, advertising, logical argument?
   c. Pressure: bargaining other than in market terms, manipulation, legal command, legal prohibition and licensing, rationing?
2. If activation fails or threatens to fail, what sanctions have the planners?
   a. Formal, veiled?
   b. Take-over of management, expropriation with or without compensation?
   c. Prison, demotion, fine?

### Campaigns

1. How much use do the planners make of specific campaigns?
2. What campaign strategies have the planners used?
   a. Crisis exploitation?
   b. Crisis creation?
   c. Maintaining an optimistic stance?
   d. The "art of the improbable"?
   e. Planner's tension?
3. How do they time their major decisions?

## Obstacles and Limitations to Implementation

1. To what extent are the planners hindered by:
   a. Illiteracy?
   b. Lack of social and fiscal discipline, theft, graft, sabotage, wholesale plan evasion?
   c. Opposition to planning in principle?
   d. The constitution and nonplan legislation (see pages 275–276)?
   e. Material self-contradiction in the plan?
   f. Their own incompetence?
   g. Lack of money or personnel for their own functions?
2. What are they doing about it?

## Correcting Mechanisms

1. How quick is feedback?
   a. Are long-range goals broken down into sequential steps on which current information is possible?
   b. Are detailed plans worked out at shorter intervals than overall plans?
   c. Are short-term reports required? Are they made on a routine basis or by personal contact? How are they treated at headquarters: ignored, exploited, or suppressed?
   d. Are periodic reviews carried out on regional, sector, or enterprise scale?
2. How rigid is the plan? At what intervals is it in fact altered?
3. Are these alterations made a priori or as the result of feedback?
4. Is the plan so flexible, owing to feedback, as to be epiphenomenal?
5. What initiative, in implementation as opposed to formulation, does the system leave to lower levels? What are the differences here between formal and informal initiative?

## RESULTS

NOTE: Most of the questions in this part are unanswerable in any scholarly way. Yet they are the most basic questions of all and are daily asked and answered by planners and politicians.

All serious judgments of the suitability of a policy or system logically entail, indeed are nothing else than, comparisons with what might have been. The depth studies must, then, however sketchily or implicitly, contain answers to them. They refer not to some ideal or radically different country but to the country as it was described by the answers to the questions under "Social Framework" (pages 265–266), and to the options it actually has or had.

## Goals

1. Were the plans fulfilled?
   a. The originally published plans?
   b. Amended versions? How recent and severe were the amendments?
2. Whatever the results, would more *laissez faire* have been better in terms of the planners' own broader intentions?
   a. Would the economy have grown faster?
   b. Would the economy have grown at the same speed but with less investment?
   c. Would the noneconomic aims have been better achieved?
3. Could different plans have better fulfilled the planners' broad intentions? Specify these plans.
   a. Would the economy have grown faster?
   b. Would the economy have grown at the same speed but with less investment?
   c. Would the noneconomic aims have been better achieved?
4. Would different types of planning have better fulfilled the planners' broad intentions?

## Side Effects

1. Apart from the country's attempt to fulfill the plan, what side effects had the plan?
   a. Were these side effects anticipated by the planners?
   b. But not part of their goals (e.g., "We had full employment, so prices rose")?
   c. Were they not anticipated (e.g., "We collectivized agriculture, so the peasants slaughtered their livestock")?

2. How do the side effects look in terms of the planners' own broader intentions?

### Evaluation in Terms of the Writer's Values

1. Were the plan's intentions good or bad?
2. Were its results, including the unintended ones, good or bad?
3. Would more *laissez faire* have been better?
4. Would different plans or policies have been better? Would different types of planning have been better?

When one runs through the list of questions set forth at the Minnowbrook Conference, it is immediately apparent that they are all biased in the direction of basic research. Many of the participants have themselves been actively involved in national government planning. From personal experience they knew that one of the great functions of applied research in past years has been to provide ceremonial legitimation of actions already decided upon by power wielders. They felt that by developing research of a more fundamental nature they would help create conditions under which, in time, applied research could become more genuinely useful than it has been thus far. Indeed, all the participants committed themselves, in their own research and work, to ask their own questions rather than be bound by questions given them by government officials. It is hoped that activities of this type will do much more than provide a larger audience for the questions here formulated. We hope to encourage other scholars to formulate better questions and engage in basic research on the ambitious efforts of national governments to guide national economic change.

### NOTE

[1] The questions in this chapter were prepared by a committee headed by Professor Wiles. The other members of the committee were Zygmunt Bauman; Nora F. Gross, research associate, Maxwell School, Syracuse University; and Tariq Saddiqi, member of the Pakistan Civil Service and graduate student at Maxwell School, Syracuse University. The questions have also appeared in Bertram M. Gross, "National Planning: Some Fundamental Questions," *The American Behavioral Scientist*, pp. 8–12, December, 1964.

# 11

# Attitudes and Beliefs on National Planning

*Michel Crozier* [1]

It is a truism that people's basic beliefs, which underlie their everyday actions and attitudes, profoundly influence the implementation, as well as the formulation, of national plans.

Indeed, national leaders and plan administrators not only recognize this but take special pride in their intuitive sensitivity to divergent and changing attitudes and beliefs as they are affected by specific plans. The growing interest in broadening the bases of consultation and participation is one manifestation of their eagerness to explore and expose these attitudes and beliefs.

Yet until now, strangely enough, there has been no serious effort (or scholarly research) to identify the many kinds of attitudes and beliefs that are relevant to the success of national planning. Nor have there been any efforts to use the tools of modern social science surveys, aside from informal personal appraisals by planners themselves, in studying these important phenomena.

The following schema has been drawn up as an aid to the systematic exploration of the attitudes and beliefs of individuals and/or groups as these may affect or be affected by national planning in any society. As it now stands, in our judgment, it could serve as an important checklist for planners to keep in mind as they appraise the feasibility and desirability of alternative plans and engage in discussions with representatives of key groups. If the personal radar sets in the minds of plan administrators are sensitive, let them be tuned in to questions of this type.

Beyond this, our schema presents categories and dimensions which could form the basis for formal surveys in particular societies over time or in different societies at the same time. In the past, surveys of attitudes and beliefs have been used for very limited purposes: as a tool in market research or in the well-known opinion polls for political purposes. With the development of national planning, we must make use of these new techniques in studying the cultural obstacles to changes and purposes sought through national planning.

The questions suggested or formulated correspond to a static analysis of the attitudes and beliefs at a given moment, but it is understood that the most important use of such surveys would be to provide a starting point for successive surveys (along parallel lines) that will permit the measurement of change.

Finally, no distinction has been made between a general opinion survey to be applied to samples of the population as a whole and analyses of specific attitudes of key elite groups (small and big business, civil service, labor leaders, political leaders, etc.). A sophisticated research design can be developed only on this latter basis.

## IMAGES OF CENTRAL PLANNING

In view of variations in the emphasis placed on the definition and structuring of planning activities in different societies, it is essential for purposes of cross-cultural comparison to broaden the analysis of attitudes and beliefs by reference to the general sphere of regulatory functions of government vis-à-vis social and economic activity.

### Perception

1. Perception of the goals underlying national planning and/or regulations, including perception of differences in the goals attributed to such planning by different groups

2. Perception of the methods used in the formulation and implementation of plans
3. Perception of the organization of planning or regulatory processes—the variety of participants, the internal relations within government and between government and extragovernment groups

## Involvement

With regard to degrees of involvement, it is essential to distinguish the case of key elite groups from that of the general population.

In the case of the former, one should try to ascertain to what extent they participate directly or indirectly in the planning process (question of fact) and to what extent they feel committed to the institutions, to the methods, and to the guidelines of planning (question of attitudes).

With the latter, one should probe only into the effective involvement people have with the planning institutions and the planning process. This could be done better by indirect means such as questions designed to measure expectations for the future, readiness to forgo immediate advantages, etc.

## Judgment

By *judgment on planning* we mean overall and conscious assessment by the respondents of (1) the idea of planning and (2) the results achieved by existing planning institutions (and, in cases where planning does not exist formally, by key regulatory agencies).

Such judgments can be elicited on the following dimensions:

1. Legitimacy of ends (Do you think the planners' objectives are legitimate or illegitimate?)
2. Legitimacy of means (Do you think the means they use are legitimate or illegitimate?)
3. Feasibility (Do you think planners use appropriate and adequate means to attain the ends they propose?)
4. Overall judgment of the institution (Do you think the planning institution has done a good, reasonable, effective job? Do you think it is a good, etc., institution, etc.?)

5. Assessment of the benefits and costs of planning in relation:
   a. To the individual respondent himself (including immediate family)
   b. To the individual's most important reference groups (such as his occupational group, the branch of industry to which he belongs, or his social class)
   c. To the society as a whole

## ATTITUDES TOWARD SPACE

National planning infers a specific form of activity occurring within, or with respect to, a space unit: a nation. National planning not only frequently proposes alterations to space but does so selectively with the result that individuals, because of their peculiar spatial affiliation, are differentially affected.

More precisely, national planning is peculiarly related to the management of the allocation of space and of the resources occupying space. Attitudes of the elite groups, planners, and the nonelite groups toward space obviously influence goal formulation and implementation strategy. Conversely, a function of planning is systematically to alter existing sets of attitudes toward spatial affiliation, cognition, and allocation.

### Spatial Identification

Here we refer to attitudes (their intensity as well as extent) of selected populations toward political space, e.g., nation, region, province, village. National planning, by definition if not always by intent, implies a degree of regulation of some aspect of society by the national government. The relative extent to which planners and planned identify with political spatial units is an important factor in the formulation of goals and even more so in the loci of the implementing authority. It is suspected that in new nations considerable planning energy must be diverted from purely economic goals to programs designed to shift spatial attitudes away from traditional segments toward the nation-state. On the other hand attitudes with respect to spatial identification may pose relatively inflexible limits to national planning.

## Organization of Space

Related to the individual sense of identification with political space is the more general attitude of how space is or ought to be organized. From a cognitive point of view this refers to attitudes as to preferred design, style, and form. Mathematics, technology, and complexity incline highly developed societies to conceive of space as organized in rectangles, precise angles, and concentrics, as large-scale and complex. A capacity to shape nature and to create models gives impetus to this inclination. In societies where life tends to conform to the irregularities of nature, attitudes as to space organization are likely to be diffuse and imprecise, small-scale, and relatively simple.

Attitudes with respect to the organization of space both within and between societies are assumed to vary widely. It is thought, for example, that the degree to which a people comprehend national planning and are therefore more inclined to view it favorably is partially a function of the sophistication of their attitudes toward the organization of space.

Though aware of the difficulties of measuring such attitudes, their significance and their effect on national planning make it worthwhile to attempt its research.

## External World

The legitimacy and comprehensibility of national planning is in part determined by the boundaries that the subjects of planning establish between what might be termed their "own secure space" and the external world. Range of cognition is an important element in the formation of such boundaries. In new nations in particular, a limited cognitive range negatively affects the comprehension and legitimacy of national planning. Conversely, a function of national planning, in developing as well as developed societies, is to extend the cognitive range and thus influence in a national direction attitudes of that portion of the respective population residing on the fringes or outside the pale of national society.

### International Environment

There is a wide range of attitudes which help to structure the individual's posture toward other nations and their nationals. The attitude of the elite and the planner with respect to this dimension is basic, for it obviously rigorously structures not only goal formulation but, more importantly, implementation strategy. Long-standing traditional affinities and disaffinities pose obstacles which planners must sometime overcome in order to carry out their plans. Problems dealing with the military aspects of national planning possibly illustrate most sharply the significance of attitudes toward the international environment.

## ATTITUDES TOWARD TIME

Planning infers a concept of time. Anyone concerned with attitudes and opinions vis-à-vis national planning must of necessity take this concept into account.

It is also essential in this connection to keep in mind the distinction between national planning in developed and developing countries. In the former case, national planning is likely to involve segmented alterations within an existing relatively stable system. In the latter case, planning is a deliberate attempt drastically and rapidly to alter culture by radically affecting mass behavior and attitudes.

Attitudes toward time are obviously related to development and to the receptiveness of a people and its elite to collective action. Still more important is the manner in which the time sense affects the management of collective action (planning). There are four such aspects of attitudes toward time which we feel most strongly affect, and are affected by, national planning. These have to do with perception of time, structuring the future, progress, and economic growth.

### Perception of Time

Here we are concerned with widely differing attitudes toward the concept of time, both within and between societies, for example, the significant difference between a society predominantly oriented toward a cyclic view of time and a society oriented toward a predominantly linear approach to time. Research is required to ascertain the nature of such varying perceptions of time and to pinpoint their relationship to the planning process and the way in which this process is itself perceived. Planned social change in developing societies implies a trend toward complexity and industrialization accompanied by increased rigidity and precision. Industrialization, mechanization, science, and large-scale organization all demand relatively exact measures of time and a high degree of human obedience to its dictates. In developing societies, particularly, the lag between the prevailing conception of time and a conception more appropriate to changing technology and organizations is likely to be of crucial significance for planners and planning.

A further aspect of time perception which merits research concerns the *fragmented* quality of time. In relatively simple societies where cyclic time tends to predominate, relatively few fundamental decisions are required with respect to the structuring of future action. On the other hand, the linear time sense characteristic of scientifically oriented societies emphasizes the end-on-end aspect of time utilization. Linear time, however, may be perceived less as a single span than as composed of time segments. Variations in time span as between different social groups, especially elite groups and nonelite groups, may significantly affect attitudes toward the future-oriented activities of government and the ways in which these are received and reacted to.

### Structuring the Future

Individual attitudes toward the future may operate collectively to determine the posture of a society vis-à-vis national planning. More precisely we are concerned here with the degree of responsibility that the individual feels for structuring (planning) his own future. A survey instrument designed to measure this attitude would ask such questions as: "What do you expect to be doing five years hence?" "What plans have you made for your children?" etc. Obviously, attitudes concerning structuring of the future will vary within a society and between societies. On the one hand, if little or no change is perceived through time other than one's growing older, dying, and being replaced by the next generation (cyclic time), there will be a corresponding absence of any sense of responsibility for structuring the future. On the other hand, a high degree of faith in the predictability of the future, a sense of linear time, together with a belief in progress, will incline both planner and planned-for to invest considerable time and energy in formulating plans for the future. We are also inclined to see some relationship between the length of time span and the degree of perceived predictability of the future. Finally, such attitudes are also likely to be major determinants of attitudes toward saving, the forgoing or sacrifice of the present for the future, which are of crucial importance in the formulation and implementation of plans or policies for economic growth.

### Progress

The concept of progress is often assumed to be a universal value. In reality, it is apparent that a number of non-Western societies do not include any such value within their traditional frames of reference. Though we are aware of the fact that there exist considerable variations in attitudes within and between societies as to perception of linear accumulative change (progress), insufficient data are available to enable us to perceive with satisfactory reliability the significance of these variations for national planning and/or future-oriented government activity.

We suspect that attitudes on the inevitability of progress exist within some societies, though probably only within specific subsocieties. Obviously, planning in a society which is predominantly of the view that progress is inevitable will differ from planning in a society where progress is "inconceivable." Equally important are attitudes toward one's own relationship to progress, that is to say, the extent to which the individual feels progress to be the product of human manipulation, including his own, as against perceiving it as a force outside his control which indirectly affects him.

Between these two extremes lies a wide range of more sophisticated or specified cases. Thus, progress may be perceived as unidirectional and constant, as multidirectional and sporadic, as unstable and reversible, etc.

## Economic Growth

This aspect of attitudes toward time is obviously related to "progress" but merits special treatment because of its peculiar significance for national planning. Economic growth, as contrasted to a more general concept of progress, refers to a human process which incrementally adds to a society's collective capacity and wealth. We would anticipate significant variation in people's attitudes as to how they themselves relate to such growth; e.g., is economic growth perceived as a bootstrap operation, with everybody pitching in? Or is it simply something that the government or another agency does, which fatalistically happens to one? A related question is the extent to which there is any perceived sense of the existence of "economic growth." Does the idea form a part of the society's frame of reference at all?

## ATTITUDES TOWARD CHANGE

Development and growth require change. Attitudes toward change are closely associated with attitudes toward action, but they can be and, in view of their importance, should be tested separately. They comprise perhaps the most important "givens" planners have to take into account. Societies will progress and planning will succeed only inasmuch as individuals and groups are ready to learn new patterns of action.

## Attitudes toward Tradition

Readiness to depart from accepted traditions is the first prerequisite of change. The tradition-bound are not found only in primitive societies, and a mapping of the areas still dominated by tradition within developed societies is urgently required.

## Attitudes toward Utopia

People departing from tradition usually can only conceive of change in a utopian, unrealistic way. Attitudes toward a utopia are therefore a very important element in understanding patterns of action in all transitional societies, and, in certain areas at least, all societies are transitional ones.

### Perception of Crisis

Change is generally accepted only when enough people are aware of a threatening crisis situation. The perceptive element behind the emergence of a sense of crisis must therefore be probed.

### Passive Adaptation to Change

Most changes do not occur with the participation of the people involved. The critical element in such situations is the readiness of people to adjust to novel situations.

### Change Proneness

Attitudes toward change can be and must be tested in their active dimensions also: the readiness of individuals to learn and to innovate, the values attached by various groups within society to innovation, etc.

### Understanding the Cost of Change

Responsible attitudes toward change necessitate a realistic appraisal of the cost of change and a readiness to pay for it which can be tested only by questions pertaining to the value of innovation.

## ATTITUDES TOWARD SOCIAL ACTION

In this section we are concerned with the attitudes of individuals and groups toward the objectives and the organization of social action. Government planning and/or regulation are themselves forms of social action which may be directed toward, or involve changes in, the prevailing objectives and/or organization of such action while remaining to a greater or lesser extent constrained by them.

### Collective and Individual Responsibility

First, between and within societies there will be differences in the measure of responsibility individuals are prepared to accept

for social, or "common," ends.  The extremes would be anarch-
ism, where no responsibility is recognized above the level of the
individual, and communalism (the indifferentiation of traditional
primitive societies, say), where no responsibility is recognized
below the level of the community.  Between these extremes lies
the bulk of modern societies in which areas both of individual
and of collective responsibility are recognized.  For any given
society, class, or individual we need to inquire where the boundaries of these two areas lie, i.e., what the things are that any
individual accepts individual responsibility for and what the
things are that he perceives as the responsibility of the community.

Secondly, collective responsibility may equally be perceived by
different individuals and/or groups in different ways:

1. Responsibility for other individuals or groups (paternalism)
2. Responsibility with other individuals or groups (the further-
   ing of shared objectives)
3. Responsibility of other individuals or groups for oneself (dependence)

Thirdly, there may be differences in perception as to the institutions in which collective responsibility is and/or should be
focused—spatial, functional, tribal or racial, religious, local, or
central, etc.

Within each of these three dimensions, differences in attitude
within or across societies are likely to be basic to the way in
which different groups or nations perceive, relate to, and judge
central, planned, concentrated action.

### Initiation

Between societies, major differences may exist as to the ways in
which collective action is initiated.  In many societies, developing and developed, the initiation of such action may be highly
formalized or institutionalized, i.e., the responsibility of particular
organizations or groups and/or individuals within these.  The
initiation of certain kinds of collective action (organization of defense, of welfare or "relief," of community development, of economic activities, etc.) may be perceived as legitimate only if carried through by some sanctioned agency or group: a village

headman, a tribal chief, a village or local council, the executives of an organization, public or private, etc. Infringement of these accepted canons may inhibit the efficacy of any collective action contemplated by governments. At the same time, the effectiveness of planning may critically depend in certain cases on altering prevailing patterns of initiation, e.g., encouraging greater devolution and spread of initiation or, conversely, greater concentration.

### Participation

What are the prevailing beliefs within a society as to the distribution and the mode of ascribed and/or legitimate participation in collective decisions (decisions taken on behalf of the "community" or society)? By "distribution" of participation we mean the number and the variety of groups and individuals entitled or sanctioned to participate in one way or another within specified areas of collective decision. By "mode" of participation we have in mind such variables as directness or indirectness, the use of elected or selected representatives, and the use of consultative or joint decision-taking techniques. In brief, who should participate in what, and how? Different political systems, e.g., varieties of parliamentary democracy (one party or multiparty), corporate democracy, varieties of totalitarianism, tend to be characterized by particular patterns of legitimate participation in decision making. These, in turn, affect the focus and organization of interest and pressure groups and the ways in which political parties, administration bureaus, or accredited representatives of industrial interests function in their roles as lobbyists. Different types of planning may alter or attempt to alter the distribution and mode of participation over a certain range of collective decisions (this has clearly been the case in France and, it would appear, in Great Britain and is probably even more sharply characteristic of planning in traditional and socially highly structured societies).

### Patterns of Organization

Planning for government action in the furtherance of development or growth often implies changes in existing patterns of organization (especially industrial organization) in the direction of increasing size and complexity. (Conversely, planning may itself be an outcome of such changes; cf. the United Kingdom in the 1960s.) Insofar as these connections are perceived, attitudes and beliefs toward scale and complexity as dimensions of organizations may exercise a pronounced effect on attitudes toward planning as such. The concern here is with the *associations* individuals make with scale and complexity. Thus, large organizations may tend to be perceived as bureaucratic, rigid, inhuman, authoritarian, characterized primarily by hierarchic rather than by polyarchic relationships, etc. In addition to the distinction between large and small scale, it would be important to analyze attitudes toward patterns of association or interconnection between organizations. These may be perceived as surrogates for large-scale organizations, as conspiratorial rather than facilitative, etc.

### Regulatory Processes

Planning is *likely* to increase the amount of conscious central regulation of economic and/or social activity. At the same time, it may significantly alter the techniques of regulation available to, and usable by, central government. Attitudes toward regulation may relate either to its volume or to its techniques. Relevant dimensions vis-à-vis the latter would be:

1. The extent to which certain techniques are perceived as *constraining* the autonomy of individual and group decisions, e.g., such techniques as fiscal and monetary policy or legal prohibitions, as contrasted with the extent to which these and/or other techniques are perceived as *infringing* on that autonomy, e.g., perhaps direct commands or physical controls
2. The extent to which techniques of regulation are perceived as discriminatory between groups or individuals (the felt equitableness of regulation)
3. The extent to which regulation is perceived as indirect and manipulative, e.g., the use of government's economic power as a consumer of goods and services and/or as an employer of factors of production

## Training and Expertise

The concern here is partly with the extent to which and the area of action within which in any society expertise is recognized and accepted, partly with the way in which expertise is perceived, for example, as closed, abstract, incommunicable, technical, rational, value-free, magical. Particular attention should be paid to attitudes toward expertise within the sphere of government and collective decision, e.g., the cult of the amateur in the British civil service, the possible overevaluation of econometrics, or the "technical" nature of economic decision making in highly centrally planned societies.

## Ends and Means

Success in social action is not related only to attitudes toward different and segmented processes of social action, however elaborate these may be. It depends also on the capacity of rational calculation concerning ends and means.

Rational calculation is possible only if the relationship between ends and means can be understood. It must be stressed that a great difference exists with regard to key elite groups and the general population. For the former, the problem lies in the capacity to achieve rational calculation. For the latter, the problem lies in their capacity to accept it.

The two types of investigations needed here are extremely difficult to handle. Any tests devised must be related to the nature of the respondent's experience. For the moment, all one can do is to propose a general framework.

There are two general types of questions which arise in connection with this dimension:

To what extent do individuals or groups take into account the means necessary for the achievement of the social or collective ends of which they approve? That is, to what extent do they ask, "What may we have to do to get $X$?" (Cf. the often-noted dissonance between the public's attitudes toward collective expenditure and those toward taxation levels.) This question may arise in situations in which there is no doubt that available means exist for the fulfillment of approved ends. Alternatively, one may inquire as to whether or not individuals or groups make any assessment of the potentialities of the means possessed by the society vis-à-vis stated or desired ends, i.e., whether they ask, "What have we the power to do?"

## ATTITUDES TOWARD SOCIAL STRUCTURE

Societies can function effectively only if their structure is stable enough to give protection to their members, but they will grow only if this structure is adaptive. Attitudes toward social structure must, therefore, be considered as a further given which planners have to take into account. The scope of the problem, however, is such that only directly relevant questions should be asked. One should not try to probe attitudes toward social structure in general but rather the degree of openness or of conservatism which these attitudes imply.

### Attitudes toward Class and Caste

Economic growth requires that class and caste should not markedly restrict individual behavior. The degree of attachment to, and the amount of protection demanded of, class and caste is thus a relevant given.

### Attitudes toward Race and Ethnic-group Minorities

With respect to racial, ethnic, and minority groups, as with class and caste, overrestrictive attitudes prevent the development of adaptive social action.

### Attitudes toward Political Parties

Where the appeal of political parties is based on rigid principles and/or on a complete, precise, and intransigent blueprint of the future, communication, compromise, and constructive problem solving become impossible.

### Rigidity versus Flexibility

Certain individuals can obtain protection from the social system only if it is rigid enough to prevent the development of situations of uncertainty. The capacity to accept flexibility in the social structure and the readiness to cope with relatively incoherent, unstructured social situations are decisive assets for innovation and change.

## ATTITUDES TOWARD CONFLICT MANAGEMENT AND COMMUNICATION

The capabilities of a society to manage conflict constitute a boundary condition for the success of planning. Some modes of conflict management are recognized as social norms by all members of a society. Others are characteristic of some groups only. Still others are completely unavailable, being either too primitive or too sophisticated. Since planning entails making decisions about conflicting interests, planners must learn to work with whatever types of conflict regulation are acceptable to, or can be learned by, those concerned. These limitations also affect the amount and content of communication and the direction and channels in and through which communication takes place. Communication, of course, constitutes another of the boundary conditions of planning.

Attitudes and beliefs about conflict management and the related modes of communication are deeply embedded and difficult to change.

### Acceptance-Rejection of Conflict

Some individuals, groups and, indeed, the cultures of some whole societies experience great difficulty in accepting in any way the existence of conflict as part and parcel of everyday social reality. They feel that to engage in conflict means simply to destroy or be destroyed. The image of conflict is that it is essentially uncontrollable, and the threat is such that conflict must be eliminated by denial or avoidance. When it does break out, it therefore tends to erupt (as expected) into primitive violence, since no social mechanisms have been evolved which can be used to channel it. To be possible at all, planning requires in the attitudinal structure of the society a certain toleration of conflict, the belief that it can be contained to a reasonable degree, and the existence of preferred modes of regulating it. No living society could, in fact, function without some institutionalized provision for conflict management, but in no society is the threat of unregulated conflict entirely absent from the attitudes of its members.

## Preferences in Conflict Management

*Win-lose.* The simplest and most common form of conflict resolution proceeds on the assumption that what one party wins the other must lose. Victories and defeats may be complete or partial, though it is presumed, in contrast to a more primitive attitude, that the losers will be allowed to survive in some culturally recognized way and at some minimum level, rather than be completely annihilated as would happen if conflict could not be tolerated at all. In this reductive sense, conflict may be regarded as regulated by a win-lose approach. This form of conflict management, however, becomes less easily available when issues become more complex, so that outcomes are less clear-cut, and when there are more than two parties involved. Moreover, win-lose methods are not available when the collaboration of the losers is subsequently required for implementation. Groups or societies in which win-lose values and attitudes prevail in conflict regulation provide settings with negative implications so far as the success of planning is concerned. Vast energies need to be diverted to cope with recalcitrance and resistance in all its devious forms.

*Competition.* The transformation of win-lose conflicts into competition is a step of the greatest importance in conflict regulation. Introduced is the principle of victory by superior performance within the rules of the game. One outclasses one's opponent; one does not damage him. One's own achievement is the criterion of success, not one's power to destroy one's adversary. Competition implies repetition and so creates a dynamic which can prolong a state of conflict without resolution and with the possibility of ultimate constructive outcomes. By contrast, the aim of win-lose fights is to end the conflict state—as soon as possible, if destruction is to be minimized. Moreover, many may succeed in a competition, which in the long run becomes depersonalized into a standard. Unless win-lose attitudes and values can become to a considerable extent transformed into competitive attitudes and values, it is difficult to see how a complex society will be able to regulate itself. Planning without competition is inconceivable.

*Bargaining.* Bargaining really assumes that both gains and losses may be made and accepted by each party to a dispute. Complex issues with many facets and outcomes and involving many parties with interests to various degrees divergent or aligned may be resolved by bargaining. Moreover, partial resolution can be accepted, with some issues left in deadlock. Some degree of skill in bargaining may be taken as a cultural prerequisite for success in planning.

*Collaborative problem solving.* Though bargaining implies compromise, it implies no more than that all parties concerned are willing to exchange limited losses for limited gains to their own best advantage while recognizing that others also must be satisfied. Bargaining is concerned with reducing the incompatibility between preformulated goals of different parties. By contrast, collaborative problem solving is concerned with the formulation of a needed common goal, which none of the parties would be able to discover by himself and which can only emerge as differences are confronted and worked through. Collaborative problem solving provides the attitudinal climate most conducive to planning success, but is the most difficult to attain, especially in intergroup, as compared with intragroup dealings. Nevertheless, some capability in this direction may be postulated as a prerequisite for undertaking complex planning tasks involving the participation of many groups.

### Communication

Communication between one party and another (whether individuals or groups) is affected in a far-reaching manner by whatever mode of conflict regulation is assumed to be operating. Attitudinal expectations are that the modes of conflict regulation in our own ingroup will be more "advanced" than in our various outgroups. The more distant the latter are, the more severe our fears. This is doubly so when an intergroup conflict is thought of as having the underlying character of a win-lose fight rather than of a competition.   When bargaining, negotiations may conceivably take a turn for the worse; we tend to take this into account both consciously and unconsciously.   Similarly, collaborative problem solving may revert to bargaining.

In win-lose fights, communication is minimal.   Information about the enemy is obtained only against his will, and he must be denied all knowledge about ourselves that might be useful to him.   The valued modes of communication are those of secrecy, deceit, and surprise.   All transactions are assumed to be in bad faith.

In competition, transactions are assumed to be in good faith, and communication is opened up in certain respects.   It is advantageous to have one's performances or the products of one's performances displayed and evaluated in regard to their properties by relevant others; one requires a reputation in order to have a worth.   But means and interests remain closely guarded.

Bargaining is concerned with private interests and how far they may be revealed and under what conditions.   Intents and means are only communicated with full openness, however, in collaborative problem solving.

## NOTE

[1] This chapter was prepared by a committee headed by Dr. Crozier.   The other members of the committee were David Armstrong, Tavistock Institute of Human Relations, London; Fred G. Burke; and Eric Trist, Staff Convenor, Tavistock Institute of Human Relations.

# Index